Also by Andrew Sinclair

THE LAST OF
THE BEST

THE LAST
OF
THE BEST

*The Aristocracy of Europe in the
Twentieth Century*

〜§§§〜

ANDREW SINCLAIR

The Macmillan Company

Library of Congress Catalog Card Number: 69-17105

First American Edition 1969
Published in Great Britain in 1969 by Weidenfeld and Nicolson,
London

The Macmillan Company

Printed in the United States of America

The author and publishers are grateful to the many publishers who
have granted permission to quote from their books, including the
following: extracts from Haply I May Remember, by Lady Cynthia
Asquith, by kind permission of the Literary Executors of Lady
Cynthia Asquith; extracts from Red Twins, by B. J. Kospoth, by
kind permission of the publishers, Macdonald & Co.; an extract from
Life and Culture of Poland as Reflected in Polish Literature, by
Waclaw Lednicki, through the courtesy of Roy Publishers, Inc.,
New York; an extract from History of the Russian Revolution, by
Leon Trotsky, reprinted by permission of The University of Michigan
Press. Copyright © The University of Michigan Press 1932, 1933,
1960, renewed 1961; extracts from Old Men Forget, by Alfred
Duff Cooper, by kind permission of Rupert Hart-Davis, London,
and E. P. Dutton, New York; the extract from Lui, by courtesy of
Bokelberg and Stern Magazine.

To
Peter Ritner,
the only begetter
of this book

Contents

List of Illustrations

❦

Prologue

'Are you born?'

Most human beings would reply that they were. Yet this question, still asked solemnly in some exclusive circles in Europe, means more than it states. It means, 'Are you born from a family which has a name that other aristocratic families recognize?' More precisely, it means, 'Is your family listed in the *Almanach de Gotha* or *Burke's Peerage* or their lesser imitators?' If so, you may consider yourself born. If not, you may not.

The mark of birth is the only one which enables the modern aristocrat to recognize his like. The true basis of aristocracy, as de Tocqueville pointed out, is land; but too many social revolutions in Eastern Europe and social reforms in Western Europe have forced aristocrats to concede the basis of their titles, leaving only their pedigrees to comfort them. The acquisition of land through wealth or of honours through politics still allows for a new aristocracy to join the thinning ranks of the old. But birth and family name still remain the final security for the last of the best in a modern world that increasingly finds less place for the pretensions of pedigree.

This book seeks to trace the history of the European aristocracy in this century from its Indian summer before the First World War through the depression and the Second World War to the present day. The book concentrates more on the history of a class or caste than on the particular definitions of the members of that class. In this way, it is more interested in generalities than genealogies.

Aristocracy once meant the government of a state by its best citizens. It soon came to mean the government of a state by its richest and best-born citizens. Thus it came to mean merely an oligarchy, the government of a state by a few men or families. And finally aristocracy reached its loose modern meaning of a group of people distinguished by birth or wealth who rank above the rest of the community, even if they have little power in the state, or even if they are no better than the rest.

Thus the concept of aristocracy has degenerated from the ideal of the rule of the best to the fact of the survival of those often least fitted to cope with the modern industrial egalitarian state. If the best still rule in the modern technocracies, their origins are usually bourgeois or plebeian. The aristocracy has lost its international and national power, retaining only some local power in Western Europe and the ultimate power of excluding from its company those whom it does not wish to see. Its interest is not to lord it over the nation now, but to lie low. *The Last of the Best* will try to show how two-thirds of a century have brought about the humbling of a close-knit European power group from the first place in Western civilization to the rearguard of the old values of that civilization.

Pedigree, like time, is merely a relative thing. Nobles with a genealogy of thirty generations condescend to nobles of twenty generations who look down on nobles of ten generations who despise nobles generated officially in more recent times. Old money looks down on new, ancient nations on more recent ones, five-year-old children on tiny tots. Thus the snobbery of ancient lineage has not been my concern in dealing with the aristocracy of Europe. I have tried to examine the history and psychology of a group of people with family names and sometimes fortunes, who consider themselves and are considered to be aristocrats, and who thus enjoy a real social influence and power.

Since there is no book dealing with the recent history of the European aristocracy, I have depended on many scraps of information garnered from research libraries and newspapers, and also on personal interviews by my researcher, Jacquemine

Charrott-Lodwidge. I wish to thank her for her untiring energy in interviewing a sample of the European aristocracy, and I wish to thank that sample for their patience and hospitality in answering her questions. I have tried to use the results of my researches and the matter of the interviews to present a whole view of what is necessarily a dispersed group of individuals living in a divided subcontinent, a group no longer international in outlook nor confident about the future. Any errors in presenting the views of the group as a whole must be my own and reflect in no way on the individual opinions of those kind enough to aid me in my work.

ANDREW SINCLAIR

Part One

THE DECLINE

One

⌐ⴸⴸ⌐

INDIAN SUMMER
1901–14

The last moments of Queen Victoria, the Duke of Argyll said, were like a great three-decker ship sinking. She kept on heaving and submerging. Round her bed gathered her son, the future King Edward VII, who had been kept waiting in a gilded corner for the throne for some sixty years; his wife and his nephew, Wilhelm II, the Kaiser of Germany; and three of the royal princesses with the royal doctor. The Kaiser supported the Queen with his good arm, the one which had not withered; the doctor supported her other side ; they remained kneeling for two and a half hours while she was dying. When she did die, the Kaiser measured his royal grandmother for her coffin and lifted her into it, assisted by the new King of England and the Duke of Connaught. The old Queen had reigned for so long that the Court had forgotten the proper procedure for burying a sovereign.

The death of Queen Victoria in 1901 in the arms of her ruling progeny and the coming of Edward VII to the British throne opened the final thirteen golden years of the international aristocracy of Europe. Monarchies, supported by powerful aristocracies, ruled in all the major countries of Europe except France, where even the Third Republic had not wholly destroyed the local power of the nobility. These monarchies, all more or less constitutional, were usually bound together by tangled ties of German blood; when a small European country such as Rumania was looking for a suitable king, it habitually picked one with the right Teutonic pedigree. The aristocracies of Europe were more national in their marriages, but international in their meeting-places, such as London and the Quorn hunt in Leicestershire, Paris and Monte Carlo, and the spas of Marienbad and Carlsbad. There were literally no frontiers for the well-born at the opening of the twentieth century. As the Duchess di Sermoneta remembered:

Our homes and our cities seemed as safe as the ground under our feet; we could not conceive our relations with people of other nationalities being anything but polite and friendly. When we wished to travel we just bought our tickets, made our reservations, and started for any part of the globe we fancied. Passports did not exist, and we changed our money unrestrictedly into any other currency we required. . . .

I remember motoring with friends somewhere in Central Europe during the summer of 1912. The driver stopped outside a small building and we asked why. 'It's the frontier,' he answered. 'I just have to show a paper about the car.' I do not even remember what frontier it was. In those days all Europe was our playground. . . .[1]

The restless Edward VII, although corpulent and aged, personally linked the aristocracies and plutocracies of his own country and all Europe by his semi-permanent peregrinations. As Prince of Wales, he had visited more private houses than any of his predecessors, including Arundel and Badminton and Chatsworth and Dunrobin and Eaton Hall and so on through the alphabet of stately homes to Wilton. His Marlborough House set had made English society accept the new rich, especially two Jewish financiers, the Hungarian Baron de Hirsch and the German Sir Ernest Cassel, who managed the prince's finances very profitably for their owner. The Austrian ambassador may have pointed out that Baron de Hirsch was not received at the court in Vienna; but the Prince of Wales still spent twelve days on the baron's Austrian estate and took part in the largest shoot ever organized in Europe, when 11,000 partridges were killed in five days, a number of slain that would still seem impressive at the time of Verdun. Thus when he achieved the throne, Edward VII was only too glad to change the style of the monarchy. 'The Court became cosmopolitan. Gone were the German stiffness and formality,

[1] Duchess of Sermoneta, *Sparkle Distant Worlds* (London, 1947) p. 7.

gone the stern interpretation of a life lived purely as a duty, gone the perpetual mourning that had for so long obscured the crown.'[2] In France, the Marquis de Castellane might hate the 'cosmopolitanism that swept over his poor country like a great leveller', but the style of the English court was contagious. Elegant Frenchmen dressed themselves in London and sent their sons to Oxford and Cambridge, while the King's French friends, Count Greffulhe and the Marquis du Lau, Marquis Henri de Breteuil and the Marquis de Jaucourt, never missed Derby Day at Epsom. The height of male *chic* in Paris was a monocle and a light British accent and the *entrée* to the salons of Neuilly, where exiled royalty and Russian nobles lived, the Queen of Naples, the Queen of Portugal, the Princess of Brazil, the Grand Duke Paul of Russia. There Edward VII stopped on his last journey back from Biarritz to murmur to Countess Greffulhe, 'I have not long to live. Then my nephew Willy will make war.'

Yet while he was alive and king, Edward VII spent some three months a year on trips of personal diplomacy among his crowned relatives and on taking the cure at Marienbad, after sometimes earning a cure at Paris. How far Edward's preference for the French and dislike of his nephew Wilhelm II led to the Entente Cordiale between Britain and France and the increasing anti-British sentiment in Germany is a matter for debate. But certainly, the royal blood shared by the King and the Kaiser led to bad blood, although the English aristocracy still preferred to send their daughters to 'finish' their education in Germany and the German aristocracy imitated the hunting dress and habits of the English as far as they could. The Kaiser regularly shot at Lowther Castle with his friend Lord Lonsdale, the effective owner of much of the English border, the reputed discoverer of the Klondike and the only peer to knock out John L. Sullivan when heavyweight champion of the world; in return, Lonsdale was invited to watch German military manoeuvres with a blithe disregard of security risks. For aristocracy, like monarchy, was an international caste that crossed the fears of generals and nations.

[2] Consuelo Vanderbilt Balsan, *The Glitter and the Gold* (London, 1953) p. 121.

The British aristocracy was, perhaps, the most admired in Europe, because it alone seemed to retain real political power in a country that was industrialized and was called democratic. Queen Victoria had largely saved the monarchy in England by adopting a middle-class canon of morality and by disassociating herself from the excesses of the smart society of London. In fact, she had blamed her son for being corrupted by the aristocracy, comparing its behaviour to the excesses of the French aristocracy on the eve of the Revolution. But her son had defended his subordinate peers:

With regard to what you say concerning the Aristocracy or 'upper Ten Thousand', I quite agree that in many instances amusement and self-indulgence, etc., predominate, but it is hard to say that all are so. I know of so many instances where those of the highest rank are excellent country gentlemen – are Chairmen of Quarter Sessions, Magistrates, etc., and the ladies attend to their duties also. In every country a great proportion of the Aristocracy will be idle and fond of amusement and have always been so, but I think in no country more than ours do the Higher Classes occupy themselves, which is certainly not much the case in other countries. . . .[3]

The House of Lords was the unique political structure, which showed the power of the British nobility to Europe. Although the Prime Ministers of England were no longer peers as in the palmy days of Newcastle and Wellington and Palmerston and Rosebery and Salisbury, the House of Lords still had a large majority of hereditary peers, despite the increasing sale of honours to the new plutocracy. These hereditary peers could always form a large conservative majority to block any reform measure of which they disapproved. Despite the increasing victories of the Liberal Party, the conservative peerage would not compromise with the House of Commons; its vote against the Finance Bill of 1909 led to a constitutional crisis and to what the First Lord of the Admiralty called 'the first step in a revolution'. The issue, according to the radical Lloyd George, was 'whether the country is to be

[3] Quoted in Sir Sidney Lee, *King Edward VII: A Biography* (2 vols. London, 1925) I, p. 170.

governed by the King and his Peers or by the King and his People'. Although Edward VII was a firm believer in the hereditary principle, he could see that he might have to curtail the peerage to save the monarchy, although he was dead before the choice was to be forced on the Crown.

To the European aristocracy, however, the position of the House of Lords seemed enviable in Edwardian days. There was no such Second Chamber in Europe, into which a steady intake of retired politicians and successful magnates and lawyers and clerics could be introduced to leaven the lump of the hereditary peerage. In the autocracies such as Germany and Austria-Hungary, the aristocracy might control the army and many of the more honorific posts in the state; but in no other democratic country was the aristocracy so powerful or so popular. In this lay the difference between the British and the European nobility.

De Tocqueville defined the essence of a stable aristocracy when he wrote: 'Land is the basis of an aristocracy, which clings to the soil that supports it; for it is not by privileges alone, nor by birth, but by landed property handed down from generation to generation that an aristocracy is constituted. A nation may present immense fortunes and extreme wretchedness; but unless those fortunes are territorial, there is no true aristocracy, but simply the class of the rich and that of the poor.' The British aristocracy, because of its love of hunting and country houses, and because of an inherited taste for improving the land and keeping on good terms with the tenants, had clung to the soil that supported it, while the law of entail had handed down landed property from eldest male heir to eldest male heir unto the ultimate generation.

The continental aristocracy, however, had often cut itself off from its country estates to gather in a court, such as Versailles or Vienna. As de Tocqueville further noted, when discussing the end of the *ancien régime* on only one side of the Channel, England was administered as well as governed by the principal landowners, while the nobles of France had lost their powers to the Crown and had kept only their privileges, which thus became intolerable to the people. The peerage in England was tolerated because it stayed on the land and gave some services as well as receiving rents; the nobility of Europe, as the visiting English aristocrats were always pointing out, often sweated its peasants and gave little in return.

In a revealing conversation with Edward VII while he was still Prince of Wales, the French leader Gambetta had explained why he had kept the local aristocracy divorced from affairs in the Third Republic. There was, he had claimed, no longer an aristocracy in France. 'There are only dukes who have no army to lead and marquesses who are not responsible for defending any "marches"; the counts and viscounts and barons have neither land nor authority nor influence.' The nobles had no desire for employment. 'They just sulk – that is their definite occupation. They are only to be met with in the army and navy, and sometimes in the diplomatic service. In those professions they look very well. . . . As a Republic, we can have only one aristocracy, that of science and merit. It declares itself without any need of titles.' When Edward VII had reproached Gambetta for being a real republican, Gambetta had replied that he considered it logical for Edward to be a royalist.

Republicanism, however, was rare in Europe; besides France, only Switzerland and Portugal were republican at the time of the Great War. The Swiss and the French Republics were long-standing; the Republic of Portugal was five years old; the English royal yacht had saved the last King of Portugal from his refuge in Gibraltar. Elsewhere, the device of constitutional monarchy seemed to be the particular European compromise, which allowed the new forces of industrialism and mass democracy to share in power with the old monarchies and land-owning aristocracies. In return for the surrender of feudal rights, the aristocrats were confirmed in their hold on their property and in their jobs in the armed services and the diplomatic corps. Constitutional monarchy was, however, something of a hollow crown in Central and Southern and Eastern Europe; there the hereditary landowners retained much more of their traditional power than in the more industrial nations of Western Europe.

The grandees of Spain, the Magnates of Hungary, the Prussian Junkers, and the Russian nobles held a veto power over political, social and particularly land reform. Such a veto power was not even possible for the British House of Lords, which appeared more politically powerful than all other hereditary European groups, but which had to give way to Lloyd George on the issue of land reform in 1909. Significantly, in the European countries where the landowners proved most retrograde and obstructive, constitutional monarchy was to disappear after the Great War, in Russia, Austria-Hungary and Germany. Yet in the Indian summer of the old aristocracy at the turn of the century, constitutional monarchy seemed the perfect umbrella to shelter industrial power and rural privilege from the storm of class war.

The success of European civilization at the time seemed to be a proof of the virtues of its social structure. The Chinese and the Romans and the Mongols at the height of their power had held insignificant amounts of territory compared to the eighty-five per cent of the land surface of the world and all of its seas under the control of the European nations. Because of the stability of the system of alliances between European countries, forged by monarchs and aristocratic diplomats who were often blood relations, the full energy of the technology and capitalism of Europe could be devoted to the political and economic conquest of the whole world. Successful imperial powers do not question the social system at home; they vaunt it to justify their civilizing mission abroad. The European aristocracy could rightly view itself as perhaps the most *international* group in its subcontinent, which depended for its total dominance of the world on not giving way to the internecine feuds that had wrecked the previous empires of its classical models, Greece and Rome.

This imperial view of themselves as people born above the potentially fatal European diseases of nationalism and militarism gave some of the aristocrats of multi-lingual empires such as Austria-Hungary and Russia and Britain an ideal of service that made their group more tolerable in the eyes of the mass of the people. In Austria-Hungary and Russia, however, the aristocrats

showed themselves particularly inept at coping with the turbulent
forces of industrialism and nationalism; under pressure they
tended to take refuge in protocol rather than in parleys. The whole
continental aristocracy, indeed, misunderstood the methods of
retaining power used by the English nobility, even when these
methods served as models for imitation.

The most potent source of influence of the British aristocracy
was through local good works, performed by some member of
each great family in the shires in a way that would have seemed
boring and almost feudally anachronistic, even to the more
obviously feudal families of Europe. Like the thanes of old, the
English still believed in feeding the lord's followers with the
crumbs from the rich man's table. When Consuelo Vanderbilt
married the Duke of Marlborough under orders from her
mother, so as to get the family billions admitted to high society in
Europe and New York, she discovered that the leftovers from the
great feasts at Blenheim were all crammed higgledy-piggledy into
large tins for distribution to the local cottagers; the young duchess
did not end the tradition, she merely had the different scraps put
into different tins so that the grateful labourers were not eating a
hodge-podge of grouse mixed with lobster soup mixed with
kedgeree.

The Victorians did not allow their children to give to charity
without performing the charity as well. Gladstone, for instance,
did not particularly wish to go round the London streets actually
picking up fallen women to regenerate; but as he wished to help
prostitutes, his chosen rescue society insisted that he put his hand
into theirs as well as into his own pocket. Similarly, the Victorian
and Edwardian peerage sent out their daughters on errands round
the estate to play Lady Bountiful, so that there was rarely a sick or
poor cottager who did not have to suffer gladly the visits of
aristocratic women. There is hardly a female memoir of the time
which does not mention an early training in local giving, trotting
about behind a 'saint' such as the eighth Duchess of Beaufort,
while she took china jars filled with rice pudding or chicken
mince out of her basket for the local poor and deserving. These

visits could expose a child to horror with the sudden vision of how the unprivileged could live. In the memory of Cynthia Asquith, the grand-daughter of the Earl of Wemyss, were set two recurring ordeals of her childhood, regular visits to the 'village idiot', which gave her terrible nightmares, and the duty of going to the Dickensian workhouse, where she gave out tea and sugar and snuff among the 'paupers'.

The grimness of this hideous, God-denying institution was indescribable. In bare, scrubbed, carbolic-breathing rooms, furnished only with backless, wooden benches, huddled, dehumanisingly garbed, men in one ward, women in another, the incongruous, mutually antipathetic inmates, some the victims of mere mischance, others of their own follies. . . . The blankness of the bare walls was broken only by framed regulations headed in huge type by the words PUNISHMENTS FOR REFRACTORY PAUPERS. . . . The only chance of preserving any individuality was to be a physical freak. The one cheerful 'pauper' able, indeed, to cut quite a figure, was a quarter-witted man, born with a third thumb, a distinction he loved to exhibit to visitors. One had to try to counterfeit admiration, even envy, but in reality that extra thumb was an object of haunting horror to me. I used to dream my own hands had sprouted. . . .[4]

In Europe, where the nobility were far more conscious of their apartness as a caste, aristocratic children were not allowed to come into contact with their inferiors, and certainly not to serve them. As Louisa de Tuscany noted, the *éducation de prince* sacrificed Christian duty for future position. The nobility had to play at being distant idols. 'My governess persisted in saying that if Marie-Antoinette had never played at being a farmer's wife she would never have been guillotined. . . . "What will the people say? What will the people think?" That was the parrot-cry we heard from morning to night, till at last we learnt to look on the people as a sort of fetish.' That mass fetish was only to be placated by a rigid code of behaviour which did not educate noble children to live for themselves, but merely to live in the eyes of the world, distant, impeccable, gracious, unfamiliar. Charity in Europe was

[4] Cynthia Asquith, *Haply I May Remember* (London, 1950) pp. 35-6.

the donation through a servant of the proceeds of a charity ball, where the family jewels and decorations were trotted out on the excuse of raising money for the unfortunate. Giving was done with great display and little contact.

The direct communication between the English aristocrats and the people was strengthened in two other ways, through unpaid local public service and through sport. While the royal families of Europe had engrossed all justice in the hands of the king's servants in order to destroy the local power of the aristocracy, the English and Scots and Irish gentry and nobility, both male and female, found themselves endlessly serving as Justices of the Peace or chairmen of some local committee or fund.

A perceptive American observer of England in 1909 declared:

The enormous amount of unpaid and voluntary service to the state, and to one's neighbours, in England, results in the solution of one of the most harassing problems of every wealthy nation: it arms the leisured classes with something worthy, something important to do. . . . When a man has made wealth and leisure for himself, or inherited them from others, he is deemed a renegade if he does not promptly offer them as willing sacrifice upon the altar of his country's welfare.

These observations may have represented only the ideal of English social life, but the important thing was that this was the ideal. Certainly, as so many of the aristocrats spent so much of their time in the countryside, their services there to the community were particularly noticed, although they lost contact almost completely with the growing industrial cities, despite occasional forays into social work in the slums of the East End of London to salve their consciences.

Yet it was sport, perhaps, and particularly racing, which gave the British aristocrats some bond with their countrymen. Over and over again, the memoirs of the time declare that the sporting Lord Lonsdale was the most popular man in England, whether presenting Lonsdale belts to boxers, leading in his racing winners, or waltzing with the costermongers' wives after their annual

[5] Quoted from Price Collier, *England and the English*, in *Edwardian England*, ed. Simon Nowell-Smith (Oxford, 1964) p. 36.

donkey races. Edward VII, whose identification with smart Society alienated some of the important conservative opinion that his mother had attracted by her strait-laced behaviour and old age, won perhaps even more popular support by the mere chance of leading in his third Derby winner as king. Of course, when sport meant the depopulation of vast areas to make game preserves by such peers as the Dukes and Duchesses of Sutherland in the nineteenth century, hatred of the aristocracy was the result, the sort of loathing with which Lloyd George used to attack the Scottish dukes and large landlords, stating that 'tens of thousands of people are turned out of their homes in order to get sport.' Sport, however, outside the unlovely methods sometimes used to make way for it, was a British national obsession and a common bond between monarch, peerage and people. As G. K. Chesterton rightly observed, the English workman then was less interested in the equality of men than in the inequality of horses.

In Europe, however, the aristocrats treated sport more as a private pleasure like the Scots dukes than as a public attraction. No European population shared in the British obsession. Thus enclosure for the purpose of racing or shooting or hunting seemed merely a despotic withdrawal of prospective farming-land from the market. Europeans could not justify their fox-hunting as Irish landlords did, by claiming that the hunt brought a great deal of local business to the area as well as destroying a pest; anyway, every Irishman surely loved a good hunter to back in the jumping-races. In the absence of this public sympathy for aristocratic sport, the Europeans sometimes seemed to be hunting people as much as birds and beasts. During the tyranny of the Magyar aristocracy in the last days of the Austro-Hungarian Empire, Bartha's *In the Land of the Kazars* gives some idea of what aristocratic hunting meant to the peasant.

The hunting periods last two weeks. There come some of the Schwarzenbergs, of the Kolowrats, of the Liechtensteins. . . . They tell each other of their hunting adventures, it was so last year, it was so the year before, . . . so will it be in the future. . . .

In order that they should tell each other all this in the smoke of

excellent Havana cigars in the flickering light of the fire-place, 70,000
Ukrainians must be doomed to starvation by the army of officials. . . .
The deer and the wild boar destroy the corn, the oats, the potato, and
the clover of the Ukrainian. . . . Their whole yearly work is destroyed.
. . . The people sow and the deer of the estate harvest. . . .

It is easy to say that the peasant should complain . . . but where and
to whom?

As that able German commentator Joachim von Dissow has
noted, it is almost impossible to exaggerate the significance which
hunting played in the life of all the European aristocracy. Until
the First World War, hunting formed an important international
link between the powerful aristocrats of the European nations.
The majority of statesmen, monarchs, ministers and ambassadors
all practised hunting – just as so many now try their hand at golf.
Despite political differences, these national leaders were bound to
each other by the freemasonry of the chase and a certain preference
for killing lesser animals in each other's company rather than killing
each other apart. From the time of Bismarck to Edward VII, important political discussions would take place during the hunt or the
shoot. The lodge could be even more important than the court.

As this was so, and as England had a great deal of power and
prestige as well as fine hunting, many of the European nobles
liked to come to England to practise their favourite and most
advantageous sport. Count Alfred Potocki, the last master of the
huge Polish estate of Lancut, tried to sum up the attraction
England held for the sporting nobility of the time. Both his
parents thought of England 'as a welcome extension of their life
at Lancut'; they were enthusiastic riders to hounds and made yearly
trips to hunt with the Quorn, the Pytchley and the Cottesmore.
Here they would meet, according to Lady Augusta Fane, a select
group of rich Americans, one of whom had married the Polish
Count Zborowski and lived locally; also present were the
Austro-Hungarian Counts Kinsky and Count Széchényi and
Count Larische, 'the owner of vast estates in Hungary, where he
was treated like a king . . . in England he was very simple,
unostentatious, and enjoyed a quiet visit to his old friends'. From

France came Prince Louis de Bourbon, the Count de Jametel looking for a local *héritière* to marry, and the Countess de Clermont-Tonnerre, who once lost her apron when falling off her horse and was too modest to think of catching her mount in breeches alone. English hunting was an international game.

For Count Potocki's family, England 'was a pattern for Polish patriots, particularly those with agrarian and political ideals. She was strong and free. Great wealth was created by the Industrial Revolution and the wise administration of her overseas Empire. Some of it went to enlarge the great country estates and to maintain a style of life similar to that lived by the Polish nobility. In the mirror of England, men like my grandfather saw the vision of a free and prosperous Poland to come.'[6] Yet however faithfully the Counts Potocki thought they were reflecting the image of England, 'a second home' to them, the English nobles who visited Lancut were somewhat shocked to see the local conditions there, with starving peasants kissing their master's riding boots as he went by on his mount, and footmen made to sleep in the corridor outside each guest's room, in case something was wanted in the middle of the night.

The differences between the British and the European aristocracies before the Great War were the differences between a class and a caste. The British aristocracy had retained real political power; the price it had paid was to make entry into the peerage relatively easy for the rich and the nationally successful. In Europe, the aristocracy had lost real political power; even such a powerful caste as the Prussian Junkers had given up all power not amenable to army influence, in order to retain the economic and social privileges of a closed caste. The Junkers preferred the righteousness of remaining outside the evolution of the modern Germany begun by Bismarck, because they did not like his fellow helpers in the business of empire – industrialists, intellectuals, liberals, bankers and Jews. The British aristocrats, however, much preferred the substance of political power to the shadow of pure pedigree. After all, it was Disraeli who had led the Tory party

[6] Count Alfred Potocki, *Master of Lancut* (London, 1959) p. 17.

into imperialism around the figure of the Queen, and who had ended as Earl of Beaconsfield, while it was Edward VII who had put the stamp of court approval on the actual ruling powers of England, the combination of the new plutocracy and old aristocracy. As the acute author of *London Society in the New Reign* observed, there had never really been an antagonism between old acres and new wealth; but the King's accession had 'completed the social sovereignty of wealth over every class in the land'.

As the ruling monarchies of the European countries very much set the fashion for their respective nobilities, the behaviour of court and country house in Edwardian England was very different from that in the contemporary German and Austro-Hungarian Empires, and it illustrated perfectly the differences between the various nobilities. English society at this time had split into numerous sets and groups; those who were allowed to join one set did not gain admission to all. The King's example gave favoured plutocrats the *entrée* to most drawing-rooms, but not to the haunts of the traditionalist Spencers and Cadogans, the last rearguard against the new ways. And in the country houses where the amorous King stayed, decorum was merely the dressing-gown to the naked truth. After the long shooting days, gambling at cards was obligatory until the King decided to go to bed after midnight ; the King, a great stickler for official observances, insisted that nobody should go to bed before him. But in the arrangement of which bedroom should be next to which, hostesses had to be sure to get the elaborate protocol of gossip correct; as an affair ripened, the weekend bedrooms of the lovers grew closer. Lady de Grey noted that pictures of lovers now adorned the mantelpieces of noble women; husbands lay hidden in drawers.

Such behaviour shocked the Germans. Daisy, Princess of Pless, had lunch with the most frequent hostess of Edward VII, Alice Keppel, before leaving for the formal Court of Berlin. She could not believe her ears when three or four of the ladies present declared openly that they had had several lovers. On the other hand, English visitors like Sir Frederick Ponsonby to the Kaiser's court in 1909 found it ludicrous to see German officers dancing minuets; but, as the Emperor explained to him, 'people did not come to a court ball to amuse themselves but to learn deportment.' Both Edward VII and the Kaiser very much cared about the proper dress on the proper occasion; but the English King would merely make an acid remark such as the fact that Lord Haldane's hat looked as though it had belonged to Goethe, while the German Emperor would have his relative the Prince von Anhalt put under arrest for a fortnight for going to a party in plain clothes rather than in uniform. Despite the Eulenburg scandals, which revealed homosexuality in court circles, the royal standard in Germany was as prim as the Victorian one had been in England.

The hierarchy of caste ruled Middle Europe before the Great War, totally in the royal capitals and constrictingly in rural districts. It was at its most extreme in Vienna, where sometimes the nobility could be even more rigid than the Emperor himself. Franz Josef of Austria might elevate twenty-five Jewish families in Hungary to baronial rank and he might consent to receive the leading Rothschild at court because of exemplary services to the state, but the Austrian nobility was horrified. It was the most distinguished in Europe from the point of view of pedigree, with its genealogical roots spreading over all Europe, from Russia to France, from Sweden to Italy, from Scotland to Spain. With this impeccable background of inbreeding, it did not feel the British need to include or expand. The shrewd Virginio Gayda found Viennese high society at this time 'fused into a disdainful little circle, closely bound to the court in time of need, impassive and indifferent to the changing times, unfriendly and opposed to things and people foreign to its kingdom'. When Viscountess Barrington visited pre-war Vienna, she noted that 'no other European country could have maintained in the early days of this century the pride of rank and class distinction which were found in the Austrian capital'.

For the Emperor to receive a Rothschild was a rarity. The court at Vienna was the most rigid in Europe with an etiquette best suited for mummies; normally, no one was admitted whose noble pedigree did not stretch back for fourteen generations. As

John Lothrop Motley observed, when he was American
ambassador in Vienna: 'An Austrian might be Shakespeare,
Galileo, Nelson, and Raphael in one person; he would not
be received in good society if he did not possess the sixteen
quarterings of nobility which birth alone can give him.' For fear
of not being recognized as part of the noble caste, the Austrian
aristocrats all imitated each other like well-bred monkeys. They
had the same way of walking slowly with bent shoulders and of
talking with the right drawl; they loved play and frivolity and the
same jokes; they even had the same profile, so that their frequent
gatherings in their great houses in Vienna or in their castles in the
country were occasions when each noble Narcissus could look
round the faces in the ballroom and see nothing but repeated
variations upon himself.

The Austrian nobility had remained very rich and very isolated,
which did something to explain the careless happiness of their
lives. All great families had a country castle surrounded by a
hunting forest. If agriculture was not an aristocratic passion as in
England, hunting seemed to be a hereditary need. The Habsburgs
were even meant to have chosen Vienna for their capital because
of the superb stags of the neighbourhood. No castle was complete
without its soaring walls covered with thousands of skulls and
branching antlers, a fair commentary on the noble love of the
chase of deer and women. As for work or contact with the people,
there was very little. 'The Austrian aristocracy,' Gayda wrote in
1915, 'contents itself very often with being merely a magnificent,
leisured race; not only great wealth but small minds full of arrogance and prejudice abound within it; it resembles a golden
casket heavily set with diamonds and perfectly empty.'

Yet this irrelevant nobility retained incredible feudal power
with little responsibility. Some of the family properties in the
Austro-Hungarian Empire were small kingdoms. The Esterházy
princes held 735,000 acres in Hungary; the Schwarzenbergs
possessed 360,000 acres in Southern Bohemia including twelve
castles and five thousand peasant families; the Liechtensteins,
the Pallavicinis, the Károlyis, the Andrássys, and twenty other

families had more than 250,000 acres apiece. The great Hungarian Magnates may have been more concerned in the actual business of government and less exclusive than the Austrian and Bohemian nobility; but they were just as autocratic and feudal on their own estates. If these princelings had cultivated their lands or had been concerned about their peasants' welfare, the situation might have been tolerable; but, in fact, they preferred the chase and acted like Taine's aristocrats who 'protected wild beasts as if they were men, and persecuted men as if they were wild beasts.' A systematic depopulation of the villages coincided with the increase of the game preserves; a wider gulf grew between the peasants who remained and their masters, whom they hardly saw.

The income of the Austrian government from the land tax dropped by one-fifth in the decade after 1893, while enclosures for hunting grew and the nobility refused to pay its fair share of taxes. A few aristocrats went into business and became even more hated as monopolists, particularly in the Sugar Cartel; but most stayed near the court or on their estates, caste-bound in the armour of privilege, more and more hated and envied and isolated and exposed. 'What esteem can this nobility pretend to,' Princess Catherine Radziwill asked, 'when it is hardly able to read and write, when it has learnt nothing and still believes itself in an age when it was sufficient to have had ancestors to be feared and considered?'

Yet the true degeneration of the contacts between the privileged and the people of Europe was best shown in the ceremony of the Lavatorio during Holy Week at Madrid. Then the King of Spain received twelve beggars in the Royal Palace and washed their feet in front of twelve of the Spanish dukes, each carrying a tray of food for the beggars to eat. In more Catholic times, the beggars had been real enough; but the stench of their unwashed feet had so nauseated the King that now he only washed the feet of the best-scrubbed beggars in Madrid. They were not even allowed to eat their meal in front of the charitable dukes, as tradition demanded; the trays were now whisked away with the food untouched; it was then put into parcels to be carried home by the beggars. So the Lavatorio had declined into a mere parade of humility, designed to spare the King and the dukes a maximum of discomfort and tedium. It was no more full of true Christian purpose than a cross made of gold and diamonds.

There were exceptions to the rule of caste among the European nobility. Some Middle European aristocrats had the patriarchal informality of the Bavarian Count von Loewenstein-Scharffeneck, who felt a particular bond between himself and his peasants, although he was related to every ruling house in Europe. His son's autobiography gives a clear indication of how far apart some of the old German nobles felt from the forces making modern Europe, and how much they clung to a nostalgic tie with place and past and people who knew how to defer to them.

My father was on friendly terms with the peasants. There was no celebration of any kind in the village at which he was not present. He drank and threw dice with them, and listened to all their stories of personal pleasures and grievances. One of the fundamental principles of my education was: 'Only one class is related to, though not equal to, the nobility – the peasants; of course only as long as they acknowledge the nobles as their masters and do not rebel!'

Of the working classes it was said that they were 'red', and always in revolt against the landowners, the monarchy, and the Church; therefore they were profoundly evil, and it was an absolute necessity that they should be kept in subjection. Still – as my father used to say in later years – they are better than the commercial classes. Those were the worst of all. They were without exception criminals – and were bound to be so from the nature of their calling. 'Why?' I asked him once when I was ten years old. 'That's very simple,' he replied. 'The rascals make their living by selling dearer than they buy. Is that honest?'[7]

The British aristocracy, however, knew that its only chance of surviving as a real power lay in joining with the leaders of the commercial classes. In a nation of shopkeepers the biggest merchant is the lord – or can soon expect to be. Between 1886 and 1914, some two hundred people entered for the first time the ex-

[7] Prince Hubertus Loewenstein, *Conquest of the Past* (London, 1938) pp. 17-18.

clusive set of fewer than six hundred peers already entitled by
hereditary right to sit in the House of Lords. Less than a quarter
of these new peers came from the old landed families, more than a
third represented industrial wealth, while another third had
ennobled themselves through the law or service in the Empire or
in the armed forces. Never more than one in three of the new
peers bothered to acquire country estates, something which had
been obligatory in the early nineteenth century. And even hereditary peers who owned great estates were selling off large areas to
tenant farmers in order to invest in the new industrial wealth of
England. As early as 1896, more than one peer in four was lending
the prestige of his title to the board of a company in return for his
director's fees; the great promoter, E. T. Hooley, bought titled
names on to the boards of his companies by bribing the noble
lords for cash down.[8]

Not only was the English peerage open to new recruits from
industry and government service, but it also liked to help its
finances by marrying heiresses and its looks by marrying actresses. While the closed caste of the European nobility often
scoffed at such common and dilute aristocracy, the British peerage
shrewdly sought for new millions and new blood. When Consuelo Vanderbilt married the Duke of Marlborough at the
command of her mother, she knew perfectly well his purpose in
this marriage of convenience. Marlborough even brought over an
English lawyer to negotiate the marriage settlements; his later
wife wrote that the lawyer 'who had crossed the seas with the
declared intention of "profiting the illustrious family" he had
been engaged to serve devoted a natural talent to that end'. Her
dowry was calculated at two million pounds sterling. Other
British peers sought their fortunes in American marriages,
especially after Edward VII had shown a decided preference for
ladies of American background, murmuring that he thought the
American women could all teach the English duchesses manners.

[8] For details on the financial affairs of the English aristocracy, I am indebted to
F. M. L. Thompson's excellent work, *English Landed Society in the Nineteenth
Century* (London, 1963).

'Failing the dowries of Israel and the plums of the United States,' one observer wrote, 'the British peerage would go to pieces tomorrow.' He even hinted that there should be a tariff on American heiresses and rich German Jewesses, to prevent too much export of capital from their countries of origin.

Only in France in the nineteenth century was there a parallel rush of nobles after rich foreign heiresses. In the Belle Epoque, three princes, five dukes, three marquesses, fifteen counts, and four barons married between them twenty-nine American heiresses with known dowries totalling at least $28,000,000 – an average of nearly a million dollars a head to acquire a French title. In the scandalous case of Anna Gould, whose first dowry was variously estimated at anything from $12,000,000 to six times that sum, her second husband the Prince de Sagan had to fight for her like an *apache* in the gutter with her first husband, Count Boni de Castellane. As Miss Gould's marriage contract kept her fortune separate from her husband's, and as she refused to marry him in a Catholic church because it was too difficult to divorce him in case she was unhappy, de Castellane had a lot to lose, and lost it. Usually, the American heiresses were no innocents abroad. If they were marrying titles, they knew they were being married for their money and took care to protect their chief asset.

The unique contribution of the British peerage to the history of Europe has been its ability to compromise with changing times instead of resisting them. Almost alone of the feudal classes of Europe, the hereditary British aristocracy has kept real power by incorporating the newly powerful. It first recognized the industrialists on both sides of the Atlantic by giving them titles and marrying their daughters, an example followed by the French. Now it seemed to recognise the beginning of the communications revolution that would make actors the fleeting aristocracy of the industrial masses, and it began to marry actresses frequently. In the thirty years before 1914, fifteen British peers and four peers' eldest sons married on to the stage; their wives included Belle Bilton, Rosie Boote, Sylvia Storey, and Camille Clifford of the Gibson Girls; in all the centuries before, only eleven peers had married players. And finally the British peerage still had a real imperial role to play that gave it a world-wide influence and experience far beyond the range possible to most of the European aristocracy.

The Governors-General of the Dominions had to be peers, preferably hereditary in origin. The Viceroy of India had also to bear a title, so that he could equal in importance the Maharajahs. The peers in imperial service learned a terrible sense of control and duty that was rare in Europe. What German princeling had the power of Lord Curzon over hundreds of millions of Indians, or could call on a subcontinent to try his record with the words, 'Let India be my judge?' What Italian count could reply as Lord Cromer did to the complaint that he did not look after the old Egyptian aristocracy, 'That is not true . . . I do look after them, for most of them are at this moment in jail?' Of course this imperial hauteur could be returned, as when the Indian prince Victor Duleep Singh referred to Queen Victoria as 'Mrs Fagin' for receiving the Koh-i-noor diamond stolen from his family.

Much of the British aristocracy before 1914 was useful and used, locally and nationally and imperially. Much of the European aristocracy at this time was better bred and worse employed. This erosion of political power seemed almost a wilful form of hara-kiri. 'It never occurred to me in those days,' wrote Prince Hubertus Loewenstein, 'to wonder what was my father's profession. When I was still quite young I was taught that decent people did not need any. Only a plebeian follows a profession; a gentleman passes his time – my father used to say – by being either a diplomatist, an officer, or simply himself.' The armed forces and diplomatic corps of the European monarchies were, indeed, more aristocratic than those of Britain, which had an upper middle-class foreign service and officer corps outside the Brigade of Guards. Yet with such restricted avenues for opportunity, how could the European aristocrats be expected to make careers without offending the rigid conventions of their caste? They could merely sneer at the British peers for not being true aristocrats at all, their quarterings dubious although their arrogant hold over one-quarter of the globe was undubitable. Yet such imperial greediness was hardly noble. As Montrond told the Duchess de Duras, the animal that most resembled man was the Englishman.

The boorishness of the British peerage at this time was rightly despised in Europe. Outside the small circle of the 'Souls' and their children, an aristocratic circle which put politics and wit above hunting and wealth, the peerage followed the invincible philistinism of the House of Hanover and Saxe-Coburg-Gotha. Even if it did not imitate the Marquess of Queensberry in hounding Oscar Wilde to prison, it ostracised Wilde completely when he came out; Lord Alfred Douglas, however, was partially forgiven for his title. Since Charles II, no cultured king interested in the arts had sat on the throne; all Edward VII's good manners could not disguise his lack of learning. He found an apple-pie bed funnier than a *bon mot*, shaving-soap on someone's trifle wittier than oral froth. He feared intellectuals, perhaps because kings do not like feeling inferior to anyone; such brilliant politicians as Lord Rosebery and Lord Salisbury took care to talk racing and diplomacy and gossip in the royal presence. The peerage, too, preferred to remain comfortably in complacent ignorance. 'As a class, we did not like brains,' confessed Frances, Countess of Warwick. 'We acknowledged that it was necessary that pictures should be painted, books written, the law administered; we even acknowledged that there was a certain stratum whose job it might be to do these things. But we did not see why their achievements entitled them to our recognition.'

The contrast with the attitude of society in the Proustian world of the *Remembrance of Things Past* is blatant. Proust may have written at the end of his masterpiece that he 'had frequented people in society enough to know that it is they who are the veritable unlettered, not the working electricians'. But at least Proust's well-born and ill-educated socialites paid lip-service to art and literature and music. The Duchess de Guermantes knew enough to adore Balzac along with other fashionable lesser fry. Even Wilhelm II of Germany insisted on writing ballets as well as

trying to run the German navy; he wanted a finger in every pie
to pull out the aristocratic plum. Consuelo, Duchess of Marlborough, could sneer at the thoroughbred aristocratic Austrians
'like greyhounds, with their long lean bodies and small heads',
who were generally more educated than intelligent and who
expressed 'their thoughts in so many different languages when
they had so few thoughts to express'. But, at least, the Austrian
nobles were educated and multi-lingual in a Habsburg Empire that
needed multi-lingual talents. They had the tools of learning, even
if they sometimes lacked the innate skills needed to use those tools.
The British aristocracy of the period did not even bother to learn
its own language well, let alone anyone else's; an invincible
insularity led it to make a virtue out of its ignorance by claiming
that a sportsman was a better chap than a swot.

Yet if there were differences between the British and the European aristocracies, these differences could be reversed for individual
cases. There were vile English landlords, particularly in Ireland,
and progressive democratic large land-holders in Europe, particularly among the Scandinavian aristocracy. Three-quarters of the
British peerage remained very much on their estates and were
called, because of infrequent attendance in the House of Lords,
'backwoods peers'; while all the ambitious nobility in Germany
and Austria-Hungary and Russia expected a state job and rank.
There is hardly a Russian novel of the turn of the century which
does not deal with poor aristocrats jockeying for status and
power at St Petersburg. Where an alliance with industry did
not offer the way to recoup falling agricultural income as in
Britain, court influence and intrigue was the best method to
achieve a sinecure and a steady salary in cash.

Fundamentally, the monarchies and the aristocracies and the
Roman Catholic Church were among the last international
groupings left in the increasing nationalism of Europe. As Count
Alfred Potocki wrote, 'The European nobility, linked by ties of
blood or marriage, was in effect a big family, sharing interests
which overcame national prejudices and political antagonisms.
The Austrian Empire provided a perfect example of this state of

affairs. Most of the great families in its constituent countries, though representing different and often conflicting national policies in Vienna, were on terms of friendship.'[9] That friendship was evident in the travelling habits of the aristocrats, who passed much of their time abroad outside their favourite watering-places and inside the palaces of cousins, who had to be visited.

As mass nationalism grew in each country, the aristocrats prided themselves on their superior position in the international class of the nobility which recognized no boundaries outside those of pedigree. The hereditary landowners were on their estates before the wars of kings and religions had made a mockery of ancient frontiers. The Holy Roman Empire had no political existence in the twentieth century, but it still possessed its nobles, who were also meant to be German or Austrian or Italian. In fact, although not as consciously perceptive as the Nobleman in George Bernard Shaw's *Saint Joan*, the European aristocracy had a suspicion that overmighty nationalism might be its downfall. Just as the kings of Europe had once used the urban middle classes to break down the authority of the feudal barons, so the national states might use the conscript industrial masses to break down the old international freemasonry of the surviving aristocrats. 'Men cannot serve two masters,' Shaw's Nobleman said to his Chaplain. 'If this cant of serving their country once takes hold of them, goodbye to the authority of their feudal lords, and goodbye to the authority of the Church. That is, goodbye to you and me.'

Despite increasing strikes and class hatred, European society at the beginning of this century still seemed too stable to be destroyed even by a war between the nations. For the strategists on the General Staffs of Europe planned only on the contingency of a *short* war, like the German ones of 1866 against Austria and 1870 against France. A long war, which might break down the social order, had not been fought in Europe since the time of the French Revolution and Napoleon; and then the French had lost, with the disease of republicanism contained within the boundaries of that unlucky country. The French aristocracy was, indeed, in a curious

[9] *Master of Lancut*, p. 29.

position, unique among the powers of Europe. There was no French monarchy, and the House of France itself imitated the lax English peerage by being above 'the narrow prejudicing of the Almanach de Gotha.' Thus the French aristocracy, deprived of the principle of hereditary monarchy, had to be even more rigid in its manners to distinguish itself from the republicans who beset it. In France, therefore, the most exaggerated form of the psychology of aristocracy that linked many of the landowners of Europe could be seen, a combination of outward arrogance and of hidden fear towards the people which only showed itself in extreme situations.

The curious story of the Duke de Caderousse, whose mad tricks were the talk of Paris before he died young, displays the aristocrat's contempt and terror of the inevitable growth of democracy better than anything else, because he was unbalanced enough to act out the obsessions of his class. As he stepped out of his carriage in front of the Café Anglais, he let a gold louis fall in the mud. He then stopped a ragged man and told him that, if he could pick up the louis in his teeth, he could keep it. The man knelt, grubbed with his face in the mud, bit at the louis, and stood up, furious at his humiliation. The Duke de Caderousse then declared that the man must hate him for being made to get the gold coin in such a way. Yes, the man said, the duke was a pig who ought to be killed as in the French Revolution. The duke agreed with him, but added that he did not wish to die just yet. However, to relieve the man's feelings, he held up a thousand-franc note and offered it to the man, if the other would hit him as hard as possible in the face. 'I deserve it,' the duke said. The man split the duke's mouth open and knocked him into the gutter. The duke rose, gave the man the note, bowed low and thanked him with the words, 'Perfect. Good evening and good appetite, my friend.' He then joined his guests, including the Prince Napoleon, in the Café Anglais and fainted in front of them, his face dripping blood.

This arrogance towards inferiors usually expressed only in the humiliation of waiters and servants, this love of violence

usually displayed only by the massacre of beasts and birds, this
morbid wish for a final bloody solution to a potential class struggle
so evident in the behaviour of the aristocracy on the eve of the
Great War, rarely came into the open. For the aristocratic ideal of
behaviour had as its premier virtue, control of self. '*What* are
nerves?' an old Sicilian princess said to the Duchess di Sermoneta.
'Just want of manners!' However far the actual aristocrats fell
from the ideal of *noblesse oblige*, that code was still taught to their
children, with its requirements of dignity and taste and restraint,
with its sense of hierarchy and tradition and due place in the
works of God and man. Yet perhaps none of the aristocracies of
Europe before 1914 could match the fierce pride of position of the
Spanish *hidalgos*, whose poverty left them with nothing but a
fanatical devotion to rank and the Catholic Church, so that they
seemed involved in a veritable crusade for the illusion of privilege
in a country stripped of all imperial grandeur and left only with its
Quixotic illusions.

According to a shrewd contemporary observer, the code of
manners of the high society of the time was so recognizable that it
permeated both sides of the Atlantic, let alone the Channel:

Good breeding is an absolute Freemasonry, and although an Obolensky
may not hold the same theories of life as a Stanley, his outward bearing
will be essentially the same and only differ in small and insignificant
matters of detail. So, say a Jay, or a Winthrop, or a Willing, or a
Crowinshield, or a Stuyvesant will be recognized at once as one of
themselves, say by a Douglas-Hamilton, a Chimay, a Colonna, or a
Furstemburg [*sic*], and so on. They all belong to the same family with
only mere insignificant surface differences.[10]

That international family learned how to recognize and imitate
each other at certain places at certain times. Even the insular and
superior English were forced by their overeating to migrate to
the fashionable continental watering places. 'Dinners of eleven
courses were the order of the day,' one aristocratic memoir pointed
out, 'and it would be difficult to realize now, when three or four

[10] J. O. Field, *Uncensored Recollections* (London, 1924) p. 333.

courses are considered sufficient, how society could tolerate and partake of, without serious injury to gastric organs, this extravagant form of living. No wonder that Homburg, Kissingen and Carlsbad became a necessary aftermath of the London season.' And Marienbad, too, when Edward VII went there. Alain Resnais' brilliant filming of Robbe-Grillet's script of *Marienbad* caught all the baroque formality and amorous intrigue of the place in its heyday; it only missed the frenzied courting of nobility which always took place. The English King liked to pretend he was *incognito* there in order to repair his health and pursue the many adventuresses who were pretending to take the cure because most of the wealthy men in Europe were really taking the cure. But everyone recognized the King of England wherever he went and begged for introductions or decorations; in his wake, he brought along the Kings of Greece and Bulgaria, and all of the nobles and politicians who needed his goodwill. 'Really there was very little difference essentially, between Marienbad and the vomitorium of the Romans,' comments one of Vita Sackville-West's characters. 'How strange that eating should play so important a part in social life!'

Edward VII also made Biarritz fashionable, although it never rivalled the notoriety of Monte Carlo. The Casino there had been opened in 1871 by an émigré from Baden-Baden, when the new German Empire had swallowed up local autonomy and had imposed laws against gambling. It was the Casino or 'devil's palace' that made Monte Carlo the centre of the most luxurious part of the international aristocracy and *demi-monde*. The greatest gamblers were the Russian Grand Dukes, Alexis and Vladimir, soon to be followed after the Great War by the Grand Duchess Anastasia, who preferred the informality of Monte Carlo to the rigid behaviour of her German husband's Court. Gambling brought every travelling aristocrat in Europe to Monte Carlo at one time or another, and gambling attracted Otéro and Cléo de Mérode and the other great *cocottes* of the time. Gold plaques worth five pounds were used at the tables until 1914 in deference to the heavy betting of the most numerous players, the English.

'These finely engraved coins made one feel so rich,' Lady Augusta
Fane wrote in nostalgia; 'paper money does not give at all the
same feeling of wealth. There was such a jolly rattle and glitter
when the golden counters were pushed to one by the croupier's
rake.'

In the last few years before the Great War, the jolly rattle and
glitter of the life of the international aristocracy gave an even jollier
death-rattle as the glitter grew. A curious prescience of approaching disaster seemed to make the aristocrats behave in a more
feverish and conspicuous manner than before. In England, this
'vortex of gaiety' sucked all society into a round of lavish hospitality and extravagance, while fear of the future even made the
gay Edward VII prophesy just before his death in 1910, 'My son
may reign, but my grandson never will.' The money for this last
spree was realized by the largest unforced land sale in recent
British history. Fearful of rising death duties and supertax and
Lloyd George's popular assaults on the 'land monopoly', some
800,000 ancestral acres were put up for sale in the five years before
1914; the sales raised the sum of £20,000,000. Such a wholesale
dispersal of estates by what seemed to be the most stable aristocracy
in Europe could only have been an indication of its terrors.
Violence in English social and political life grew even after the
capitulation of the House of Lords to the Commons in 1911,
when the Liberal government had the new King's promise to
create as many peers as necessary to overcome the Conservative
majority in the Lords. By this politic promise, George V seemed
ready to save the hereditary monarchy even at the cost of shopping
the principle of a hereditary peerage.

Moreover, the many strikes of seamen, dockers, miners and
railwaymen against working conditions often had peers as their
targets, because the aristocracy had become heavily involved in
owning large companies. On one notorious occasion, Ben Tillett
got a meeting of strikers on Tower Hill to repeat after him, 'Oh
God, strike Lord Davenport dead.' Even the ladies so venerated
in pre-war times could descend to arson, suicide and other crimes
in their search for votes for women. The militant suffragists

were already fighting a war in time of peace; as one of them wrote, 'The suffrage campaign was our Eton and Oxford, our regiment, our ship.' Undoubtedly, the Liberals' attack on the peers fanned the flames of militancy both among the proletariat and the suffragists. And when the Lords prevented the passage of a Home Rule Bill for Ireland in 1912, they seemed deliberately to be provoking anarchy across the Irish Sea during the two years of their delaying power, more to protect the landed interests of their relations in Ireland than to save the Protestant minority in Ulster. As Sir Edward Carson armed his Ulster Volunteers for the show-down against Home Rule, he found himself supported by what Margot Asquith called 'all the brains of all the landlords in Ireland, backed by half the brains of half the landlords in England'. An Irish Civil War initiated by the 'Orange aristocracy' of Ulster was postponed only by the opening of the European conflict.

On the eve of the Great War, England was not alone in suffering from social turmoil. Both of the other great polyglot empires, Austria-Hungary and Russia, were racked by internal dissension. In Austria-Hungary, this inner malaise was a direct cause of its mobilization against Serbia – the first step in the eventual march towards world war. The Habsburg Empire had long conducted a weak foreign policy as a reflection of its internal dissensions; now it wanted a strong foreign policy as a compensation for those dissensions. On Machiavelli's principle of conducting wars abroad to bring about peace at home, the old rulers at Vienna had come to the desperate verdict summed up in the phrase, 'Better a terrible end than an endless terror.' The octogenarian Emperor Franz Josef was heavily under the influence of the anti-Russian Prince von Montenuovo, who supported the German alliance at all costs. Moreover, the foreign minister Count Berchtold was quite arrogant enough to force war on Serbia to save the Austrian monarchy and aristocracy, for he was what Princess Catherine Radziwill called him, 'the perfect type of an Austrian aristocrat – proud, haughty, and more or less convinced that the Almighty, in creating him, had had some quite special views and intentions as to his future'.

The trouble with the court circles of the Habsburgs was that, in reality, Berlin and Budapest had to agree with Vienna before any foreign policy could be pursued. Because Austria-Hungary was a dual monarchy, Budapest had the right to influence diplomacy and the powerful Count Tisza, who became Prime Minister of Hungary in 1913, made the wishes of the Magyar gentry and aristocracy the most powerful internal influence in the Habsburg Empire.

Tisza was a conservative and a sincere believer in the historic mission of the Magyar nobility, which numbered one out of ten persons in Hungary, and which had most of the pretension and none of the spirit of compromise of the British aristocracy. Although only six per cent of the Hungarian population was represented in parliament, Tisza worked against both democratic reform and unity under the Habsburgs. He wanted the Magyar landowners to continue in their traditional role as the oppressors of the ten million non-Magyars beneath them, Slovaks and Germans and Rumanians and Ukrainians and Serbo-Croats, while they should also represent true Hungarian patriotism against all comers, including the power of the Habsburgs. Tisza thus sought to use the Magyar nobility to prevent an alliance between the Habsburgs and the oppressed peasant minorities of Hungary; equally, he wanted to buttress the nobility against any effort by Germany and Russia to dismember Hungary in the name of pan-Germanism or pan-Slavism.

Thus briefly before the Great War, a champion of aristocracy in Budapest played a vital role in the initial Austrian decision to mobilize against Serbia, after the assassination of the Archduke Franz Ferdinand at Sarajevo. Tisza knew of Austria's long-standing desire to destroy Serbia and he only reluctantly agreed to go to war because of pressure from Berlin, since he clearly saw that aristocratic Hungary had to lean heavily on aristocratic Prussia to survive against its dangerous partner, Austria, and more dangerous enemy, Russia, the eternal friend of the Slavs. But Tisza did finally accept the war; as he wrote three weeks after the outbreak of hostilities:

Twenty bitter years I was oppressed by the idea that this Monarchy, and with it the Magyar nation, were doomed, for the Lord means to destroy those whom he deprives of reason. During the last few years things began to take a turn for the better. Again and again joyous events awakened a hope of new life: a hope that history will not after all coldly dismiss us. Now, in these momentous days, the decision will be reached.[11]

Thus the leader of Hungary allowed the Habsburg monarchy to bring on 'its mortal crisis to prove that it was still alive'.

Aristocratic reaction also played a minor, but significant, role along with pan-Slavism, when Russia decided to mobilize in 1914 on the side of Serbia. The Tsar had a passionate belief in the sanctity of his own autocracy, and, although he had had to concede various powers to the Duma after the Revolution of 1905, he was always willing to listen to those who preached a return to the medieval precedent of the single ruler supported by his feudal nobles. Stolypin, the Chairman of the Council of Ministers who tried to carry out the modernization of Russia with Witte, had said that he could not update his country without 'twenty years of peace, at home and abroad'. In this policy, he had been backed by his successors, Kokovtsov and Sazonov, and by the pro-German Rasputin with his huge influence over the Tsarina. As the Tsar had full final control over foreign policy, his pro-German entourage had his ear, while the pan-Slavs were out of favour. 'A lot of nonsense is being talked about war,' Rasputin declared in 1913. 'Can you really fear that our patriots will go to war?' But the sufferings of fellow Slavs in the Balkan Wars made Kokovtsov and the pro-German clique about the Tsar lose influence, both in St Petersburg and among the Russian aristocracy. The clamour for an attack on the 'patchwork monarchy' of Austria-Hungary grew. For the Russian aristocracy which dominated the Duma felt itself racially different from the Western aristocracies, Slavic rather than Magyar or Teutonic or Latin.

The dismissal of the moderate Kokovtsov in January 1914 was a victory for aristocratic reaction; 'he was let go like a

[11] Quoted in Sir Lewis Namier, *Vanished Supremacies* (London, 1958) p. 115.

servant,' one of the Grand Dukes said. The anti-Germans, led by the future Commander-in-Chief, the Grand Duke Nikolai Nikolaievich, influenced the Tsar to switch from hostility towards England to hostility towards Germany and Austria-Hungary. Repeated strikes by the St Petersburg workers in the summer of 1914 made the aristocratic reactionaries fear even more a repetition of the Revolution of 1905. Their best refuge from the volcano threatening to erupt beneath them was to unify the Russian peasantry and people under the Tsar in a crusade to help the oppressed Slavs against their hereditary enemies, the Teutons. Or so thought the Tsar's reactionary advisers in exactly the same way as the Viennese aristocrats advised a unifying war against the Slavs. Brief bursts of patriotic enthusiasm, with vast crowds kneeling before the Tsar in Palace Square, proved only a temporary solution for a permanent ill. The Russian reactionaries should have remembered the recent lost war against the Japanese, and should have wondered if the *ancien régime* would outlast another defeat. But, for the moment, as a contemporary magazine wrote, the outbreak of war 'like a magic knife divided the two halves of the year . . . bringing the nation to its senses. What had appeared unattainable in time of peace, was achieved.'

In the German Empire, the aristocracy also had a considerable part to play in making the decisions that led to a world war. Between 1871 and 1917, all the Chancellors of the German Empire belonged to the aristocracy, as did the majority of the State Secretaries. In the same period, nearly two-thirds of the members of the Imperial cabinet bore aristocratic names. In the last year before the war, the Prussian state government numbered seven aristocrats among its ten members. Although there were pitifully few aristocrats to be found in economic affairs or the law or science or business, they dominated state and provincial and national government, the army and the diplomatic corps. Three-quarters of the Prussian Herrenhaus, which possessed an absolute right of veto, was composed of aristocrats, and one-quarter of the Prussian House of Representatives. Eight of the ten leading officials in the Ministry for Foreign Affairs were nobles in 1914, while all but

four of the thirty-eight embassies were also manned by aristocrats. The German aristocracy, particularly in Prussia, was in a
position of some practical power on the eve of the First World
War.

The psychology of that aristocracy contained some dangerous
elements. The rulers of Germany considered the Slavs an inferior
people, fit only to be peasants within a Greater Germany; the
call of Germans, who formed a superior caste of landowners
among Slavic populations, was one of the reasons for the policy
of the *Drang nach Osten*. This feeling of superiority in German
Kultur made the Hohenzollern monarch and his advisers feel that
they were the natural heirs to the shaky Habsburg empire. Here an
old dream played a role, the nostalgia for the Holy Roman
Empire, in which Prussia would once again create a *Mitteleuropa*
stretching from the Baltic to the Adriatic. In 1905 the German
Chancellor had written to the German ambassador in Moscow,
suggesting an agreement about the division of the spoils, should
Austria-Hungary collapse. Pan-Germanism and the revival of the
Holy Roman Empire, which would give a reality to the hollow
titles still held by certain aristocrats of that fictitious entity, was the
hope of a strong group in Germany, and a factor in its policy.
The spectre of the Germans absorbing Austria and reaching the
Mediterranean at the port of Trieste was enough to drive the
French even further into the Russian alliance, particularly when
the Morocco crisis showed that the Germans were no longer
prepared to leave the Mediterranean as an Anglo-French lake.

Nostalgia for the Holy Roman Empire might have been sup-
portable in Germany, if the nation had not acquired the industrial
power to make that nostalgia into a reality. The aristocracy of
Europe might have survived for decades in the peaceful years of
the Concert of Europe, if Germany had not determined to become
much stronger than any other European nation. Germany meant
to exercise the power given to it by its central position and
technological strength. Here the aristocratic dream of the revived
Holy Roman Empire coincided with the industrialists' dream of
a vast captive European market for German goods, while the

excessive militarism of Germany that was the contribution of the Prussian Junkers found a popular following among the German masses, who sensed that their future prosperity lay in their country's expansion.

The mixed love and hatred felt for England by the Kaiser and his aristocracy provided another factor in Germany's decision to go to war. Anger at the naval superiority and empire of England helped to provoke the naval armaments race and increased tension between the countries before 1914, while admiration at the stability and might of the maritime island power caused an increasing exchange of visits and marriages. The Kaiser had English blood himself and, as one of his biographers puts it, 'the desire to be an English gentleman was alternating all the time with the desire to be a Prussian prince – and each conspiring to frustrate the other'. The wife and daughters of Admiral von Tirpitz had been to Cheltenham Ladies' College and the family employed an English nanny. Anglophilia in aristocratic Prussia was matched by respect for Germany in aristocratic England. France might be an official ally, but she was neither trusted nor admired by the well-born British. As one of them wrote :

Before the summer of 1914, few Englishwomen went to France except to buy clothes in Paris, or to escape from the cold to the Riviera, but a great number of people – in fact all those who could afford to do so – sent their young daughters to be what was called 'finished' in Germany. This not only led in some cases to Anglo-German marriages, which were on the whole happy and successful, it also caused many young people in this country to have a most affectionate feeling for Germany. This being so, the outbreak of war in 1914 seemed to stun many of my friends.[12]

Because of innumerable personal contacts with Britain as well as the studied ambiguity of British foreign policy, the Kaiser and his advisers could never quite believe that their 'cousins' would intervene on the side of Latin France and Slavic Russia, instead of maintaining a profitable neutrality as in the war of 1870 because of a certain Anglo-Saxon blood kinship.

[12] Mrs Belloc Lowndes, *A Passing World* (London, 1948) p. 22.

Yet it was finally the militarism of Germany which led it to declare the world war. The authority on this subject, Gerhard Ritter, notes three aspects of the phenomenon of militarism, that soldiers are not sufficiently subordinated to civilians, that warfare and the military mentality have too much social prestige, and therefore, that technical military needs play too great a part in political decisions. Bismarck's deliberate policy of buttressing the declining Junkers and emasculating parliament and dragooning the people had resulted in rampant militarism in pre-war Germany. Soldiers were not subordinate to civilians, but only to the Kaiser, who was both Head of State and Commander-in-Chief. Military ways enjoyed the highest social prestige, uniforms were the most prized articles of dress, and past service in the armed forces was a necessity for promotion in most professions. This bellicosity was so widespread that it even had a popular following.

Aristocrats are usually militaristic, because bearing arms is their hereditary function and reason for title; but only in pre-war Germany was the worship of helmets and brass bands made into a popular idolatry. Even the pacific parliamentary members of the Social-Democratic Party were unable to stand out against the tide of militarism and had to give up their opposition to war for fear of seeming unpatriotic to their own followers as well as to conservatives. Karl Marx himself had exulted in Germany's civilizing mission in Slavic countries. How could German socialists, then, oppose a just war? They did not, but voted overwhelmingly for the war credits needed to sustain the government on the outbreak of hostilities. Their reason was patriotism, not socialism, even if the German Chancellor could be prescient enough to foresee that a world war would benefit the socialist party because it was the peace party. 'The power it stood to gain,' Bethmann-Hollweg added, 'might even be enough to topple a few thrones' and the aristocracies which those thrones sustained.

In these ways, the aristocratic mentality helped to bring about the decisions taken in Austria-Hungary and Russia and Germany, which led to the First World War. This war was also the last European dynastic war. It began with the murder of an Austrian

Archduke at Sarajevo by a Serbian nationalist ; the irony was that the victim was pro-Slav because of a morganatic marriage with a Czech countess. When the war ended, a few thrones were indeed toppled by socialism or nationalism in Russia and Turkey, in Austria-Hungary and Germany. The militaristic psychology of the powerful aristocracies of the day and their obstruction of social reform had helped to bring about their own downfall. Some aristocracies in Eastern Europe were to hang on until the Second World War, but essentially the long-term interests of hereditary landownership stood or lay down with royalism. And both the kings and the nobilities beneath them chose to destroy themselves. As Bebel had correctly predicted to the aristocratic opposition in the Reichstag, 'The great break-up will come; and it will not be brought on by us, but by you yourselves.'

In fact, the aristocracies may unconsciously have sought a quick death because they already saw themselves doomed to a slow death by the forces inexorably shaping the modern world – industrialism, urbanism, nationalism, technocracy, mass communications, mass education and mass conscript armies. Only the British aristocrats, who were from a trading nation, and the French aristocrats, who were living under an industrialized republic, and the northern Italian aristocrats, who had sometimes obtained their titles from banking and were often based outside Rome in the old city-states of Florence and Venice and Milan and Genoa, seemed ready to adapt themselves to an elegant survival in the industrial and urban world. Nationalism, of course, damned the international illusion of aristocratic kinship, as the war hatred between the Allies and the Central Powers grew and wiped out all feeling of hereditary solidarity. The power of the technocrats, who were to become the new functional aristocracy of the twentieth century, was only nascent as yet; but the decisive intervention of the United States in the last dynastic war of Europe was to show how technology and its masters were destined to rule large estates and their masters. The rise of mass communications and media would reach even the feudal backwoods of Eastern Europe and would reveal to the peasants that things had changed elsewhere, while mass education would free them from their superstitious loyalty to noble and Church. And as for mass conscript armies – the invention of the French Revolution which flowered in the First World War – they were so large that aristocrats could no longer command their millions; not only men, but increasingly officers had to be drawn from the middle classes and even the proletariat, because in the first year of the war alone, much of the European aristocracy would lie dead in the mud.

Yet in the summer of 1914, the aristocrats of Europe still felt that they held power in a subcontinent that dominated the whole world. A few hundred men of good families had traditionally spoken French to one another and had settled the affairs of the various empires and nations without much reference to the wishes of the masses. What had been might well still be, because no one actually knew the alternatives. After more than forty years of European peace, a long war resulting in the destruction of many of the constitutional monarchies and aristocracies was unthinkable. 'War,' Bergson wrote in a brilliant phrase, 'was probable but impossible.'

So the aristocrats confidently went to war to exercise their profession and to tempt the fates. They were uncertain about the results of the fighting; but then, they were even more uncertain how long they could contain the internal pressures of a continuing peace. The forces of modern life already seemed to doom them, even though it was impossible for them to consider their creeping destruction in a rational manner. So they took refuge in a certain action, the fighting of a war which might solve something, although wars never solve very much. And they judged from their past experience – the most unreliable of guides to the future – that because there had always been a hereditary and powerful aristocracy distinguished particularly in wars, there would always be one in the future. In the Hungarian parliament, Count Albert Apponyi greeted the news of the declaration of war with the joyful cry, 'At last!' A short blood-letting seemed a good temporary expedient for internal difficulties; few forecast a long war, except Lord Kitchener.

Thus hope and complacency masked the underlying insecurity of the European nobility at the outbreak of the Great War. Fighting was a noble game to them; the holocaust to come was outside their experience and their expectations. 'My generation,' wrote Sir Edward Cadogan, 'went into the First World War lightheartedly. The senile denizens of White's Club were not alone in believing we should win the war in a week.' The reality of the trenches was inconceivable for most people. War was as remote as a newspaper paragraph read at the breakfast-table. Princess Marie Louise, who had been divorced by her German husband and was living again in England, described this feeling :

The shadow of a possible war and all the horrors of modern weapons were unknown to us young people. It is true there were wars in Egypt, the Sudan, and South Africa, but all these were being fought in far-distant lands and did not seriously affect young lives, so we danced, sang, and no doubt flirted in a mild manner, through those carefree years of long ago. Then came 1914, and all was changed.[13]

In hindsight, many of the aristocrats were to see the last few pre-War years as a mad dance of death; but this was only in hindsight. 'We were compelled to die,' Count Ottokar Czernin said after the end of the Habsburg Empire. 'We could only choose the manner of our death, and we chose the most terrible.' But before 1914, the collective disaster waiting for the aristocrats in the future was only suggested by the individual assassinations performed by the nihilists and anarchists and nationalists – the regular killing of the Tsars by their subjects, the murders of the Empress Elizabeth of Austria at Geneva and of the King of Portugal and his elder son in Lisbon, or the bomb thrown at the royal coach during the wedding of King Alfonso of Spain, a bomb which killed some twenty people including the Marchioness Torlonia and her niece who were standing on a balcony to watch the procession. As aristocrats knew, the fringes of royalty could be dangerous. And indeed, the simple assassination of one Austrian Archduke began all the troubles of the aristocracy of Eastern Europe.

Perhaps the most remarkable prophecy of doom came from

[13] Princess Marie Louise, *My Memories of Six Reigns* (London, 1956) pp. 133-4.

the soured Marquis de Castellane, who published his memoirs in 1911 and reckoned that the end was coming anyway, because French high society had dropped a few of its barriers to admit the rich and the famous and the merely witty. Cosmopolitanism had already ruined France for the marquis. What distinction was there left for the aristocracy to save?

We are assisting at the most extraordinary and exaggerated social licence that an old nation has ever beheld. Each one wishes to be in another's place: there is no rank left of any sort; no respect is paid even to age. . . . We have ceased to mount, we are rushing downhill, endlessly, without a moment's intermission. Where will this mad career stop?

It will never stop. An avenging God will place His foot on the neck of our princesses; the orchid will grow side by side with the dandelion; and we shall once more be conducted into the court of beggars, the court of the halt and the lame, the only court that will be left standing in the wide world.

I see the France of the future looking like this: at the top, a calf, the calf of gold, broken down, a driveller and a dotard. Above this malevolent, though slumbering beast, a huge hornet's nest, in which venomous insects have come swooping down from the four corners of humanity and swarm, rabidly despoiling all those whom they cross on their path.[14]

Twenty days before Sarajevo, the Duchess de Rohan put off a long voyage to China with the remark, 'The war, alas, is too close.' And in Rome, the Count Greppi, almost a hundred years old, reproved the petulant Princess Rospigliosi for complaining about her footmen. 'Try to tolerate it,' he said. 'When there are no more servants, there can be no more Society . . . I met Nietzsche in Switzerland and he told me, "The twentieth century will be essentially the century of war." So, my dainty Princess, what will become of Society?'

[14] Marquis de Castellane, *Men and Things of My Time* (London, 1911) p. 189.

Two

THE GREAT DEATH
1914–18

Except for the French Republican army, the armies of the great powers which fought in 1914 were led by officers whose code was aristocratic if their pedigree was not. The strongest of the armies, that of Imperial Germany, had the most aristocratic officer corps. Historically, the forces of the Kingdom of Prussia had been staffed by the sons of the Junkers, who had acted as a First Estate and a body of Teutonic Knights round the person of the king, their 'Supreme War Lord'. The three victorious wars of unification fought between 1864 and 1871 had given that officer corps a sense of invincibility and power; for had not the officers round their Kaiser been the architects of one nation? The exclusion of Austria from the Germany which Prussia had brought together, had given the Prussian army total control within the framework of the national army; their aristocratic habits set the tone of the whole military establishment.

Despite the pressure of rich manufacturers' sons and experienced non-commissioned officers to join them, the aristocrats resisted as far as possible the entrance of non-Junkers into higher ranks in the forces. What Prince Friedrich Karl of Prussia had observed in 1860 was still true fifty years later: 'The nobles dominate our corps of officers, in the sense that they believe commissions are really meant for them alone and that *bourgeois* are only admitted on sufferance.' Despite the need of finding many new officers to command the expanded army of 1913, more than half of the higher ranks of the Prussian officer corps were still noble, and half of the General Staff. Elite regiments, such as the Guards and the cavalry, tolerated hardly an officer without a title; they were always stationed in the most comfortable and chic places. When the Inspector-General sent in a report in 1909, complaining of the low level of education among young Prussian officers compared to French ones, the reply from the Chief of the Military Cabinet was in the tradition of the Junkers. He did not mind that his young officers were ignorant 'so long as the supply of character keeps up'. Moreover, there was 'no comparison to be made between the level of education in the German corps of officers and that which obtains in the French officer-corps where so many captains and lieutenants have been promoted from the ranks'.

Prince Friedrich Karl's essay on 'The Spirit of the Prussian Officer' had also summed up the ideal code of the German officer, which granted him a position of privilege inside society as the representative of a state within a state.

The honour of the Prussian officer is honour raised to the very highest power. No prince or King can escape its influence or its dictates. It is more exalted than they are, although they may not all be aware of the fact. The man of honour takes orders willingly and needs no visible punishment. Honour alone is his task-master; conscience his judge and his reward. It is not for pay and awards that he serves. An award or decoration flatters him but adds nothing to his merit in his own eyes or in those of his equals. The Prussian officer today still thinks that the most he can do is his duty. [1]

In fact, the Prince had been so enthusiastic about the ideal of an officer that he had disliked the aristocratic vices of the corps, 'the so-called noble passions and their corresponding vices, viz. brawling and drunkenness, gambling, and that tendency to excess and the life of the *Landsknecht* which holds such attraction for Germans generally'. Also deplorable to the prince had been the recurrent feature of 'snobbery based on noble birth, the pretension of superiority over other corps and other classes, with a tendency to take it too far in all directions'.

[1] K. Demeter, *The German Officer-Corps in Society and State, 1650-1945*, translated by Angus Malcolm (London, 1965).

It was a Field Army two million strong, led by men with these ideals and these vices, that the aristocratic von Moltke the Younger sent in eight armies under eight noble commanders to fight on two fronts in 1914. The commanders were the Crown Prince of Germany, who was to be fought to a standstill at Verdun, the Crown Prince Rupprecht of Bavaria, the Duke of Württemberg, von Bülow, von Kluck, von Hausen, von Heeringen, and von Prittwitz und Gaffron. In addition, ten other army corps were under aristocratic command. The rapid victories won by the German armies in the West until they reached the Marne, and then in the East once the Junkers Hindenburg and Ludendorff had taken over the Russian front before taking over the entire German war effort, seemed to prove the worth of the aristocratic principle of command. It was trench warfare, the machine-gun, barbed wire, massed artillery and gas that killed off in weeks the aristocrats who had taken centuries to breed. When the German right wing stalled in front of the British Expeditionary Force at Ypres, Moltke's successor, von Falkenhayn, sent in the four reserve corps of war volunteers, which contained the flower of German youth and the material for future officer corps on the old pattern. They were butchered in a sea of mud and blood, while they for their part butchered the first volunteers and the old regulars of Britain; one survivor of the battle was the plebeian volunteer Adolf Hitler.

By November 1915 one-quarter of the regular and reservist officers in the Prussian section of the German army was dead; they could not be replaced by the same quantity of aristocratic material. Also the officer corps was expanding fast; the regular officers of 1914 amounted only to one-twelfth of the total number who received commissions during the course of the war. The Military Cabinet tried to stick by the old social standards and refused to allow efficient sergeants to be commissioned at higher than the hybrid rank of *Offizierstellvertreter* or Deputy Officer; but military necessity triumphed over ostrich respectability. Officers had to be found 'wherever one could hope to find anything suitable!' By 1917 one General was reporting that the best of the front-line officers were elementary schoolteachers, while the far-sighted General Staff was withdrawing the few surviving aristo-cratic officers out of the trenches to form the nucleus of a new officer corps, which could maintain the old traditions and keep order if the war were lost.

The holocaust consuming the German aristocrats, who volun-teered practically to a man in order to serve the fatherland, did not spare the other aristocrats of Europe, who were also forced by traditional honour to volunteer in the most murderous war in the history of the subcontinent. The Russian army had been modelled largely on the German army. Until the reforms intro-duced after the Revolution of 1905, seven officer schools and fourteen Junker schools produced an officer corps that came overwhelmingly from the Russian and Baltic aristocracy. The officers of the Guard, who were responsible for the security of the Tsar, were drawn almost entirely from the nobility and held privileges of seniority and treatment over the officers of the Line regiments. The more educated officers from the *bourgeoisie* tended to cluster in the engineering and artillery regiments; they were dissatisfied with the discrimination against them, almost as dis-satisfied as the intelligent non-commissioned officers, who could never hope for promotion. Even the mild reforms in the training schools before 1914 did not change the relationships between Russian officers and their men, which mirrored the attitudes of the old landowners towards their serfs, nor did these reforms reduce the tensions between Guard and Line officers. As Trotsky summed up the situation:

The ill-will and friction between the democratic and aristocratic officers, incapable of reviving the army, only introduced a further element of decomposition. The physiognomy of the army was deter-mined by the old Russia, and this physiognomy was completely feudal. The officers still considered the best soldier to be a humble and unthinking peasant lad, in whom no consciousness of human per-sonality had yet awakened. . . . The authority of the officers rested upon the exterior signs of superiority, the ritual of caste, the system of suppression, and even a special caste language – contemptible idiom of slavery – in which the soldier was supposed to converse with his officer. [2]

Even more than in the case of the German army, mobilization swamped the traditional officer corps of Russia in the mass of troops. Badly-trained reserve officers from doubtful backgrounds commanded peasant soldiers, who had poor weapons or none at all. Russian tactics, as employed at their most extreme by the ruthless Grand Duke Nikolai Nikolaievich, consisted of the assault *en masse*, by which the weight of human bodies was meant to compensate for lack of shells and bullets. In the war, the Russians lost two million dead and more than two million prisoners out of a total army of some fifteen million. This disorganized rabble was no more than the peasantry mobilized, and, after three years of being butchered, the peasants began going home to seize the piece of the land which agitators promised them in 1917 on the fall of the Tsar. Aristocratic attitudes survived among the officers and were transmitted to all newcomers to high rank; but when civil war broke out between the Bolsheviks and their opponents, most of the officer corps found itself on the side of the Whites as the defenders of status and privilege. Although there were Bolshevik high officers from the nobility such as Tukhachevsky and Kamenev, the old Russian officer corps foundered in the vile campaigns of the Kornilovs and Krasnovs and Denikins and Wrangels, who could hardly hope to stop a mass revolution with the shibboleths and punishments of yesteryear.

The officers of the Austro-Hungarian army in 1914 stood half-way between the aristocratic bias of the German and Russian armies, and the *bourgeois* bias of the armies of France and England and Italy. 'Vienna,' a contemporary noted, 'does not, like Berlin, give you the impression of a city whose daily life revolves about an armed man. In the cafés, the public places, the streets of Vienna, the officers are quieter, more moderate and tolerant in their behaviour than in Germany.' The ruling circles of the army were

[2] Leon Trotsky, *The History of the Russian Revolution*, translated by Max Eastman, (Ann Arbor, Michigan, 1932) p. 253.

split between two small worlds, a caste of aristocratic officers from great families who were determined to support the court and the Catholic Church, and a class of high-ranking officers promoted for reasons of merit or policy by the Emperor and given the honorary titles of *von* or *Freiherr*. The second class of officer actually ran the army more than the aristocrats, who were, however, far better at the art of political intrigue and thus more powerful in the Higher Command. The Emperor himself, conscious of the need to attach to his *person* a devoted group of officers, who could protect him against social or nationalist revolt, seemed to prefer those who had no great attachment to hereditary lands, something which might make them more Magyar or Bohemian or Polish in their sympathies than Habsburg. As Hermann Bahr pointed out, the Habsburg Empire needed as its ruling group 'not an aristocracy. Within its ranks are aristocrats and *bourgeoisie*. One can enter it from any class. Only, one must first break with one's class, deny one's nationality.' This done, a man could become part of the new aristocracy that ruled the Austrian half of the Habsburg Empire by the Emperor's favour, attached to him and not to lands and positions inherited from a feudal and pre-Habsburg past.

Except in the purely Hungarian or *Honvéd* regiments, all the officers spoke German, whatever their country of origin. They were frequently transferred from one place to another, from Hungarian to Croat to Polish to Ukrainian camps, in order to keep them loyal to the Crown and to prevent them from liking any garrison town overmuch. As a military machine, the army was well-led, if badly equipped. On the outbreak of war, the same phenomenon appeared as in Germany, a rush of aristocratic volunteers to the colours under the prodding of the Catholic clergy, who saw in victory the strengthening of the old order. Yet, despite the rush, the massed troops demanded multitudinous commanders from all parts of society. There was not enough blue blood to be spilt. The High Command under General Conrad von Hötzendorff, however, was still old-fashioned enough to entrust the Archduke Karl, the heir to the throne, with command of the German-Austrian army which fought in 1916 in the Carpathians.

Under the Third Republic in France, the *bourgeoisie* held a position of increasing power in the French army, particularly after the Dreyfus affair. Since the time of Louis Napoleon, the government had increasingly blocked openings for aristocrats in all careers outside the army. As Paul Bourget made one of his characters say in *L'Emigré*:

Every career was barred to the future Marquis de Claviers-Granchamps. Yes, barred. Foreign affairs? Barred. My father, at least, would have been accepted by the Empire. Today we are no longer desired. The Council of State? Barred. The Administration? Barred. Can you see a noble acting as Prefect of a Department? . . . The Army alone was left to me. I studied at Saint-Cyr, although not without difficulties. There, at all events, I knew the joy of not being isolated, of feeling that I was a Frenchman like the others, of not being exiled from my own age, from my generation and my country. . . .[3]

Thus two in seven of the Class of 1878 at Saint-Cyr were of noble origin; Weygand wrote in his memoirs, 'They told me that the Army was the thing for nobles without a fortune.' But with the Dreyfus affair, when a Jewish officer was wrongly accused of spying by the real culprit, the aristocrat Esterházy, officers from the nobility were held back deliberately from promotion by the government, which was scared of an officer corps that was becoming too monarchist and right-wing to be tolerated in a republic. Yet stagnation in peace had made the officers reactionary. Many of them had mouldered at the rank of lieutenant for fifteen years and at captain for twenty; the number of candidates presenting themselves at Saint-Cyr had halved; bitterness and boredom within the officers' messes had expressed itself against 'the red donkeys' who had dared to support the republic. In retaliation, the government set officer to spy on officer, promoted the *bourgeois* anti-clericals and Masons and anti-monarchists, until Captain d'Arbeaux could declare that 'conversions to a new ideal were both numerous and exceptionally

[3] Tr. Kenneth Douglas; in De La Gorce, *The French Army* (London, 1963).

violent! The neophytes burned what they had adored, gave up church attendance, flocked to the Masonic Lodges and paid homage to the Republic.' General André put the cause of the change even more bluntly: 'Promotion in the Army is in the hands of Parliament.'

This new policy was so disastrous to military morale that it soon collapsed, when secret files on clerical officers were found in a Masonic Lodge. Two threats brought about an understanding between the government and the officers, despite the disestablishment of the French church by the state. First was the threat of social revolt; the government increasingly had to use troops against strikers. Secondly, there was the increasing military threat of Germany, which led the parliamentary Deputies to vote more money to strengthen the army, and which destroyed the antimilitarist sentiment in the administration. The pacifists lost their influence; the left wing became Jacobin again.

With the promotion of colonial French officers like Joffre, who had stayed out of the Dreyfus affair and its aftermath by serving in the China Seas, compromise army leaders were found to satisfy both the government and the officer corps. Before the outbreak of war in 1914, a new ideal was beginning to show itself in the French officer corps, which fell back on the old ascetic codes of Catholicism and nobility. First put forward by the well-born Lyautey, the theory maintained that military service obliged officers to fulfil their social and moral duty to the utmost, in the colonies as well as at home. This ideal of moral duty and dedication to service, in which the French officer was to be the *best* citizen rather than most aristocratic warrior, restored morale and made it possible for the French officer corps to fight the war united under the flag of republican France. Letters from Catholic and aristocratic officers at the front show their surprise and delight at being appreciated for their courage by their fellow officers, sometimes from proletarian backgrounds.

The British army at the outbreak of the war was both small and unaristocratic by birth, despite Lord Kitchener's complaint that it was 'the preserve of gentlemen who dislike having to take

their own profession seriously.' The British Expeditionary Force
which went to France numbered a mere four divisions. The
chief merit of the English aristocrats in the first months of the war
was to use every influence they possessed to get themselves into
France and action as quickly as possible. Their rush was based on a
misconception. 'It was generally felt,' the later Lord Norwich
noted, 'that war was a glorious affair and the British always won.'
In one case, a woman friend of the Minister of War was approached by two ladies to use her influence to get their husbands
sent to the front; a mother whose son got into the fighting
quickly was called 'lucky'. 'That he would probably be killed or
seriously injured did not seem to occur to her. . . . In those days
society, using the word in its narrowest sense, still appeared to
live in the atmosphere of the Boer War. There had been tragic
losses in South Africa, but it had not been war.'

Harold Macmillan, one of the few survivors among the early
volunteers, used his family's influence to become gazetted to the
Reserve Battalion of the Grenadier Guards. His comment in his
recent memoirs on his use of that influence is ironic. 'It was privilege of the worst kind. . . . But, after all, was it so very reprehen-
sible? The only privilege I, and many others like me, sought
was that of getting ourselves killed or wounded as soon as
possible.' In this bullocking towards the shambles, the pedigree
beast was in front. The case of the late Duke of Bedford was rare
enough to be noteworthy. He had had an unpleasant time in the
territorial army, where he had met again 'the Eton bully type'
from whom he had just escaped at school. Thus he was not prepared to go through the 'disheartening torture' of obeying the
orders of those he despised. He served in the Young Men's
Christian Association and became an evangelical social worker;
as a result, his father refused to see him again and tried to dis-
inherit him; he lost 'home, money, friends and the chances of
marriage'. Not to fight in 1914 was almost as drastic a decision
for an aristocrat as to fight.

The British ladies also went to war. They not only sacrificed
their men, but also they put together the pieces. Contemporary

accounts of London note that almost every woman in Society was doing some form of war work, usually in the field of nursing the wounded. Most of the great London houses were converted voluntarily into hospitals, and many country houses into convalescent homes. The Duke and Duchess of Sutherland gave up both their house in Portman Square and their castle of Dunrobin; many followed their example. There seemed to be some cathartic relief in playing Florence Nightingale with more or less efficiency; it was as though a tradition of service in the local village had suddenly become a patriotic duty for the nation.

On the continent, aristocratic women did not plunge into the hospital business with quite the background in voluntary work of the British ladies. They did run hospitals in their *châteaux* and *palazzi*, but rather more in the delightful manner of Cocteau's Princess de Bormes in his best novel, *Thomas the Impostor*. In describing the princess's motives for setting up a private ambulance corps and turning her Paris home into a hospital, Cocteau hit at a root cause behind aristocratic action. Where it was not a duty to do something, it had to be chic.

The war appeared to the Princess all at once like a theatre of the war. A theatre reserved for men only. She could not bear to live on the margin of something happening; she saw herself excluded from the only spectacle which counted from now on. ... She was madly in love with fashions, whether frivolous or serious. The fashion was danger; she was dying of calm. Youth spending and squandering itself to the point of jumping out of windows, while she was chafing at inaction. She would have liked events to help her, sustain her, like a crowd helps a woman to see fireworks. [4]

So private ambulances and a hospital were produced to satisfy the Princess de Bormes' hunger to act at war. But her *protégé*, the poor Thomas the Impostor, playing at being the aristocrat de Fontenoy, achieved the final reality on the cross put over his dead body in Flanders; his epitaph bore his assumed noble name and the true sentence, *Dead for us.*

Away from the trenches, the war appeared unreal to many

[4] Jean Cocteau, *Thomas L'Imposteur* (Paris, 1923) pp. 18-19.

more than Thomas, pretending to possess a better name than he had received at his christening. Some used the war to acquire titles like the rich American William Waldorf, who became Viscount Astor 'for political and public services', which meant that he had bought his title by giving a lot of money to hospitals and party funds. Others used the war to make fortunes by profiteering, a prerequisite for buying a title. Others such as Lady Clodagh Anson treated air-raids like thunderstorms and 'a frightful nuisance'; she refused to leave her bed on the theory that it was better to die comfortably, rather than get a chill by squatting in a shelter. Few, though, had the gall of the mistress of the great house of Knole, who wrote to Lord Kitchener telling him not to put the estate carpenters in the army. 'Do you realize, dear Lord Kitchener, that you are ruining houses like ours?' To keep them going was 'a national duty, just as important for us as keeping up the army and our splendid troops'.

Patriotism was also given as the reason for another aristocratic habit, the urge to entertain. 'Behind shuttered windows, hilarious parties took place nightly, with rather an hysterical emphasis on "giving the boys a good time".' Lady Diana Manners, probably the most beautiful woman in London, wrote of her circle's 'salutary delirium' at 'dances of death' flowing with wine; there 'the young were dancing a tarantella frenziedly to combat any pause that would let death conquer their morale'. Duff Cooper, later her husband supported the frenzied gaiety of those who seemed to be living a life of heartless fun in the war capitals; it was their duty to give harmless pleasure to the officers on leave and to pretend to ignore the murdering of most of the adult males of their class.

There were always some on leave; and over them all was hanging the shadow of death. How splendidly our youthful spirits resisted the gloom and terror which that shadow is wont to cast! It may well be that the near presence of death enables us to form a truer estimate of its importance. The nineteenth century had been, especially in England, a period of great security, and sudden death was so rare that it came to be regarded as the greatest of all calamities. These four years of war, with casualties more numerous than ever before or since, familiarized us with the spectre. We did not feel our losses the less because we wore our mourning more lightly. Among my own friends it became a point of honour never to show a sad face at the feast. And if we wept – as weep we did – we wept in secret. [5]

Margot Asquith went to Ypres with a party to put crosses on the graves of the sons of the Duke of Richmond and Lord Lansdowne. The cemetery there ended her illusions over war, with its dripping bits of wood stuck on hundreds of huddled graves, marked only with names scrawled in pencil being washed off by the rain. A Tommy digging a fresh grave was asked who it was for, and he replied without stopping his digging, 'For the next. . . .'

The mounting casualty lists and bloody grind of the war ended the gay pretences and fond illusions of the aristocracy. 'What was there to come of age for,' one of Lord Curzon's daughters asked, 'with the gaunt spectre of war ever present, and the blood-soaked trenches claiming more and more of my generation?' Not only were the men dead or wounded, but also the fiction of the international solidarity of the feudal class. Those of divided loyalties had to choose, and they usually chose their country of birth. Sir Rudolf von Slatin, the son of a distinguished Viennese Jewish family, had risen in the British army to the rank of Inspector-General; at the outbreak of the war, he was offered the post of viceroy of Central Africa. He set sail for Vienna with the noble words: 'I have the proud honour to be a British general. As such I must return home in time of war.'

Rabid nationalism was everywhere triumphant. The First Sea Lord of Britain was the German-born Prince Louis of Battenberg; he was forced to resign, as he had once served as an officer in the little army of Hesse; he wrote to Winston Churchill, 'At this juncture my birth and parentage have the effect of impairing in some respects my usefulness on the Board of Admiralty.' Churchill accepted his resignation in a letter, acknowledging that the old forgiveness for pedigree was over. 'This is no ordinary war, but a

[5] Duff Cooper, Lord Norwich, *Old Men Forget* (London, 1953) p. 51.

struggle between nations for life or death. It raises passions between races of the most terrible kind. It effaces the old landmarks and frontiers of our civilization.' By 1917, even the King of England felt forced to change the name of his dynasty from Saxe-Coburg-Gotha to Windsor, while the Battenbergs changed their name to Mountbatten. As this was a time when the music of Mozart and Beethoven was considered treasonable and dachshunds traitorous, even royalty had to bow before the storm.

In Austria-Hungary, exactly the reverse hatred was common. At the outbreak of war, the Serbs were the most evil people on earth; soon they were joined by the Russians, French, Belgians, and especially the English, the perfidious cousins. 'Mind you never tell anyone that your grandfather was Lord Pirbright!' the Count von Loewenstein-Scharffeneck told his sons, after the local mob had sacked the house of an Austrian cavalry officer who had dared to speak French in the streets. The Count himself shared in the chauvinism, praying, 'Thanks be to Thee, O Lord, that thou hast made an end to idle peace,' and composing poems such as the one beginning, 'On the banks of the Thames, ye shall lie at our feet.'

The fact was that the monarchies and aristocracies had completely lost power in their own countries to the generals, the politicians, and the propaganda machines. By 1916 in Germany, Hindenburg and Ludendorff had taken over effective power and were imposing a form of 'war socialism' on the nation, in order to ration food and ensure a regular flow of war materials to the front lines in East and West. This ruthless exploitation of all human and material resources was very much in Ludendorff's Junker concept of war; but it failed in its most important task, the uplift of the weakening morale of the German troops and civilians under growing hardship. In France, Clemenceau, and in Britain, Lloyd George, gained more and more power from the need for a final authority in military decision, while the unsuccessful armies of Austria-Hungary and Russia increasingly showed up the failure of the old aristocratic ways of running wars.

Yet in this domination by nationalism and military decision, the European aristocrats found time for certain niceties as a tribute to the past. English noblewomen caught on holiday in Germany at the outbreak of the war had been politely returned, in gratitude for country-house visits to England in better days. The German Emperor and Empress kept up a minor correspondence with their relations, the British royal house, over matters such as war widows and congratulations for family anniversaries. Even among the Junkers, war hatred was less strong than among the middle classes, because a long tradition of fighting and sacrifice made the enemy into another practitioner of the art of war – if he was an officer and a gentleman. The later Lady Listowel, the daughter of a Hungarian nobleman, reported that no English people were interned in Hungary during the war, while their English nanny stayed where she was; 'it was a civilized war' in Budapest, even if there was little to eat besides bread and potatoes. And such unfortunates as the Hungarian Princess Elisalex von Clary und Aldringen, who had married a Belgian aristocrat, found herself a refugee in England in the Duke of Portland's house, where little reference to the war was made for fear of the divided loyalties in the guest's heart. A certain common suffering made nationalism still seem ridiculous to such polyglot and refugee aristocrats. 'We all pooled our thoughts and hopes and fears for our dear ones on all fronts,' the Princess wrote of her stay at Welbeck, 'and suffered together and for each other.' For, as Noël Coward once pointed out, the privileged also suffer like anyone else.

The privileged at home, however, were suffering less than the men in the trenches. The gigantic losses and bad discipline of the Russian army under the personal command of the Tsar led to an attack by the Russian aristocrats on the pro-German clique at court. Some Russian Grand Dukes put Rasputin to death early in 1917; as the poet Blok noted, the bullet which killed Rasputin 'reached the very heart of the ruling dynasty'. Soon the Tsar himself lost all support and was forced to abdicate, while the aristocrats rushed to join the new civilian government in order to preserve their power. Trotsky later analysed the process in Russia with admirable precision:

The nobility sees the cause of all its misfortunes in the fact that the monarchy is blind or has lost its reason. The privileged caste cannot believe that no policy whatever is possible which would reconcile the old society with the new. In other words, the nobility cannot accept its own doom and converts its death-weariness into opposition against the most sacred power of the old régime, that is, the monarchy. The sharpness and irresponsibility of the aristocratic opposition is explained by history's having made spoiled children of the upper circles of the nobility, and by the unbearableness to them of their own fears in face of revolution. The unsystematic and inconsistent character of the noble discontent is explained by the fact that it is the opposition of a class which has no future. But as a lamp before it goes out flares up with a bright although smoky light, so the nobility before disappearing gives out an oppositional flash, which performs a mighty service for its mortal enemy. [6]

The Kerensky government, which seemed to offer some haven for turncoat aristocrats, was soon overthrown by the Bolsheviks, as the Russian forces streamed back in rout to the cities and the fields, putting to death the noble officers and landowners who stood in their way. The example of the Bolshevik attack on privilege was contagious; there were mutinies in the French army at Verdun and in the Austrian army on the Italian front, with soldiers shooting their officers and singing the 'Internationale'. Both the French and Austrian mutineers were unsuccessful. The French army was held together until victory, and the Austrian army did not collapse until the German one did. The Italian army also had much trouble from its troops after its defeat at Caporetto; but it survived. Only the British army seemed untouched by socialist propaganda, perhaps because the habit of obeying commands without question was still acceptable in a stable nation, which had not yet learned to hate the principles of authority and hierarchy.

The German army was finally defeated by the disaffection at home and by the failure to receive enough supplies to withstand the Allied troops, who had been reinforced by the intervention of the Americans. Part of the reason for the German army's collapse in 1918, however, was the soldiers' resentment at the

[6] Trotsky, op. cit., p. 77.

aristocratic attitudes still aped by members of the officer corps, when the horrors of years of trench warfare should have reduced all men into a dirty democracy of dying. Erich Remarque's *All Quiet on the Western Front* tells of the fury of his hero, who is briefly on leave from the front and is disciplined by a fat army major. Throughout the common hell of the war, officers and men were segregated everywhere, even on beaches and in churches, hairdressers, theatres, lavatories and brothels. Feeling against the German officer corps had risen so high by 1917 that Ludendorff had to send out a memorandum to all officers to behave more democratically. There was no brotherhood of fighting men in the trenches; belly in the dirt under shrapnel fire did not muddy the insignia of rank. Even when the German troops were starving by the summer of 1918, some of the officers still gave expensive dinners on black market food, despite the warnings of Ludendorff that they were calling down the deluge. It was scarcely surprising that when young reservists were being rushed to a gap in the front just before the Armistice, they were met by the retreating troops, who jeered at them, 'Strike-breakers!'

To the aristocrats, the social turmoil that spread across Eastern and Central Europe after the Russian Revolution was incredible. In weeks, centuries of tradition were swept away. In Germany, General Groener played a leading role in the Emperor's abdication, when he told the Emperor that the army commanders would not support the Emperor against the homeland and that the soldier's oath to the Emperor meant nothing any more. The Emperor then abdicated, theoretically dissolving the General Staff which owed allegiance directly to him; but the General Staff under Hindenburg remained intact without its 'Royal Shield', carefully leaving the odium of conducting peace negotiations to the civilian government, in order not to seem implicated in the collapse of the monarchy nor in the terms of a shameful peace.

In Austria, the nobles had treated the war placidly, certain that their way of life could not be interrupted; but once the army had dissolved, they refused to rally round the new emperor Karl. He had, at least, fought and had nearly been killed in the front

line, observing that it was 'a dreadful feeling to send thousands
of others to their death at a safe distance', and also observing that
not a single archduke had been killed or wounded in the war.
The archdukes were equally absent when not one loyal regiment
could be found to protect the last Habsburg emperor in the palace
of Schönbrunn; even the two bodyguards of nobles, the *Arcièren
Leibgarde* and the Royal Hungarian Noble Guard, melted away to
defend their own estates from the social revolution bursting out
everywhere. The last pair of *Leibgardisten* fell asleep at their post
outside the Emperor's door, for they were never relieved. The
final bodyguards of the Emperor on the eve of his abdication
were the boy Cadets from the Military Academy; the last of the
Habsburg monarchs was left in command only of uniformed babes
and sucklings.

Even the surviving aristocrats on the winning side could find
little joy in the Armistice. 'After so much bitter loss,' one wrote,
'it was unnatural to be jubilant. The dead were in our minds to
the exclusion of the survivors.' Eugénie, the ex-Empress of France,
even found herself sorry for her old foe, the German royal family,
which had caused her exile in England; she did not wish the
Kaiser to fall a victim to the anger and disillusionment of his
people, as she herself had fallen. 'No one,' she pointed out to
Princess Marie Louise, 'who has experienced a revolution would
wish even her worst enemy to undergo all the horrors that it
entails.' Lloyd George refused to allow the King of England to
offer asylum to the Russian royal family; the result was that the
Tsar and his household were eventually butchered. The British
King, however, took steps to guarantee the safety of the Austrian
Emperor Karl, who had explored ways of reaching peace in 1916,
thus earning Anatole France's accolade as 'the only honest man
who occupied an important position during the war, but he was
not heard'.

Brecht once wrote that, whoever won a war, the people always
lost. But the monarchs and the aristocrats also lost the First World
War. They were right to be overcome by melancholy and
thoughts of the fallen among the cheering and waving and

drunken crowds of Armistice Night. The Middle Ages had now ended in the most backward parts of Europe, although some landowners were to hang on for another two decades until the fighting of the Second World War. Except perhaps in England and Scotland and Hungary, heredity was now to mean very little in terms of power in Europe. The sons of the aristocrats were dead or wounded, their daughters were forced to be spinsters or marry commoners, their estates were often ruined by devastation or revolution or taxation. The feudal nobility, which had risen to power as the king's warriors, fell as the king's warriors in the last dynastic war.

Of the two great films made on the First World War, one dealt with the nasty shambles of dying from the point of view of the ordinary soldier. In Pabst's *Westfront, 1918*, the meaningless butchery of the war among the machine-gun fodder in the ranks was revealed in all its messy dying. The German soldiers had lost against increasing odds; they had no time for the high jinks of heroism. Renoir, however, in his classic film, *The Grand Illusion*, saw the war in a wider context, as the end of the European aristocracy in the face of the industrial masses and their manipulators. The relationship between the German commander of the prisoner-of-war camp for officers, von Rauffenstein, played by Erich von Stroheim, and the French Captain de Bœldieu, played by Pierre Fresnay, gives a remarkable insight to the fall of the nobility in the last war of privilege.

Rauffenstein has been the commander of an air squadron and is very much modelled upon the character of the real Baron Manfred von Richthofen, the great air ace. Richthofen was a Silesian baron who left the mounted Uhlans for the air force, attracted by the ruthless chivalry of air warfare – the joust of individual against individual above the mass slaughter below, the skill of the lone hunter against the dangerous hunted. He brought down eighty Allied aircraft and filled his air squadron with the same breed of efficient killers, sometimes with pedigree and always with discipline and daring. His enemies were treated as victims in the air and as gentlemen if they survived behind the German lines

after they had crashed. When Richthofen himself was eventually
shot dead in combat, the Royal Air Force buried him with full
military honours. A British air ace delivered the final toast to his
memory: 'He was a brave man, a clean fighter and an aristocrat.'

Such a eulogy could also be pronounced over the fictional
character of Rauffenstein in *The Grand Illusion*. He is presented
as the last of the old school, a gentleman so absolute that he will
tolerate no familiarity with anyone except his equals in pedigree,
an officer so stiff-necked that he wears a steel corset to support his
bad wounds; Bœldieu, on the other hand, has become friendly
with his fellow officers in the prisoner-of-war camp, particularly
with the Jewish businessman Rosenthal and the proletarian
Maréchal. Rauffenstein's first words to Bœldieu are that he is delighted to see the Frenchman again; they chat together in English
about girls they have known in Maxim's before the war and about
mutual friends and cherished horses. When Bœldieu later asks
Rauffenstein why the camp commandant receives him alone,
Rauffenstein answers that they are both titled and both career
officers. Bœldieu then points out that Maréchal and Rosenthal
are also officers and good soldiers; no aristocrat can stop the
democratization of the army.

RAUFFENSTEIN: I do not know who is going to win this war, but
I know one thing: the end of it, whatever it may be, will be the
end of the Rauffensteins and the Bœldieus.

BŒLDIEU: But perhaps there is no more need for us.

RAUFFENSTEIN: And don't you find that is a pity?

BŒLDIEU: Perhaps!

After this conversation, Bœldieu agrees to play a sacrificial role
in the escape of Rosenthal and Maréchal, who represent the
industrial future of France, just as he represents its agricultural
past. For this reason, he chooses to play a flute like a mocking
Pan and draw the attention of the German garrison while the other
two get away. He climbs up high on to the fortress, with
Rauffenstein begging him to surrender before he is shot. Bœldieu

refuses, so Rauffenstein shoots him with a bullet in the stomach. In hospital, Rauffenstein asks the pardon of the dying Bœldieu; he had aimed at the other's leg. Bœldieu politely replied that he would have behaved in just the same way and that it was a hard shot, as the light was bad and the distance great. Then, speaking with difficulty, he sums up the position of the whole European aristocracy in the Great War that ended its power:

BŒLDIEU: Of us two it isn't I who should complain the most. I, I'll be finished soon, but you ... you haven't finished. ...

RAUFFENSTEIN: Not finished dragging out a useless existence.

BŒLDIEU: For a man of the people, it's terrible to die in the war. For you and me, it was a good solution.

RAUFFENSTEIN: (*bowing his head*) I have missed it.[7]

[7] *La Grande Illusion*, directed Jean Renoir, scenario C. Spaak, translated by Andrew Sinclair and Marianne Alexander (London, 1968).

Three

Three

A PATCHWORK QUILT OF SHOCKING TASTE: 1919–39

Between the two World Wars, the surviving aristocrats were forced to choose the guillotine or the slow garotte or a wasting disease. Communism was dedicated to the destruction of the feudal classes at once; revolutionary fascism to their eventual strangulation; and *bourgeois* democracy to their bleeding away through death duties and income tax. With one of these three alternatives of government imposed upon them, the aristocrats had to shift as they could to last a little longer.

Sometimes as in Hungary and Poland after the Armistice, the aristocrats seized back most of their old feudal power and privileges after a fierce battle against Bolshevik forces. More often, they continued to exist under a weak *bourgeois* democratic government, which failed to deal with the problems of post-war reconstruction. This economic chaos after 1919 gave Mussolini and the original Fascists the chance to seize power in Italy in the early twenties; from the Italian example other fascist movements drew their strength, until Hitler's fantastic success with the Nazis in Germany made the Third Reich the model for National Socialism in the late thirties. Both Mussolini and Hitler blamed the failure of capitalism in their countries on *bourgeois* democracy, not on the remaining representatives of the aristocracy; they agreed with the Marxists that the industrial countries of the West had already passed through the stage of feudalism. Thus both major fascist leaders could make a deal with the aristocrats in the early and feeble days of their régimes. They both proposed the same compromise, that fascism would not interfere with the large estates of the aristocracy and would guarantee fair prices for crops, if the aristocrats would accept the replacement of the *bourgeois* élite by the new élite of fascism. Thus the European aristocracy came to terms with the new order in those countries taken over by revolutionary fascism; like any other group, it put its survival above its sense of honour.

Outside Spain, fascism was essentially a movement of the young veterans from the First World War, who wanted to keep alive their sense of *camaraderie* under danger and their involvement with immediate action. It was the consequence of the mass mobilization of a subcontinent, which destroyed the old values of honour of the small regular armies. The leaders of fascism were from a new generation; Mussolini came to power at thirty-nine, Hitler at forty-four, the Belgian Degrelle was in his early thirties and Codreanu in his late twenties. These leaders were not tainted by the failures of the past; their appeal was to a unified society, in which the classes would not fight each other but join together in a hierarchy of service to the national state.

Fascism could appeal to workers and peasants, as in Hungary and Spain and Rumania; for it was a revolutionary movement until it seized power, when an inevitable reaction began. In order to keep up the momentum of action despite the compromises with vested interests demanded by the logic of exercising power, some of the fascist régimes were forced into wars of conquest abroad, which were to bring them down in the end. Those which did not keep up the fascist dynamic sank back into old-fashioned military dictatorships based on the support of reactionary bankers and landowners and the Church, such as Franco's Spain. Where the aristocrats threw in their lot with the fascist régimes in eastern Europe, they were doomed by the result of the Second World War. The aristocracy was, after all, fighting a holding action after 1918; it failed to put a brake on Nazi schemes of conquest and thus was to be totally destroyed behind the final lines of the victorious Red Army.

In a sense, fascism was always a graft on the existing social structure; but it took different forms in different nations. In Poland and Hungary, large landowners controlled huge areas, although the fascists were powerful in the state; in both countries, the landowners could combine with the fascists to attack the new capitalists, some of whom were Jews. For fear of a Bolshevik revolt, most of the land in Rumania had been distributed to the peasants after the Great War; but the monarchy of King Carol II and the aristocracy and the government borrowed many features from Mussolini's Italy without changing the structure of society at all – something which encouraged the rise of a proper revolutionary fascism under Codreanu, which briefly took power in 1940. In Czechoslovakia and parts of Yugoslavia, powerful fascist parties showed themselves to be efficient butchers, once the Nazi advance had brought them to power; but they had no social programme other than excessive nationalism, a mere thirst for power which caused them to butcher all who stood in their path, whether aristocrat or *bourgeois* democrat or Jew.

Mussolini set the pattern for the first decade of fascism; all the would-be leaders of similar national movements travelled to Rome; just so, all roads had led to Rome in the great days of the Roman Empire and the Papacy. The Italian example taught all European imitators the value of co-operation with the existing right-wing powers, the big businessmen and the landowners. The tycoons and the aristocrats had to be won over during the dangerous years of the rise to power and the consolidation of power. In his early days as Duce of Italy, Mussolini even felt the need of claiming noble antecedents to give himself status. He said that the blood of aristocrats from Bologna flowed in his veins; his noble ancestors could be traced back to the thirteenth century. Only after a decade as dictator, and jealous of Hitler, did Mussolini feel powerful enough to claim a descent from 'generations of humble peasants' – the chief supporters of his régime.

Mussolini first distinguished himself as a Socialist, going to jail for fighting for the peasants against the 'share-croppers, tools of the landlord class'. After becoming a nationalist and a corporal in the Italian army during the First World War, he set up veterans' associations of *fasci* to exploit the political and economic chaos in Italy after the Armistice. Inflation after 1919 ruined the shop-keepers and *rentiers* and small landowners, but the aristocracy was not particularly affected. Italian nobles tended to emigrate to the South of France, when conditions or disorder in rural Italy grew too bad.

For Italy was still overwhelmingly rural. More than half of the Italians lived on the land; of these, only one-quarter owned the land which they tilled, while nine-tenths of the landowners possessed less than one-seventh of the soil. Large and medium land-owners held most of the fertile places in Italy and employed millions of agricultural labourers at starvation wages, particularly on the estates of the Neapolitan and Sicilian nobility in the South. The Italian army had been kept together after the disaster of Caporetto only by promises of land redistribution; when these promises were not kept, the massed peasants occupied the waste land of the large estates of absentee aristocrats near Rome and in the South, also in some of the more productive parts of the Po Valley. Strikes in the cities organized by the parties of the Left proved how much the democratic government had lost control, as the official army began to break up into private armies under the orders of large industrialists and landowners, the communists, the nationalists led by such men as Federzoni and d'Annunzio, and the fascists led by Mussolini. A civil war virtually broke out in 1921 in Emilia and Romagna and Tuscany.

Fear of a Bolshevik revolution in Italy was so great that the various powers of the court, the Church, industry and property had to find a strong man who could both appeal to the masses and control the splintered forces of the Right. Mussolini was that choice. His power over the veterans' groups brought him support from the industrialists who first gave him money for propaganda and organization; the aristocrats began by backing rival nationalists, but they went over to Mussolini when the nationalists joined the Fascists.

Mussolini's party elected deputies to parliament and stirred up violence until Mussolini was asked by the King to form a government, although the Fascist March on Rome was a miserable fiasco. Mussolini gratefully acknowledged the King's help by turning to him in homage as the man 'who refused to adopt useless and reactionary measures, who prevented the outbreak of civil war, and who allowed the mighty tide of fascism to flow into the dry veins of a Parliamentary State'. Mussolini was always supported by the militarist Duke of Aosta and the Queen Mother, who persuaded her son to live in Mussolini's shadow as the best way of preserving the Italian monarchy. Like most of the pessimistic Italian aristocrats, however, she spent her time in amassing bearer bonds against the day of exile; she had no intention, she said, of living uncomfortably, even as a mere Signora Savoy. When she managed to die still a queen of Italy, she gratefully made Mussolini her executor.

Mussolini was an extraordinary pacifier of class tensions; he delayed the fall of the Italian monarchy for two decades, while the aristocracy still holds on to much of its lands. Fascist trade unions made the agricultural labourers accept whatever conditions the government imposed, including lower wages; instead of expropriating the landowners, Mussolini secured their backing by scrapping death duties and resettling landless peasants on reclaimed land such as the Pontine Marches. He won what Hermann Goering complained that the Nazis could not win in their early days in Germany, the approval of 'men of property and education'. There was no redistribution of land under fascism, merely 'the battle for wheat' to increase food production without changing ownership of the soil. Photographs of the Duce himself wielding a sickle or sweating on a tractor seat seemed to allay the peasants' rebellion against the rural aristocrats. The countryfolk felt that Mussolini and the government were particularly theirs and that he would do well by them in the end. He had the gift of raising hope without a set term for its satisfaction. He even brought about a successful concordat between Church and State, which put the priests behind Fascism in their country strongholds.

Adventure was Mussolini's method of keeping his popularity. When the mad sister of an English peer grazed him with a bullet, he went on to make a speech to the crowd from his balcony with the comment, 'Perfidious Albion! We must not change the day's programme.' He married off his daughter Edda to Count Galeazzo Ciano in great style, and he put his son-in-law in charge of foreign affairs. He made the King into an emperor in Ethiopia, and he intervened in the Spanish Civil War on the side of Franco and the old order. Adventure was all right as a policy, as long as Mussolini did not take it too far. His survival depended on avoiding a military defeat, because he had not really attacked the old power-structure of Italy, based on the Crown and the generals of the old school. There was an alternative right-wing shadow government, if Mussolini should falter. But he was no longer allowed by his ex-pupil, Adolf Hitler, to duck the choice of all for Fascism or nothing. He was dragged into the Second World War on the coat-tails of the Nazi leader, now become his master, and his evil genius.

Hitler's rise to power had far more to do with a political situation, in which the aristocratic core of the army played a major role. When the Kaiser had abdicated, the German General Staff had officially ceased to exist; for it had taken a military oath directly to him. But the General Staff had decided to continue in the service of the idea of the State, whoever might represent the State in the future. In the chaotic Germany of 1918, the high-ranking officers resolved to preserve the traditional honour of their corps as the sole principle of authority. Although soldiers' councils were springing up on the Bolshevik model, the officers managed to keep enough authority to march their troops home. Thus they could believe the legend that they had never been defeated in the field, but had been stabbed in the back by treacherous civilians behind the front. The General Staff offered to support the weak new socialist government of Ebert against any terrorist *putsch*. For, as General Groener wrote in his memoirs, 'We hoped to transfer through our activity part of the power in the new state to the army and the officer corps; if we succeeded in this, the best and the strongest element of the old Prussia was saved for the new Germany, in spite of the revolution.' Even after the Allied victory, the aristocratic core of the German army refused to accept defeat, but resolved to become a state within a state until it could rise again in the service of a trustworthy government.

The General Staff, however, could not hold the army together. The officers and soldiers just went home with their arms. Soon they began to form *Freikorps* or unofficial groups of veterans under leaders who seemed to share the character of the old *Landsknechte*, adventurers ready to be hired by any political cause. The discontent of the soldiers, who found only hunger and unemployment at home, fed on the ideas of radical and nationalist agitators, such as ex-Corporal Adolf Hitler in Munich. The *Freikorps* were useful to the government and the General Staff in putting down left-wing risings such as the Spartacus revolt; but they made violence part of the political way of life in the infant German democratic state. As the anonymous author of *The Tragedy of Germany* lamented in 1921, 'The instincts of an unlicensed soldiery dominate today the whole of our public life. The hand grenade . . . the revolver and the rubber truncheon take the place of argument, murder has become the recognized instrument of politics.'

In such a situation, the aristocrats could do no more than hope to survive. While the Allied hunger blockade went on, food was their chief concern; they starved like the rest of the people. When the Duke of Mecklenburg-Schwerin was asked by the King of Denmark what he would like for a Christmas present, he replied, 'Any kind of food.' In Bavaria, the young Hubertus, who became Prince Loewenstein, was living in a bare flat when the family footman came back and settled down to serve as if nothing had changed. He wore the same blue livery with crested buttons, set Meissner china on the table and announced: 'Your Illustrious Highness, dinner is served.' Then he adjusted the chairs of all the noble family at table and served a few turnips and potatoes. Such a formal charade seemed a good thing to the princeling, saving him 'from becoming a complete savage, from sinking into absolute barbarism – a phenomenon not infrequent among the nobility once they have got below a certain point.'

The disgruntled aristocracy joined with the Junkers, the industrialists, the big businessmen, the officer corps, and the veterans' organizations to form a threat to the Republic that was greater than the communist menace. The lack of food and jobs, the shameful terms of Versailles, the boredom of a difficult peace after the heightened horrors of war, made the right-wing *Freikorps* twice attempt to seize power, partially aided and abetted by certain army officers. The number of right-wing conspirators among junior members of the officer corps made von Blomberg say, 'With Prussian officers correct behaviour had been a point of honour; with German officers it must be a point of honour to be sly.' In 1920, a Junker leader called Kapp tried to take over the government with certain *Freikorps*; the army refused to fire against ex-soldiers, but a general strike put an end to Kapp's pretensions. In Munich, Hitler's infant National Socialist Party acquired a weekly newspaper through the help of Army secret funds, also strong-arm men from military ranks through the aid of Captain Röhm. When Hitler tried, however, to carry through a premature *putsch* in Munich in 1923, he was badly defeated by the police and the army, which began to recover something of its old code of manners under the leadership of the aristocratic von Seeckt.

The Pomeranian nobility had produced von Seeckt and he sought to restore a military career to the landowners. By 1930, more than three in ten of the officer cadets commissioned came from the nobility, despite efforts by the Social Democrats to provide for the suppression of educational privileges in the corps of officers and for a quota of officers to be commissioned from the ranks. But von Seeckt and his successors continued to restore the old idea of a noble élite in command of the army. By 1932, nearly half the cavalry officers, and one-fifth of the staff and infantry officers came from the nobility, making up almost one-quarter of the whole officer corps. It was perhaps curious that such an aristocratic military group, unique in Europe, should eventually choose to help an Austrian ex-corporal on his way to the dictatorship of all Germany. Yet, as the acute Social Democrat Leber noted, the Nazis had succeeded in winning over many of the young soldiers because they offered ideals which the Republic had not; for the Republic was scared of exactly what the Nazis wanted, 'the recollection of imperial glories, and patriotic language'.

Hitler was slow to win support from the high-ranking officers and landowners and big businessmen; for these traditional right-wing groups tended to back the rival National Party. Hitler's supporter, the ex-air ace Hermann Goering, introduced Hitler to some of his contacts in upper-class circles; these included the former Crown Prince and Philipp Prince of Hesse, who had married the daughter of the King of Italy, also Fritz von Thyssen and other industrial barons as well as influential army officers. A politic alliance in 1929 with the National Party led by the press lord Hugenberg allowed Hitler to steal many of its backers and much of its publicity, before he turned to destroy it in the end. The respectable German right wing was, after all, prepared at the last resort to follow anyone from anywhere who could guarantee it what it wanted.

The Junkers had agreed to give their nominal backing to the Weimar Republic only after President von Hindenburg had insisted that the government should pay them large grain subsidies throughout the twenties; when Chancellor Brüning and his successor von Schleicher refused to continue the subsidies through the corrupt *Osthilfe*, Hindenburg dismissed them one after the other, thus facilitating the rise of Hitler to the Chancellorship. So the Junkers directly contributed to the instability of the Weimar Republic through their selfish demands. The only 'Comrade' Prince to come out in support of the Republic testified, 'Most of the Junkers I met were German Nationals, but there were also a few Nazis among them. The few who were members of the Republican parties, and were thus deserters from their caste, were regarded as suffering from some nervous complaint.'

In bad times, nothing succeeds like excess. It was Hitler's excessive promises and visions which attracted large followings among the youth, then among the conservatives and nationalists in Germany. He became the prophet of action in the discontented sloth of the great depression. Fascism was not an aristocratic movement; it was a revolutionary movement of the frustrated, who hoped to become part of a new élite which would replace the failed managers of *bourgeois* society, including the surviving aristocrats. But fascism was equally a movement in which the aristocrats might hope to survive, unlike in the opposing revolutionary movement of Communism. For while the Communists wanted to destroy the aristocrats, the fascists wanted to incorporate them into the *Volk* and into the organic whole of the nation, particularly when the nobility represented an ideal of racial inbreeding. Aristocratic leaders of fascist movements such as Prince von Starhemberg's Austrian *Heimwehr* and Sir Oswald Mosley's English Blackshirts were rare; aristocratic support of successful fascist movements was normal. Perhaps this was why, at the famous Coburg wedding of 1932, when Princess Sybille married Prince Gustavus Adolphus of Sweden, a message from Hitler was read out, thanking the House of Saxe-Coburg-Gotha for its support for the Nazi movement. Rather a Black government than a Red one.

The psychology of the aristocratic supporters of Hitler has been best explained by Friedrich Christian Prince zu Schaumberg-Lippe. He was brought up to believe that hierarchy and order were the keystones of German society. His first tutor tried to convince him that 'he must learn that all men are equal and noble birth is only a fiction if not accompanied by merit'. He was inoculated in the virtues of a military career. He was told 'at every opportunity that a man of high birth who is not a soldier is but a wretched fellow'. He played tactical manoeuvres with fifty or more friends at once; he was taught to believe that the only holy war since the Crusades was the fight against Marxism. Another tutor filled him with the recklessness of Nietzsche, while a third warned him that, even with the downfall of the monarchy, he owed his services to the German people. 'Your life belongs to others,' his final tutor stated. 'It is your damned duty and debt always to think of this and act accordingly.'

Such was the upbringing of the Prince zu Schaumberg-Lippe, his training in the concept that service to the state justifies all sacrifices. The aristocracy still had a duty to lead, even if its social standing was tarnished by its refusal to fight for the monarchy in 1918. According to the prince, the German aristocracy had different attitudes to Hitler in different regions. The wealthy aristocrats felt threatened by Hitler's rise as well as superior to his humble origins; thus he had little support in the beginning from the Rhine area, Southern Bavaria, Vienna, and Berlin. But the poorer aristocrats of Schleswig, Pomerania, East Prussia, Mecklenburg, Brunswick, Westphalia, Styria, Carinthia and the Tyrol were generally behind the Führer. Yet even when the aristocrats disapproved of Hitler, few could be found to disapprove of the more cautious Mussolini.

The attraction of the Nazi Party for most of the aristocrats lay in its appeal to their spirit of service rather than to materialism, and to its concepts of the leader and the led. 'There could never be a peaceful co-existence,' the prince wrote, 'between real aristocracy and the unnatural assertion that all men are equal.' The members of the 'real aristocracy' had to uphold many of Hitler's precepts – the duty of war against the enemies of the people and the nation, the need to fight for the principle of worth against greed, the call to revise the iniquitous Treaty of Versailles and secure the freedom of the German people at home and abroad, and the creed of strengthening the family and the farmers as the core of a truly national life.

In the aristocratic club which the prince attended, General Hasso von Manteuffel would declare that Hitler should be helped, exploited, and not followed openly. The prince ignored this advice and went to see Hitler personally to ask him whether there was any room in the Nazi Party for aristocrats. To the prince, Hitler seemed to have the gestures of a *grand seigneur*, the physique for putting the shot and throwing the discus, and 'peaceful eyes which seemed to look into eternity'. Hitler replied ambiguously, saying that the prince rightly belonged to those who were monarchists from their very roots, thus the prince might not give more than his support to the Nazis. The prince then went away to write political pamphlets stressing the need for a leader in Germany, and the need for the whole nation to obey that leader when he appeared. To the prince, his whole education had fitted him to follow Hitler on the day that Hitler could prove by his deeds that he was indeed chosen to be the Führer.[1]

Yet for every aristocrat who served the Nazis joyfully, there was another aristocrat who served them warily. Ferdinand Prince von der Leyen, seeking to explain why he became a reserve officer in 1935, revealed much of the wish to compromise with a nasty political situation that leads men into a wrong, if not an evil, choice:

I belonged, as did my family, neither to the Party nor to any seemingly harmless organization and, although I am not by nature a 'passionate' soldier, the firmly united army seemed to me as it did to many others to be the last bulwark, which might check the incoming flood of characterlessness and protect those who did not belong to the Party. . . . And yet men such as I made a fundamental mistake then: we overestimated the spiritual capital and strength of character of the professional soldiers.

The Prince von der Leyen was to reproach himself later for not resisting the Nazis other than tacitly, even when he knew of the concentration camps.

Horrors should not be forgotten, human nature remains the same. Even if only very few were directly responsible for murdering Jews, the others were not deaf and blind. . . . There is no collective guilt of evil commonly committed, but we should all be rebuked for the good that was omitted.[2]

Outside the group of aristocratic plotters who were eventually to attempt to overthrow Hitler once he began to lose the Second World War, the attitudes of the two princes gave a fair picture of the wild enthusiasm or the mild acceptance shown by the

---

[1] Friedrich Christian, Prinz zu Schaumburg-Lippe, . . . *verdammte Pflicht und Schuldigkeit* (Leoni am Starnberger See, 1966).

[2] Ferdinand, Prinz von der Leyen, *Rückblick zum Mauerwald* (München, 1966).

German aristocrats in the face of Hitler. Yet the appeal of National Socialism was to the mass as well as to the upper class. Support for the Nazis also came from the millions who found a patriotic utopia embodied in the Nazi vision of a classless society of *Herrenvolk*, the dominant race in Europe. Yet the Nazis made an equal appeal to a nostalgia for the old Prussian values and the 'ideal chains' of an aristocratic society before the defeat in the First World War, a golden age of honour and order before the wrangling and greediness of the politicians of the Weimar Republic. Thus the Nazis could attract both those who wanted a classless Germany of the future and those who wanted a restoration of the ordered Empire of the past; with a Hitler speaking for a Hohenzollern, both contradictory ideals seemed possible in his cloudy harangues.

In fact, National Socialism was soon to cement its alliance with big business and big landowners, although Hitler was to talk more and more of the classless state, as the practice of Nazism diverged further and further from his explanations. As late as 1941, when the new élite of Nazis and generals and tycoons completely ran the war machine, Hitler could declare:

What distinguishes the present from what went before is simply this: then the people were not behind the Kaiser. . . . Then the leaders had no roots in the people, for when all is said and done it was a class state. . . . Today the National Socialist community of the people takes its place at the front, and you will notice how the Armed Forces from month to month become more National Socialist, how they increasingly bear the stamp of the New Germany, how all privileges, classes, prejudices and so on are more and more removed; how, from month to month, the German national community gains ground.

Such was the egalitarian nation Hitler hoped to create and deliberately did not. He rose to power by a series of alliances with the old vested interests and found out that he could not survive in power without strengthening those alliances. Big business began to support Hitler, when it became evident that he could pull in the votes where the National Party failed to do so; his programme of rearmament was particularly attractive to the steel barons of the Ruhr, who had been pressing President von

Hindenburg to become a dictator even before Hitler became chancellor. At first the tycoons had been split between supporting as chancellor the Westphalian aristocrat von Papen or General von Schleicher or Hitler; but the increasing success of the Nazis at the polls after 1930 made the tycoons turn against von Schleicher in favour of a government led by von Papen and Hitler. Hitler, given his chance, soon eliminated his rivals. Von Papen was easily pushed aside. General von Schleicher had threatened Hitler that the army would shoot him if he came to power illegally; but once President von Hindenburg had summoned Hitler to become chancellor, it was Hitler who had von Schleicher shot, along with another general and the head of Hitler's own storm troops, Röhm, and some four hundred lesser fry. He accused them of joining in a secret French conspiracy to get rid of him; in fact, he was eliminating his most serious rivals, with the short-sighted connivance of the officer corps, which allowed the murder of two of its generals in order to secure the doubtful benefit of the murder of the head of Hitler's private army.

The reason for the army's backing of Hitler was its dislike of the Republic and Hitler's ceremonial act of obeisance in March 1933, to old Field-Marshal President von Hindenburg. At the *Tag* at Potsdam, Hitler began his chancellorship by bowing low before the President in the traditional manner of ancient Prussia. Moreover, Hitler had won over the exiled Kaiser and his second wife, Princess Hermine von Schönaich-Carolath, who became a passionate supporter of Hitler after he had vaguely hinted at restoring the Hohenzollerns. As a result, the army high commanders thought that they could manage him; in fact, he was to manage them. His selection as the new War Minister, General von Blomberg, was a convinced National Socialist and soon sent out a secret directive that aimed unsuccessfully to put an end to the aristocratic manners of the officer corps. This stated:

The old practice of seeking company within a particular social class is no longer any part of the duty of the corps of officers. Our social habits must be permeated by the realization that the whole people forms a single community. There is no warrant for preferences based on nothing but social origins and education. If this means our dropping a few individuals who cannot rid themselves of their traditional social outlook, it may be hard on those affected; but it must be done. [3]

It was not actually done, because the officer corps had a certain solidarity and even succeeded in having the names of the two murdered generals restored to the honour rolls of their regiments. But Hitler was winning the real victories against the independence of the army command. When old von Hindenburg died, Hitler had himself declared president as well as chancellor. And he made his War Minister von Blomberg compel the whole army to take the oath 'before God' to the new Führer and chancellor; the officers did so, even when it offended their sense of Christian traditionalism. Hitler followed up his advantage by increasing the power of his new private armies, the security service and the Gestapo under Himmler; this led to more friction with the officer corps, which found that Hitler's mania for ranting and conquest was a two-edged sword, admirable when it re-equipped a new German military machine prepared for war, despicable when it tried to use that army for irrational adventures and ruthless extermination of lesser races.

There was no room for a code of honour in Nazism other than loyalty to the Führer, and the officer corps stuck by its own code of honour. However hard he tried, Hitler could not replace good officers with good Nazis who made bad officers. In addition to his suspicion of professional soldiers who were not his devoted followers, Hitler had a violent aversion to officers that dated from his days in the ranks. He knew well that they despised him as a 'Bohemian corporal', while he despised the 'gentlemen' who wrote *von* before their names and had never served as privates at the front. The Junker code and Hitlerism were sometimes allied by circumstance, but always opposed by nature.

The Junkers out of the army on their Prussian estates also did a deal with Hitler, which was to prove fatal to them and their sons after twelve years. By the farm laws of 1933, the Nazis agreed not

[3] Quoted in K. Demeter, *The German Officer Corps in Society and State, 1650-1945* (London, 1965) pp. 368-9.

to touch the estates of large landowners, even though this meant betraying their plans to resettle landless labourers on their own farms. By refusing to expropriate the Junkers in return for their support, Hitler was unable to resettle his land-hungry peasant followers except where land was bought or reclaimed. His answer to the problem, already set out in *Mein Kampf*, was a war of expansion, which could give the German peasants all the farms they wanted in the conquered countries of the Poles and the Czechoslovaks and the Russians. Although the Nazis successfully controlled agricultural production and marketing and bound the peasants to the soil in a medieval way, the larger grain-producing estates of the Junkers flourished under the Nazi régime, which soon gave up its ideas of peasant socialism for fascist imperialism. Thus the Nazis committed the Junkers to a future war of expansion to solve the land-hunger of Germany; and the Junkers, by trying to preserve too much from the Nazis, lost everything to the Red Army.

Equally, Nazi promises to help artisans and small businessmen in a middle-class economy of directed socialism soon gave way to an open alliance with the tycoons in order to prepare for war. Hitler's policy by 1936 was mostly nationalism and a little socialism. Nordic religion and social harmony between labourers and employers were underplayed as ideals in favour of fascist imperialism, racialism and élite rule. Small groups in the Nazi party, big business and the military, working in their own spheres for the same end, the rearmament of Germany, produced moderately high employment, a successful foreign policy of daring, and the weapons needed to turn Hitler's dreams of force into fact. He himself, in order to create a new aristocracy of will rather than of birth, set up *Ordensburgen*, based on the old castles of the Teutonic Knights, where trainees for the Nazi élite lived in absolute obedience and learned discipline, party ideology, 'racial sciences', military tactics and the strategy of expansion to the East; the final training castle was actually the old castle of the Teutonic Knights in Marienburg in East Prussia on the very frontier of the lands to be conquered. In the interim, Hitler used the old aristocracy which supported him; more than one-quarter of the members of Hitler's cabinets were aristocrats compared with one-tenth under the Weimar Republic.

In a curious way, Nazi ideology was the perversion of the nobility's obsession with good breeding. Racism is, after all, the lowest common denominator of the aristocratic urge to feel oneself better *born* than the rest of the human species. The aristocrat disdains the masses of mankind outside his small hereditary group; the racist loathes the rest of men outside his large hereditary group. Hitler's claptrap about the superior Aryan race was merely a maniac's version of the old nonsense about the superiority of the blood royal, this time applied to a whole people. The arguments for the excellence of white skin and blond hair were merely the same sad stuff as the arguments in favour of blue blood, writ rather larger. Hitler's trumpeted classless society was a society in which every German was classed as an aristocrat and everyone else as a slave. Hitler's wish to replace the old German aristocracy with the new Nazi élite was mixed up with his wish to breed eugenically a new race of supermen, whose deeds would outdo the aristocratic legends of Siegfried. Instead of the nobility of the past, Hitler wished to create a nobility of the future, bound by blood and duty to the Führer as once the Counts were bound to the Holy Roman Emperor.

Elsewhere in Eastern Europe, fascism was bound up with this same perversion of the aristocratic ideal of pure breeding and authority over inferior races. It fed on the dislocations and frustrations produced at the end of the Great War. Nowhere were these irrational forces stronger than in Austria in 1919. It had been bad enough in Vienna before the war, far worse than in London or Paris or Berlin. Then, conditions had warranted a social revolution that did not come until the break-up of the Habsburg Empire. For a quarter of the city population had lived with a whole family in one room, while some 150,000 people had used the *bettgeher* system of leasing a bed in shifts. The Magyar aristocracy had deliberately kept food prices high for the benefit of their estates; meat had cost more than any worker's budget could afford and the importation of cheap meat from the Argentine had been forbidden; thus the average worker's diet was contained in the proverb of the Adlersgebirge weavers, 'When the water-soup and the potatoes have been eaten twenty-one times the week has gone.'

The Austrian working class was already suffering the worst evils of primitive industrialism, including the sweated labour of children; the war and the Allied 'hunger blockade' after the war made its sufferings intolerable. The Allies wanted to starve the new moderate socialist government of Austria into accepting the dismemberment of the empire under the terms of Versailles. All at once reduced to a petty landlocked nation of six million, Austria found herself with a huge and unnecessary bureaucracy, an excessive professional class, and only enough land to feed a third of her population.

The Viennese aristocrats, who had done nothing to help the Habsburgs in their downfall, were very lucky not to lose all themselves. The break-up of the Habsburg Empire had been caused as much by a choice against the feudal rule of German and Magyar and Polish aristocrats as by outside pressure and a choice for democracy and national independence. But in Vienna, the nobles' complacency and disengagement from politics allowed the moderate socialist government to pluck them rather than destroy them. All Austrian titles were abolished; one Count of the Holy Roman Empire still goes round with a visiting card stating that he was knighted by Charlemagne and unknighted by Dr Renner, the socialist leader. The socialists had promised to expropriate the great property owners; but nothing was done in the end, except the virtual expropriation of landlords in Vienna through low fixed rents and the imposition of heavy taxes on luxuries. The socialist government was too weak to proceed against the vested interests, which would certainly be backed by the right-wing veterans' organizations such as the *Heimwehr*, already in contact with veterans' groups in Italy and Germany.

Moreover, the socialists could not trust their own little federal army, which rapidly became as pro-Habsburg as a republican army could decently be. There was also the fear of a Bolshevik revolution, given the horror of living conditions in post-war Austria. Between the red devil and the deep blue sea, the socialist government could not provoke its enemies by outright assaults; it had to try to diminish their power slowly. Thus it was a tribute to the strong and clever policy of the municipality of Vienna that Baroness Ravensdale could visit the city in 1929 and decide that Viennese society was dying a lingering death. She admired the splendid new tenements, schools and hospitals; but she argued that the Burgomaster, by taxing the rich so crushingly, was killing the goose that laid the golden eggs. His reply was that this did not matter, as long as the taxes lasted until the population was healthy and well fed and well housed; then the people could look after themselves.

During the socialist government of Austria in the 1920's, the aristocrats retired from politics, shutting up their palaces in Vienna to save paying taxes for their servants and to keep out of the way of the city mob. An observer of this decade said that the aristocracy had no desire for a Habsburg restoration; it contented itself 'with boycotting the Republic, its public services and institutions, and in indulging in a pious hope that this misbegotten Republic will one day be seen to be in every way unworkable without the leadership of the former great families.'[4] That pious hope was rapidly to be realized by the upsurge of fascism in Austria; the core of the movement was the *Heimwehr* led by the aristocrat Prince Ernst von Starhemberg. He both raised and armed his private battalions of the *Heimwehr*, while the government merely looked on. Funds came through from the Nazis and from Munich and the Ruhr; obviously Hitler, an Austrian himself, was hoping that the success of fascism in both countries would lead to their eventual merging in a Greater Germany. He did not calculate, however, on the extreme nationalism of Prince Starhemberg, who supported the authoritarian and clerical-fascist régimes of Dollfuss and von Schuschnigg between 1933 and 1938. It was the respectability of Prince Starhemberg which gave the *Heim-*

[4] G. Gedye, *Heirs to the Habsburgs* (Bristol, 1932) p.28.

wehr the support of the Church and the leading bourgeois political party of the time, and which allowed it to share in power through an alliance with the politicians. The authoritarian governments of Dollfuss and von Schuschnigg were never as severe as the Nazi régime, despite the horrible massacre of a thousand Viennese workers in 1934 by federal and fascist forces.

Yet the success of the National Socialists in Germany led to a split in the *Heimwehr*, encouraged by Hitler. The Styrian section backed the Nazis and an *Anschluss* with Germany, while Prince Starhemberg co-operated with the nationalist and conservative Austrian government. Mussolini, fearful of a German presence on the Alps, backed Starhemberg and helped him to organize a counter-terror, the Fatherland Front recruited from patriotic Austrian right-wingers, who drove the National Socialists back. Mussolini again prevented Hitler from taking over Austria, when the Austrian Nazis murdered Dollfuss in 1934; and von Schuschnigg, the new Chancellor, cleverly isolated Starhemberg from Mussolini and the Fatherland Front when the Prince seemed likely to loose his own *putsch*. A congratulatory telegram from Starhemberg to Mussolini at the successful end of the Duce's Abyssinian campaign provided Schuschnigg with the opportunity of excluding the fascist Prince from the government and the Fatherland Front. This was tragic for the independence of Austria; when Schuschnigg collapsed in front of Hitler in 1938 and accepted all the Nazi demands, there was no right-wing leader with a private army to fight for Austrian independence against the supporters of a National Socialist Greater Germany.

Schuschnigg, himself an Austrian aristocrat, was as unable to cope with Hitler's threats and ruthlessness as the German generals of the old school, whom Hitler had just disgraced. Threatening Austria with invasion, Hitler brow-beat Schuschnigg into handing over the police to an Austrian Nazi. The result was that local Nazis took to the streets of Vienna in their tens of thousands without fear of counter-attack; they mobbed the middle-class Jews, always a useful target in a riot, and their nationalist and left-wing enemies. The situation became so desparate that Otto of

Habsburg, the youthful pretender to the Austrian throne, wrote from exile, reminding the chancellor of his old oath of loyalty to the Habsburgs when Schuschnigg had been an imperial officer, and offering to serve as chancellor in Schuschnigg's place, if such a step would save Austria's independence. Schuschnigg preferred to ask the Austrian left wing to save him; but it had been too crushed and disarmed by his own authoritarian state. Thus Hitler mobilized on the frontier, using a plan called Special Case Otto, ready against the emergency of Otto of Habsburg's return to the throne.

In this crisis, fearful of another intervention by Mussolini to save Austria, Hitler sent Philipp Prince of Hesse to Rome to flatter the Duce into staying put. Hitler claimed that Austria and Czechoslovakia were plotting to restore the Habsburgs and send twenty million men against Germany; this farrago of nonsense was delivered by its princely bearer; Mussolini considered the situation and decided to throw Austria to the wolves, as he needed Hitler's backing for his imperial dreams in the Mediterranean. France was caught between a change of governments; in England, the Foreign Secretary, Anthony Eden, had resigned and had been replaced by the amenable Lord Halifax. Hitler had nothing to fear.

The Austrian Nazis took over the government and invited the Germans to enter in triumph. Hitler made a conqueror's return to the capital where he had starved in his youth, and delivered one of his harangues from a reviewing stand opposite the Hofburg, the ancient palace of the Habsburgs. He had, after all, achieved the nostalgic dream of the German aristocrats, the reuniting of the German-speaking peoples once again in a Greater Germany, somewhat similar to the area of the Holy Roman Empire. Von Papen, exiled by Hitler as ambassador to Vienna, wrote of Hitler 'as being in a state of ecstasy'.

So Vienna became a provincial capital of the Third Reich and the last remnants of its imperial glories were gone; Habsburg princes were sent to Dachau. A poor Austrian, jumped up in Germany, had wiped the name of Austria off the map; it was now known as Ostmark. The Jews were set to menial tasks, were bullied and jailed, and were wholly looted. The palaces of the Rothschilds were stripped; Baron Louis de Rothschild was able to buy his way out of the country by turning his steel mills over to Hermann Goering. Schuschnigg was degraded and sent to various concentration camps, although he was allowed to marry by proxy Countess Vera Czernin, a brave woman who chose to share her new husband's life in the concentration camps. By an irony of fate, Philipp Prince of Hesse joined the ex-Chancellor of Austria in the concentration camps in 1944, when his wife, the daughter of the King of Italy, had been done to death by the SS after the Italian King had deposed Mussolini and had gone over to the side of the Allies.

In Hungary and Poland, the issue between a government of the left or the right was solved quickly and bloodily after the end of the First World War. In both countries, after a brief period of Bolshevik successes, the old régime counter-attacked and held on to power until the Second World War. In Hungary, some of the aristocrats tried to lead a mild left-wing revolution – the last flare-up of the lamp going out, as Trotsky described it. Count Michael Károlyi became the radical Premier in 1918 and Archduke Josef willingly dropped his titles to become plain Josef Habsburg in the new order. But revolution in the Kerensky style was not enough; it had to be all or nothing. The vicious red terror of Béla Kun succeeded Károlyi's government, only to be succeeded in its turn by the more vicious white terror, which eventually ended in the establishment of the stable Horthy government. Admiral Horthy himself backed the old Catholic Magnates of Hungary and only claimed to be a Regent for the missing Habsburg dynasty. His Premier from an old Transylvanian princely family, Count Bethlen, even went as far as restoring the aristocratic House of Magnates after 1925, giving great political power back to the nobility and certain members of the House of Habsburg.

In fact, the Horthy régime was old-fashioned and relatively

moderate, gaining the support of landowners and Jews and sometimes the left-wing against the radical and racist excesses preached by the Hungarian National Socialists. Little was done about land reform in Hungary, although about one-tenth of the available arable land was redistributed in the 1920's. Yet even so, more than one-third of the fertile areas of Hungary was owned by the Church and some 1,500 Magnates. Prince Esterházy still owned 180,000 acres of good land alone; the Pallavicinis and the Károlyis and the Semseys held on to vast areas; conditions were so feudal on these estates that the Hungarians called them 'kingdoms in miniature'. Curiously enough, these great Catholic Hungarian families were no longer dominated by their agricultural interests, because of their heavy investments in industry and banking. They usually supported a Habsburg nostalgia, co-operation with entrepreneurs of all races, a limited suffrage, and a lingering of the old ways on their estates and in the society of Budapest. Their opponents were usually the Protestant gentry and the petty *bourgeoisie*, who easily fell for the National Socialist doctrine of race hatred, and who saw their opportunity in the promised despoiling of the Magnates and the Jews.

Although the ex-Habsburg Emperor Karl twice tried to return to the throne of Hungary, he failed on both occasions. The aims of the Catholic Magnates were less to restore the Habsburgs than to use the imperial myth as an excuse for a foreign policy which sought the old frontiers of Hungary; for two-thirds of the state had been lopped off after the First World War. This demand to revise the boundaries of Hungary was partially the tenacious effort of a ruling class to divert peasant and industrial discontent at home into adventure abroad. The Magnates also regretted their old estates lost behind the borders of the new nations created out of the ruins of the Habsburg Empire; although they were lucky to hang on to power in Hungary more than in any other state of Central Europe, they still wallowed in their nostalgia for their great days under the Habsburg Empire. A fanatic Hungarian patriotism which united all Magyars was a great catalyst against the divisions of rich and poor.

In 1932 with fascism on the rise everywhere in Europe, General Gyula Gömbös, the son of well-to-do Swabian peasants, became prime minister and moved the reactionary Hungarian government more in the direction of Mussolini's Italy. Although Gömbös preached an attack on aristocrats and Jews, he continued to rule in concert with both groups. What he did do was to change the tone of the régime towards demagogy and away from aristocratic paternalism. He put down radical fascist organizations such as the peasant Scythe Cross; he did not object to it hating communists, but to it hating gentlemen. In the Arrow Cross movement, however, several Hungarian aristocrats were among its founders and made it quite respectable among the Magnates; the fascist Count Sándor Festetics could order his peasants to vote him into parliament in 1935, using his *seigneur's* authority from the past to try and set up a new Hungarian order. The Arrow Cross, however, needed a more dynamic leader from a more obscure background, the ex-officer Ferenc Szálasi, to gain prestige and eventually power in the last days of pre-communist Hungary, when Szálasi was to begin the attack on the great estates which the communists were to continue until the power of the Magnates was to be obliterated.

The experience of Poland between the world wars was also reactionary rather than fascist under the national hero Marshal Pilsudski, the victor over the Red Armies. Pilsudski was prepared to put through enough land reform to satisfy the peasants, but he had no intention of wiping out the Polish aristocracy; in fact, he was prepared to bolster that aristocracy when it would make the Polish nation stronger. Pilsudski used expropriation against the aristocrats when they were German as in West Prussia, which had fallen to Poland after the Great War. There the German landowners were dispossessed and tens of thousands of Polish farmers were resettled on the Junker estates. In more Polish areas, Pilsudski moved warily; but he was prepared during the great depression to seize 125,000 acres from the largest landowner in Poland, Count Zamoyski, in lieu of taxes, and also many of the estates of the Countess Branicki. Peasants were settled on these

large tracts of land taken from two of the most famous families
in Poland, whose ancestors included the heroic Jan Sobieski.
Such measures convinced the aristocrats, isolated as they were
even in Warsaw from the world of government and business,
that Pilsudski was arbitrary in his methods and that land reform,
as Princess Virgilia Sapieha reported, was 'useless and unjust';
surely the peasants were destined by God to stay on the land run
by the old aristocratic families.

In Galicia, however, where the Polish aristocracy was a small
minority set over a large rebellious Ukrainian majority, Pilsudski
backed the Polish nobles to the hilt. They were the representatives
of the Polish state in an area where there were too few Poles;
if there was expropriation to be done, it was at the expense of the
Ukrainians. The Polish aristocrats in Galicia, always fearful of a
peasant uprising, had been the most faithful subjects of the
Habsburgs in the old days of the Austro-Hungarian Empire;
Princess Catherine Radziwill described them as 'subserviently
faithful to the Habsburgs, who have toadied to them, caressed
them, exploited them, and allowed them all the liberty which
they cared to have'. In exactly the same way, the Galician
nobility was subserviently faithful to Pilsudski, who toadied
back to them for the same reasons as the Habsburgs, and allowed
them to keep small private armies to cow the Ukrainians.

Pilsudski did resettle some 3,000,000 landless Poles on some
500,000 new farms; but he did not displace the old aristocracy
where it could strengthen the Polish nation. Even in the depths
of the agricultural depression, which ruined this nation of food-
producers, nobody blamed the old Polish patriot, who had
allowed feudalism to linger on oppressively in the Polish countryside. Conditions had not changed on the great estate of Lancut,
when Count Alfred Potocki received Mary Curzon, Baroness
Ravensdale, in the 1930's. As the Baroness wrote of the Count:

The peasants collected acres of sugar-beet for him, and kissed his feet
as he passed by on his horse. I was a menace to him inquiring into the
wages and earnings of these poor mortals on the land and in the
factories. The low standard appalled me. The peasants' horses were so

thin that I could not drive in Alfred's coach and four past these creeping animals without feeling ashamed of his wealth. The gigantic house teemed with servants – one slept outside my door. It had so many *salons*, so many dining-rooms, that we used different ones on different days of the week. Valuable French works of art, pictures and porcelains adorned the walls, mostly of the period of Marie Antoinette. [5]

Potocki, convinced that the Polish nobility was a popular and progressive body of patriots, kept his illusions too late. Like the last French Queen and all his aristocratic friends, Potocki lost every scrap of his estates in 1944, 'expropriated and divided for the benefit of the People', whom he seems to have benefited so little.

In Czechoslovakia, the government also applied Pilsudski's policy in West Prussia, because the aristocracy was predominantly German and Hungarian in a country which was mostly Czech and Slovak. Bohemia and Moravia had been regions where the big estate and the game preserve had flourished; after 1919, more than one-third of the country was requisitioned with forced compensation; legally nobody was allowed more than a maximum of 700 acres of soil. This land reform seemed reasonable in areas where one-third of the soil belonged to less than one in a hundred landowners; but as the expropriated landlords bore names such as Clam-Gallas, Liechtenstein and Schwarzenberg, Czech social justice could seem to be anti-German nationalism. The seized land was, indeed, primarily given to the Czechs, which seemed a method of establishing watchdogs among the Sudeten Germans.

The large landowners themselves went so far as to complain to the League of Nations in 1922 that no Germans had sat in the Constituent Assembly voting on land reform, which was merely a revenge against a defeated minority enclosed within the frontiers of a new and persecuting state. When the Czech government then seized the forest lands on the German frontier in the interests of national security, aristocratic and Sudeten indignation boiled over. In racial terms, the frontier forests had been German for

[5] Baroness Ravensdale, *In Many Rhythms* (London, 1953) p. 118.

centuries, and here noble and peasant felt as one. As the town of Graslitz announced, 'The attack on German home land will meet the united resistance of the whole German population, since our German people is bound indivisibly to its soil and its woods, and will never divorce itself from this inheritance.' In this way, the aristocracy's defence of its privileges was to provide Hitler with an excuse to rape Czechoslovakia in 1938, on the pretext that land reform was oppressing the whole Sudeten people.

Yet the Czech government's attack on the aristocrats appeared more severe than it was. The Schwarzenbergs were left with some 70,000 illegal acres; other large proprietors among the Sudeten Germans were also left with great estates in the frontier districts; even the minority Catholic Church was allowed to remain a large land-holder in Protestant Czechoslovakia. Although titles were officially abolished as in Austria, the nobility continued to use its titles without trouble. As it happened, the democratic Czech régime's attack on the Catholic alien aristocracy of the new state was to make that aristocracy seem the champion of the new minority groups who had been the old masters, and to prepare Sudeten opinion for the mystical organic thinking of Nazism with its emphasis on German ties to soil and pure blood. In fact, when the Nazis took over Czechoslovakia, their New Order would have no place for those aristocrats who had fought for Germany and themselves by clinging on to their land. The Schwarzenbergs themselves opposed Hitler, as did the Esterházys, whose estates lay both in Hungary and Czechoslovakia; both these great families were far-sighted enough to see that their survival had more chance under democracy than under fascism.

Elsewhere in Eastern Europe, the aristocracy did no better than in Czechoslovakia; even under the most reactionary of governments as in King Carol's Rumania, land reform and the end of the Class Voting system were necessary in order to steal the Bolsheviks' thunder and to raise up a wall of nationalist property owners against a communist attack. Yet the aristocrats remained powerful; with their compensation money, they bought their way into the banking system and salted away funds in Switzerland against the day of exile and lived a life of flagrant luxury. The few in high society in Bucharest existed extravagantly in their American cars and Paris fashions; it was the same in Belgrade and Athens. Although Rumania acquired the trappings of the fascist state, it was really no more than a gloss on the old system, and Codreanu's radical Iron Guard was suppressed by a traditional ruling class and new plutocracy that wanted peace to pursue their *douceur de vivre*. Yugoslavia also went through a major land reform; but the state under King Alexander and Stojadinovic was like Rumania, superficially fascist but really reactionary, except in Croatia where fascism helped to sustain the rebelliousness of the Croatian peasants. In Greece, where the monarchy was thrown out in 1923 and recalled in 1935, the government remained reactionary, land reform was mild, and the radical left and right made little progress.

As land was the basis of a stable aristocracy, the degree of land reform in Central and Eastern Europe between the world wars showed the actual power retained by the nobility. In Germany and Italy, the nobility kept titles and land and local power at the price of conceding political power to the Fascist and the National Socialist Parties. In Hungary and Poland, the nobility retained most of their lands and national power. In the other nations set up on the fall of the Habsburg and Hohenzollern and Romanov Empires there was sweeping land reform, but no proscription of the aristocrats, who still held limited power in certain areas of national life. In all, some 70,000,000 acres of arable land were redistributed, or one-fifth of the total area of farming land. The liquid capital thus available to the old aristocracy was reinvested in banking and industry and escape funds abroad. Yet as the nobles lost their land, so they lost the basis of their feudal power and respect; and they became distinguished only by their titles and perhaps by their manners from the new plutocracy of capitalism and fascism.

Radical fascism did, indeed, preach the destruction of the aristocracy and a classless national state; but once in power, the fascists always found it easier to accommodate themselves to a lesser or greater degree with the aristocrats. The nobility of Central and Eastern Europe can, perhaps, not be reproached too much for compromising with triumphant fascism; at least, a deal was possible with this new élite, while a communist régime meant certain devastation. It was, of course, a fatal compromise in all the areas which fell behind the line of march of the victorious Red Army at the end of the Second World War; to be a noble *and* a fascist was to be doubly a class enemy. Yet in Western Europe, a politic alliance with reaction or fascism could mean an anachronistic survival of power for the nobility. This was particularly the case in Spain and Portugal.

Portugal decided to ignore the twentieth century and remain resolutely in its agricultural past. Although Dr Salazar rose to power after a military march on Lisbon in the style of Mussolini, the Portugese dictator decided to postpone the nightfall of the old ways, as the Surrealists once put it, indefinitely until the next instalment. The republican governments had abolished titles, Salazar restored them. Portugal became the haven for most of the exiled royalty of Europe; and Salazar gave judicious help to the nationalists during the Spanish Civil War so that he could be sure of a friendly right-wing power in Spain. Nazi help to Franco was conveyed through Lisbon harbour with the utmost smoothness; under such a reactionary régime, the aristocracy of Portugal could be sure of remaining in its semi-feudal state.

In Spain, however, the decades between the world wars were full of violence and sudden change. In 1923 rebellions in Morocco and Catalonia led to the end of the Spanish parliamentary government and the dictatorship of General Primo de Rivera, whom King Alfonso XIII of Spain once miscalled 'my Mussolini', but who was no more than a military dictator seeking to keep order and continue the industrialization of agricultural Spain. The aristocrats with their huge estates in Central and Southern Spain were hardly likely to be disturbed by a régime in which court etiquette was so strict that the Queen went bathing at Santander escorted by two armed guards in full uniform, who had to follow Her Majesty into deep water up to their necks. 'It was a most extraordinary sight,' wrote the Duke of Sutherland, 'the sort of thing one might expect in Ruritania.' The great depression ended this anachronistic idyll; Rivera resigned and the King soon withdrew into exile, when the municipal elections of 1931 showed that the Spanish cities had turned against the monarchy.

The Republican ministries of the next five years were traditional opponents of the Church and the great landed estates. Although the Church lands had been confiscated in 1837, the Church hierarchy was considered the ally of the aristocracy, even if the village priests sometimes lived a life as poor as Christ's own. The new government was attacked from both left and right, with the anarchists firing churches and the monarchists plotting a *putsch* to bring back the King. The government retaliated by attacking the anarchists and by abolishing all titles of nobility, for all Spaniards were now called free and equal. State payment to priests was to stop, and land reform was to begin in Andalusia, Estremadura, and some provinces of Castile and Murcia. All untilled estates were to be taken over and redistributed to the peasants. The large estates in Galicia and other parts of Castile were, however, untouched; the Minister of Labour called the measure 'an aspirin to cure an appendicitis', since it would hardly provide for the irrigation that had formerly made Spain one of the most fertile provinces of the Roman Empire.

Yet, even so, the Spanish aristocrats were right to fear the agrarian reform law as a deliberate attack on the feudal nobility. The leading intellectual and orator of the Republican government, Manuel Azaña, was absolutely lucid about the government's actions and intentions. In a brilliant speech on 8 September, 1932, he proposed to parliament the additional expropriation without compensation of three hundred large landowners. He used these words:

We conceive the Republic as a work of reconstruction for the whole of Spanish society, of destruction for the old parties of this society, of everything which is rotten, harmful and archaic in the State, so that we can build on these ruins a new society. We have the will – and I think no republican can give the lie to us – to create a class of rural workers living off their own work, of the direct exploitation of the earth, and that cannot happen without breaking the chains of landed property that have bound Spain down for so many centuries.

So, it is absolutely certain that the nobility constitute a social fact which prevents the progress of the Republic and the Revolution. If we recognize this, we will suppress this social fact. I know well that this is daring, this is revolutionary, this is an upheaval. That is why we are doing it.

The Republic must destroy all large landed estates which do not know how to develop and which are the basis of the economic power of a social class which can put the biggest check on the progress of the Republic.

With such a hater of landed power and privilege in the key post of Minister of War, the aristocrats had every reason to fear that the first agrarian reform law was only the thin end of a wedge that would split them for ever from their lands. Thus they resolved to retaliate with Azaña's own official weapon, the Spanish army.

The Spanish army was an army where there were only ten men for each officer; many of those men were mercenaries from Spanish Morocco. The officers were patriotic reactionaries, their eyes fixed backwards on the glories of the Spanish Crown and Church in the old days of empire. In the same way as German officers, they felt more loyal to the mystical idea of the state than to the Republic, which seemed to oppose that idea. They were split in sympathy between the nascent fascist Falange, usually supported by the *bourgeois* officers, and between the two different pretenders to the throne, supported by the aristocratic officers; those from wealthy families normally backed Alfonso XIII and were known as the monarchists, while the Carlists from the poorer aristocracy were ranged behind Don Alfonso Carlos. The abortive *putsch* of General Sanjurjo in 1932 – mostly plotted from the Seville house of the Marchioness de Esquivel – united much of the aristocracy behind the conspirators; 145 of the nobles and officers were deported to a penal colony, including two princes of the House of Bourbon.

Spanish fascism provided more effective plotters against the

Republic than the aristocracy. Mussolini subsidized and armed the fascist rebels within the army, and the right wing made increasing gains at the polls against the government. From 1934 onwards violence grew worse. Agrarian reform was so slow that villagers in the Estremadura began to take over the neglected estates, and the government did not dare to stop them. The army under the equivocal General Francisco Franco was called in by the government to crush a rising of miners in the Asturias. Officers of the Civil Guard and Falangists began killing each other in the streets; the police officer who slew the fascist Marquis de Heredia was himself killed and buried on the same day as the right-wing leader Calvo Sotelo. This double murder was the signal for the monarchists led by the Count de Vallellano to leave parliament and flee with most of the aristocracy from Madrid to the relative safety of their country estates, knowing that the republican mob would soon get out of control. And, indeed, when the army officers began the successful *putsch* in Morocco and in various Spanish garrison towns that opened the Civil War, city mobs did attack all the aristocrats they could find.

At the opening of the Civil War, the Spanish aristocracy survived best in the broad belt of land running from the Portuguese frontier north of Madrid to the French frontier at the Carlist stronghold of Navarre. In that most Catholic area, the rebellious nationalists committed atrocities on the poor and cowed the peasants and townsmen into submission. But in the Basque and Catalonian country, near Madrid and in the South, the rich and the nobility and the clergy were decimated. The palaces and the churches were sacked; private or clerical wealth was presumed to be a confession of guilt against the poor. The Republican government and the anarchists killed with the fervour of crusaders for a classless utopia. Like the old French revolutionaries, they wanted to wipe out the last traces of privilege in blood. Those aristocrats who did not get away to nationalist areas were butchered and their property confiscated, although in many rural areas the peasants only killed their immediate and hated boss, the factor, rather than the more remote owner of the land. This official obliteration of the old régime made the Nationalists even more ferocious and united the army, the Church, the monarchists and the Carlists in 'a certain class desperation, a greater knowledge of the really disastrous consequences of defeat than existed on the Republican side.'

While the Spanish Civil War ran its bloody course for three years, the western democracies washed their hands of the affair, as the Italians and the Germans intervened on the side of the Nationalists and the Russians aided the Republicans. What had begun as a war between Spanish clericalism and aristocratic militarism on one side and Spanish democracy on the other ended as a war between the rival totalitarian ideologies of Europe, fascism and communism. No more perceptive than the generation before the outbreak of the First World War, the nobles played away the last years of the thirties, largely unconscious that the prelude of the Second World War was being fought in Spain. On the Riviera, the Duchess di Sermoneta received her French and German and Italian and American friends from the *beau monde*. 'We heard of Toledo being taken and the Alcazar relieved, but it was like the muttering of distant thunder. We played golf all day and bridge in the evening.'

When an English peer's daughter, the Honourable Jessica Mitford, ran away to besieged Bilbao with her pro-Republican future husband Esmond Romilly, a destroyer was sent by Anthony Eden to bring them out. She was English enough to complain about a Basque beating his dog over the face with a whip, only to receive a tirade from her husband on how much the aristocracy took refuge from the real problems of their time in an easy sentimentality over pets and prettier things. He said:

What right have you got to try to impose your beastly upper-class preoccupation with animals on these people? . . . Don't you know how the English people of your class treat *people*, in India and Africa and all over the world? . . . You'll see plenty of horrible sights, bombed children dying in the streets. French people and Spaniards don't give a damn about animals, and why should they? They happen to think people are more important. If you're going to make such an unholy fuss about dogs you should have stayed in England, where they feed the dogs steak and let the people in the slums die of starvation. . . . [6]

In the western democracies, indeed, the aristocrats remained wrapped in their own preoccupations with their particular way of life, which seemed to survive the radical changes that fascism and communism were imposing elsewhere in Europe. Proust noticed that in post-war France, a new Society sprang up in Paris with a 'prodigious aptitude for breaking up class distinctions. The springs of a machine which had been strained were bent or broken and no longer worked, a thousand strange bodies penetrated it, deprived it of its homogeneity, its distinction, its colour.' Some aristocrats such as the Prince de Faucigny-Lucinge, the Prince Georges Ghika, the Duke de Luynes, the Viscount de Noailles, and the Counts de Beaumont and de Fels, welcomed the new celebrities of the stage or screen or literature or bohemia, as these new breeds displaced them from the society columns of the newspapers; they were repaid by the ironical gratitude of those they helped, recorded in Jean Cocteau's film *Blood of a Poet* by the shot of an aristocrat clapping politely from his box as the poet dies on stage. On one celebrated occasion, a gentleman insisted on talking literature to the Duchess de Noailles, confusing her with the poetess Anna de Noailles until she was forced to answer, 'You are mistaken, Monsieur, I am only the Duchess.'

The rest of the old nobility retired more and more to its estates to nurse its bitter sense of hereditary superiority. Louise-Marie Ferré in 1936 found that the *noblesse* was a class with the character of a caste, military in outlook and obsessed with heredity; it numbered some 60,000 families who pretended to nobility, many of whose titles came from a 'personal fantasy'; it was 'a cardboard aristocracy, not a parchment one'; only some 800 families actually came from the ancient nobility. Yet the urge to acquire the monosyllable *de* before a name was so strong among *arrivistes* that they were prepared to break a provision of the criminal code and falsely claim nobility in an effort to distinguish

[6] J. Mitford, *Hons and Rebels* (London, 1960) p. 117.

themselves in levelling France, thus manufacturing false titles to cover up the real factory goods which were the basis of their wealth. Yet had not even the sceptical Voltaire been beaten to a pulp by a noble's bullies for the pathetic snobbery of adding *de* in front of the greatest name among the *philosophes* of the *ancien régime*?

The nobility was, however, distinct from the 'two hundred families' which the Popular Front accused of ruling France in the thirties. These were the great banking and industrial families, into which the nobility married from time to time, but which did not spring out of the nobility. The characteristics of the nobility noticed by Ferré were, indeed, the characteristics of a caste fighting for survival, not clawing its way into power; these characteristics included the desire for isolation, an extreme hostility towards intrusion by strangers, an excessive concentration upon genealogy and precedence and the cult of ancestry, over-strict manners and extreme politeness within the family, the education of children by governesses and tutors and private schools, a preference for the peasantry and a hatred of the *bourgeoisie*, a love of riding and hunting and the chase, and a strict Catholicism that allowed for a worldly life outside the provinces. In contrast to the *haute bourgeoisie*, a noble did not have to possess money to be considered a noble by other nobles; birth was the ultimate criterion. Apart from a few nobles engaged in diplomacy and literature and the Church, the army remained the predominant function of the aristocrat in search of a career.

The French officer corps after 1918 may have remained largely *bourgeois* with aristocratic officers heavily concentrated in the cavalry regiments; but officers became increasingly conservative and cut off from national life, putting on the manners and beliefs of those rural aristocrats and reactionary elements in society who had done the least to adapt themselves to modern France. Therefore the officer corps easily fell prey to right-wing propaganda in the 1930's and was greatly penetrated by anti-republican groups such as the *Cagoule*, which supported a military dictatorship to solve the problems of the slump. The Popular Front government of the Jewish Léon Blum, indeed, represented the high point of the estrangement between the officers and the government; psychologically, they were more sympathetic to fascist doctrine from Italy or Germany than to French republican tradition. Yet when the army was to collapse in 1940, considerations of aristocratic honour would make a few officers obey their conscience rather than Marshal Pétain and follow de Gaulle into exile and resistance.

Although the fascists in France were split, as elsewhere, into supporters of a conservative or a radical solution to France's problems, their chief philosopher, Charles Maurras, put forward a defence of the hereditary aristocracy in his *Action Française*, which is unique in fascist doctrine. For him, competition in society was the great evil. The only way to eliminate that competition was to breed people politically and physically and economically for the jobs which society needed them to do. A corporative state without competition would live tranquilly under those bred to be monarchs or aristocrats. Hatred of the new technocrats and businessmen of France made Maurras indulge in a nostalgia for the *ancien régime* which was out of place in European fascism.

Maurras seems to have been so obsessed by racial purity and hatred of Jewish financiers that the pure blood of the inbred *vieille noblesse* appealed to him as a French ideal. Certainly, the *Action Française* took an almost masochistic interest in listing rich Jewish families which had married into the old titled families; three Rothschild women had married three French princes in the nineteenth century, while four rich sisters called Haber had married a marquis, a viscount, and two counts. Even so, the French *noblesse* had remained concerned enough with pedigree to give it high place in Maurras' vision of the new order coming to France. In fact, when that new order was to come under the Vichy government, the reactionary French right wing with its monarchist and aristocratic leanings would find itself more and more driven into resistance by the radical and racial excesses of the Vichy government, pushed on by the evil genius of Laval.

In the constitutional monarchies of the Low Countries and of

Scandinavia, the aristocracy survived in societies of increasing democracy, as it was almost unnoticed. In Belgium, the brief rise of the Rexists led by the charismatic Léon Degrelle in the mid-thirties led some of the Notables, whose power had been steadily declining since the electoral reforms of 1893, and the French-speaking upper-classes of the Flemish provinces to think that they had found their strong man against the power of modern industry and Flemish separatism. Degrelle, however, soon lost their support as his political star went down, although the fascist part of the Flemish separatists survived to collaborate with the invading Nazis. In Holland, however, the aristocracy did not collaborate with the Nazis; the Crown Prince, indeed, was one of the leading lights of Dutch resistance, despite the fact that he had been a German princeling.

In Norway, titles had long been abolished; they seemed ludicrous in a country where every Norwegian considered himself personally descended from a race of kings. In Denmark, the opposite was true. There a title had been given to everyone, the title of his trade, so that each man was known as Butcher or Baker or Student before his name; only work had honour, and thus the Danes were practically free from snobbery, that great oil slick on which aristocracy floats. In Sweden and Finland, the nobility, which often bore German or Scots names because of descent from the ancient war captains of the Vasas, feared Russian Bolshevism more than anything else; this fear the Swedish aristocrats translated into a policy of profitable co-operation with Nazi Germany, and the Finns into a passionate patriotism that united nobility and people in resistance against the Red Army. The welfare state, however, was already spreading so widely in Scandinavia that the aristocracy was rapidly becoming irrelevant to society as a whole, however much it prided itself on its distinguished pedigree.

An increasing phenomenon, the émigré aristocrat, began to haunt the capitals of Europe and to cross the Atlantic. Count Harry Kessler claimed to have met the Ukrainian 'Minister's' wife in Berlin in 1922, wearing diamonds as large as pigeon's eggs on her fingers and a diamond-and-pearl necklace that hung down into her lap; he supposed that she was wearing the confiscated wealth of the entire Ukrainian aristocracy, only to find that she was the wife of the Ukrainian rebel leader, not the Soviet ambassador. Although many escaped aristocrats were penniless and became waiters and taxi-drivers, particularly in Paris, others brought their jewels and sold them off, piece by piece. There was enough of a sense of solidarity left in royalty for the English King to give the Grand Duchess Xenia and the Empress Marie of Russia some £12,400 a year; perhaps this was an attack of bad conscience for not making more of an effort to save the slaughtered Russian royal family.

Some aristocrats stayed in Russia, however, feeling themselves bound to remain in their own country at whatever cost. The Hungarian Lady Listowel found one girl in Moscow, who had become a bricklayer to forge the right proletarian background and support her mother; her background as a class enemy had prevented her from getting an education as an engineer, a career open only to proper proletarians. Yet the girl did not want to leave Russia, even under the continual terror of the Stalin régime. 'With all their faults and brutality,' the girl said, 'in twenty years the Bolsheviks have done for Russia things which my ancestors failed to do in three hundred. I belong here. Russia is my country.'

Lady Listowel's memoirs are one of the few from the inter-war years which give the feeling of an international and concerned aristocracy in the new period of passports and armed frontiers. Judith de Márffy-Mantuano was the daughter of Hungarian gentry and was brought up to worship the reactionary Count Tisza, assassinated in 1918. She suffered from the hunger of the early twenties, became a journalist, reached the London School of Economics, and married an English peer. She travelled widely, mourning the tragedy of the Hungarian nobility, while it gradually lost power in a country it had ruled for a thousand years. As her own class of nobles struggled and suffered, she felt herself a detached observer, no longer one of them. 'My dream of a career fitted much better into a free world, than into the charming

but very rigid caste system to which I nominally "belonged".'
She also observed her aristocratic friends giving way to fascism
in Germany and Austria and Italy, too ineffectual to oppose this
new and brutal order. After the *Anschluss* she described a typical
Austrian patrician, 'jam for the Nazis', who had sided with them
to save his fortune, and had then discovered the wolves were
ready to tear him down as well as the Austrian state. As for Rome,
all society life had come to depend on Caesar and his daughter.
'What mattered was no longer the old canons of behaviour, or
"right or wrong", but simply and purely how you stood with
the Régime. . . . Inside the Mussolini and Ciano family, the easiest
way was the most ancient: make love to father, daughter,
or son-in-law. It was done, and in a pretty shameless manner too.'[7]

So the travelling aristocrats watched the world of their old
code crumble beneath the forces loosed by the great depression
and by the vulgarity and time-serving of rising fascism. Some
could insulate themselves from the new ways, such as the Duchess
di Sermoneta, whose wealth and English blood and international
circle of friends could make her fairly detached from Mussolini's
Italy. To wash her hands of fascism, her memoirs claimed that she
had never gone in for politics, although politics had gone in for
her. Her passion had always been 'for pure beauty and definite
facts', things of no concern to politicians. She, too, noticed 'the
shameless display of toadying' in Roman society during the
period of the Cianos; yet she certainly felt patriotic enough to
sacrifice her gold jewellery with the Queen and people of Italy,
when Mussolini asked the nation for its gold in order to defeat
sanctions during the Abyssinian war. Later, when the Germans
were to occupy Rome, she was nearly to be arrested; but she was
on hand to welcome her friends among the liberating British
army, perfectly capable of surviving a world war with her
reputation undimmed.

It was true, indeed, that the aristocrats of the inter-war period
did not usually go in for politics, and that politics went in for them.
In nearly all the memoirs of the time, the chief aristocratic urge

[7] Judith Listowel, *This I have Seen* (London, 1943) p. 135.

to meet the people only went as far as being photographed with Charles Chaplin. Over and over again, the popular idol in the tramp's costume was snapped standing beside some simpering duchess or count. He was even persuaded to go on a wild boar hunt with the legendary Duke of Westminster. And if the aristocrats' memoirs did not include a photograph with Chaplin, then it was a photograph with Douglas Fairbanks. This penchant for film stars showed a nice appreciation of the way the world was going. Not only did the company of the stars give the aristocrats the publicity that they craved, but it also gave them the feeling that they still had contact with the new arbiters of the masses, the aristocracy of the screen. The reason why the screen idols wanted to know the aristocrats is a little more obscure; perhaps they knew their title to fame to be precarious and envied that hereditary security of a title given by pedigree rather than credits on a film. Similarly, Proust once noticed the curious fascination that the opposite worlds of high society and hardened bohemia had for each other; he explained it away as corresponding to 'the reciprocal curiosity and desire to be allies displayed by nations who have fought against each other'.

In the fluid European social world, where politics and fashion and mass communications were giving the aristocracy the choice of adapting or dying, England and Scotland seemed an island of no change, of fixed nostalgia, even if Ireland had gone up in rebellion and the Anglo-Irish aristocracy had had to flee across the sea back to their imperial motherland. The English Tories had tried to keep their rule in Ireland by killing off the independence movement through kindness; thus agrarian reform was not a problem by the time of the Irish Rebellion. The trouble in Ireland was the reverse of that in Czechoslovakia; while Habsburg imperialism had imposed a Catholic nobility on Protestant peasants, British imperialism had imposed a Protestant aristocracy on Catholic peasants. Among the leaders of the Irish resistance movement was Count Plunkett, a Count of the Holy Roman Empire, and the remarkable Constance Gore-Booth, who married the Polish Count Casimir Markievicz, and gave up hunting foxes and celebrities for the wearing of the green. 'It's all been such a hurry-scurry of a life,' she wrote to her sister from an English jail. 'Now I feel that I have done what I was born to do.'

Few other Irish Catholic aristocrats found rebellion a hereditary duty and more engaging than the social whirl. In fact, the war between the Sinn Fein and the British army merely made the social whirl a little more exciting. Lady Clodagh Anson told of driving off to dances in 'the bad times' of curfew, carrying no pass from either side because such a pass would merely give the other side a reason to shoot. War was not allowed to interrupt the hunting and dancing which continued in the great country houses, although these began getting burned down frequently, especially when one faction of the rebels accepted the partition of Ireland and had to suppresss the other faction of the rebels in a bloody civil war. Among the casualties of the long rebellion and fraternal war that resulted in the independence of Eire was the murder of the Ulster King of Arms, 'the most deplorable desertion' by the British government of the 300,000 Protestants of Eire under their leader Lord Midleton, and the burning of the country houses of the Irish Senators Lord Mayo and Lord Desart. Perhaps nothing, however, showed the determination of the aristocrats and their supporters to continue the old forms of life so much as the remark of Lord Dunsany's butler to the Black and Tans, as they left after ransacking Dunsany Castle, 'Who shall I say called?'

The final solution of the Irish problem, the partition between Eire and Ulster, satisfied few of the rebels, although it was accepted by the mass of the people who were tired of war; Countess Markievicz called the new Eire 'the Irish Freak State'. But no social revolution followed the political revolution in Ireland; the Catholic nobility still held on to their huge estates in Eire, and the Orange nobility in Ulster, while some of the Protestant aristocrats even returned after the time of the troubles to what was left of their lands in Eire. Ireland remained a backward agricultural country of disappointed hopes and wrangling politicians and hostile religions in a partitioned land. One of Lady Gregory's correspondents suggested that some one should write a play about how the generations for seven hundred years had fought to free the beautiful Cathleen of Ireland, 'and when they set her free, she walked out, a fierce vituperative old hag'.

Across the Irish Sea, however, slow change without revolution eroded the position of the aristocracy without disturbing much of its apparent social power. In fact, the massacre of the aristocracy in the First World War caused an agrarian revolution without any need for overthrowing capitalism. Death duties compelled the sale of land; sometimes a father and his heir were killed within a month of each other, and double death duties finished the estate, with the tax fixed at two-fifths of the value of the whole. In this earthquake of land sales, the Duke of Marlborough declared that the old order was doomed; The Times stated that England was changing hands. The picture was too gloomy. By 1921, one-quarter of England had new owners. The real agricultural revolution, however, was reflected in another statistic. Before the Great War, farmers had owned only one-tenth of the agricultural land of England; by 1927, they owned more than a third. The yeomen had come back to the English countryside after four centuries in the biggest transfer of soil since the magnates had risen on the spoils of the monasteries and the Royalist estates confiscated under the Cromwellian Commonwealth.

The great London houses, such as Grosvenor and Devonshire and Stafford House, were also closed or converted into hotels or offices; not only was money short, but the number of servants available had halved during the Great War and hardly increased even during the depression years. Mayfair became a centre of business, not of society life. Apart from a few great proprietors such as the Westminsters and the Portmans and the Cadogans and the Howard de Waldens, the urban landlords began to sell off their city empires, mainly en bloc to property companies. The liquid capital saved from death duties went into shares or industrial development. The rich were, after all, still rich. One in a hundred people owned two-thirds of the national wealth, one in a thousand people owned one-third of the national wealth. Mining royalties still accrued to certain hereditary owners for no service whatsoever; when the Duke of Northumberland was asked why he should get royalties on all coal mined in his estates, he could not justify himself at all.

The surviving aristocrats, however, did now feel impelled to enter business one way or another, in order to survive in times of great agricultural depression. 'Society went into trade with a good grace when the war ended,' one impoverished lady of title wrote of her venture into a *boutique*; indeed, society had to go into trade, although accepting necessity with good grace has always been the mark of the true aristocrat, as if even the inevitable needed the nod of the well-born. The adaptability of the English nobility to a changing social situation remained their chief virtue and ensured their survival, along with their nice habit of giving up their powers just in time without a fight.

In this slow change, the English aristocrats appeared to hold on to power in a remarkable fashion. This was partially due to their refusal to accept that their power was declining. It is a remarkable fact that the people who had the most children during the inter-war years were the aristocracy and the coalminers, those who had apparently the least future in the nation. Nothing was more futile and yet arrogant than the appeals made by such wealthy aristocrats as Viscount Barrington or the Earl of Rosslyn to railwaymen and miners. At Shrivenham, Viscount Barrington gave a party for the railwaymen from Swindon and ended a short speech to them with the exhortation, 'My good men, if there is another strike, don't you come out!' The railwaymen roared with laughter, and went home to do what their union said. When the Earl of Rosslyn presented medals to 320 ex-soldiers who came back to the mines which he ran, he is reported to have said to them:

Think and realize that I, who have the privilege of addressing you, am a greater democrat than any of you, and feel what a loss it would be to me, what a loss to yourselves, were you to unshackle the bonds which have for centuries tied my family to yours, and bind yourselves to a Government control without sympathy and without soul.[8]

[8] The Earl of Rosslyn, *My Gamble With Life* (London, 1928) p. 152.

In such a way the aristocrats remained blinded by their memory of the deference paid to them in the past; they almost seemed to expect that it would be the same in the future, as if somehow their hold over their tenants was transferable to modern railway-men and miners.

Yet they were not wholly wrong. Such anachronistic appeals struck chords with the third or more of the working class which continued to vote Tory. England remained the most class-conscious of societies at all levels, not in the Marxist sense of class-consciousness, but in the sense of a consciousness of the *proper* place of each individual in the whole society. Thus the aristocrats in the country districts still had a position guaranteed by their pedigree and pretensions and past. Many would have agreed with Lord Norwich's defence of class in his memoirs:

Class is a word that in this age stirs passions and provokes people to talk nonsense. There are even those who would, if they could, create a classless society. If such a society were possible it would be as useless as a rankless army and as dull as a wine-list that gave neither the names of the vineyards nor the dates of the vintages. Class is an inevitable adjunct of human nature. The aim of the lawgiver should be to render the relations between classes happy and to facilitate the passage from one class to another. When class, which is natural, degenerates into caste, which is against nature, it becomes an evil. [9]

The passage from one class to another was, indeed, facilitated after the Great War. Aristocratic wives were available ten a penny for commoners; for most of the suitable men of their class had been killed and they were not proud enough of pedigree to remain spinsters. The making of new peers also continued steadily; 280 new titles were created between 1916 and 1945, swelling the membership of the House of Lords to some 800 hereditary peers. Increasingly, Members of Parliament were ennobled for political services, and businessmen for contributing wisely to charity and well to party funds. Only nine of these new peers had wealth and land and local power that was inherited; they were easily out-numbered by the nineteen peers created by the Labour govern-

[9] Duff Cooper, Viscount Norwich, *Old Men Forget* (London, 1953) pp. 65-6.

ments to give the party some sort of representation in the House of Lords. In the Cabinets of the inter-war period, however, the land-owning interests did much better, holding on to seven cabinet positions in the Bonar Law government and dropping to a low of two positions in the two Labour governments and the National Government. There was no question of the aristocracy hardening into a caste, while it could still include the politically successful and the wealthy with such ease.

To some Members of the House of Commons, the inheritance of a hereditary peerage was a disaster, although their aristocratic connections had probably helped their career up to that point. But with a seat in the House of Lords, they could no longer serve as the elected representatives of their constituency. It is interesting that the revolutionary change of having women Members of Parliament after 1919 was mitigated by the titles held by the first women Members; although the Countess Markievicz refused to take her seat in the Commons at all, being a member of the Sinn Fein, the American-born Lady Astor broke into the exclusive male club of Westminster and did not stop from annoying its members for the next twenty-five years. In fact, as in the case of the Duchess of Atholl, Lady Astor merely succeeded to the seat which her husband had held before being ennobled – a case of inheritance through marriage. Lord Astor had tried to give up his peerage to stay in the Commons, provoking the remark from his wife, 'Some people find it hard to get titles; Lord Astor is finding it even harder to get rid of his.' Lady Astor now had the best of both worlds, a title and a seat in the Commons, which may have prompted another of her remarks when fighting for equal rights for women, 'We are not asking for superiority, for we have always had that. All we ask is equality.' The ironic fact was that peeresses in their own right were still excluded from the House of Lords by custom, although peeresses by marriage could lord it in the Commons, from which their husbands were excluded.

The fact that the younger sons of peers and titled ladies could be elected to parliament in England showed the prevalence of the belief that aristocrats were still *better* than the average man. Some

were trusted enough, such as the Duke of Atholl, to be called in
as mediators in a strike; they were felt to be above partiality and
thus able to give a just decision over the matters in dispute. But
such cases became increasingly rare; although the clubs set up to
regulate the new worlds of aeroplanes and racing cars might
still choose a peer to preside over the committee, the possession
of a title became an impassable political handicap after 1922,
until provision would be made for the renunciation of titles.
The peerage had always been strong in the Conservative Party;
yet once Lord Curzon was passed over as leader of the party
because he was a peer, and once the new 1922 Committee had
switched control of the party from the landowners to the businessmen, nothing was ever to be the same again for the old reigning
Tory political families.

The General Strike of 1926 showed both the hidden terrors
of the aristocracy and the basic stability of most of the English
people. When the trade unions came out on strike in sympathy
with the miners, who had been locked out of work to force them
to accept lower wages and longer hours, the aristocrats were more
scared of a Bolshevik revolution than seems credible in retrospect.
The Duke of Sutherland testified that many politicians thought
England on the verge of revolution; Lady Diana Manners 'could
hear the tumbrils rolling and heads sneezing into the baskets,'
so she asked her husband Duff Cooper when they could leave the
country. 'Not till the massacres begin,' was his reply. In fact,
the strike was broken in eleven days, with the aristocracy and the
middle classes turning out *en masse* to run the railways and buses,
and the unemployed given a few days' pay to risk the stones of the
strikers. A curious spirit of adventure and fun buoyed up the well-
born scabs who considered that their strike-breaking was actually
patriotism in keeping the essential services of the country running.
'Quite frankly,' Loelia Ponsonby, later Duchess of Westminster,
wrote, 'my friends and I were amused by the novelty and excitement of the strike and it was over before it had time to pall.'

Such carefree playing at industrial war by the thoughtless aristocrats and the 'sick anxiety' of the thoughtful ones at 'the brooding

menace' of the strike was balanced by the clever handling of the situation on the part of the Baldwin government. No bloody martyrdom was allowed the strikers; a concern for compromise and a refusal to start a class war dominated the relationships between the trade unions and the government, which did not listen to the aggressive vapourings of Winston Churchill denouncing the British workingmen as 'the enemy'. The King himself took the side of the miners against the coalowners' representative, Lord Durham, and helped to prevent civil strife. The Countess of Airlie heard the King say that he was sorry for the miners, and Lord Durham reply that they were 'a damned lot of revolutionaries'. At this His Majesty exploded with the words, 'Try living on their wages before you judge them!' The Crown was certainly more representative of the feelings of the people than the reactionary coalowners.

A. J. P. Taylor, in his brilliant account of the period, puts the behaviour of the strikers on a par with the voluntary mass enlistment in the First World War. 'Such nobility deserves more than a passing tribute. The strikers asked nothing for themselves. They did not seek to challenge the government, still less to overthrow the constitution. They merely wanted the miners to have a living wage. Perhaps not even that. They were loyal to their unions and to their leaders, as they had been loyal during the war to their country and to their generals.'[10] The hopeful exhortation delivered by Lord Lonsdale, when dedicating the Cenotaph in Carlisle in 1922, turned out to be true; in his speech, he had asked the war veterans to remember, 'when the difficulties of labour and other troubles arise, that you yourselves perhaps have fought for King and Country, and are yourselves pledged to King and Country, keeping the balance of your minds even'.

The balance of people's minds remained even enough in Britain to act as a counterweight to any revolutionary tendencies, even in the leadership of the trade unions and the Labour Party. When two brief Labour governments actually held power in 1924 and 1929, the issue of creating peers split the radical socia-

[10] A. J. P. Taylor, *English History, 1914-1945* (Oxford, 1965) pp. 244-5.

lists from the reform socialists led by the Prime Minister, Ramsay MacDonald. MacDonald himself softly fell prey to the sweet reason of co-operating with the powers-that-were and to the easy inclusion offered by the peerage. Not only did he stay at Easton Lodge with many of the socialist leaders, entertained by the 'red' Countess of Warwick; but he also visited such conservative strongholds as Dunrobin Castle, the home of the Duke of Sutherland. When criticized for this, he replied that 'the world is a village of glass houses through which phantasmagoria as well as men and women move.' The phantasmagoria apparently included the traditional hatred for the peerage shown by radical socialism; MacDonald, indeed, went so far as to choose Labour peers from men whose social background would make them unnoticed in an aristocratic gathering.

The temptation of power, perhaps, caused MacDonald to take the fatal step of agreeing to head a National Government in 1931; the election of that year wrecked the section of the Labour Party which refused to support MacDonald. To the horror of some conservatives like Lady Angela St Clair Erskine, he was 'now accepted as a reformed character, feasting in the houses of the few great people who have survived the results of his one-time policy.' Others, such as the Duke of Sutherland, saw him as a praiseworthy man, who put his country before his party at the price of seeming a political turn-coat. Certainly, he never could sustain the necessary sense of class antagonism, which would have kept him from co-operating with the Tories in a time of national emergency. Yet he remained enough of a socialist to refuse an earldom for himself, when he handed power over to Stanley Baldwin in 1935; although he had been excluded from the Labour Party, he still wished to be known as 'MacDonald of the people'.

As in Europe, the great depression seemed to many aristocrats to be the final disaster which would end the old order. *Through Eighty Years*, the autobiography of Charlotte, Viscountess Barrington, published in 1936, harps on these fears. She considered that all had shared equally in the sacrifices demanded by the Great War and the depression, but that the upper classes were the chief sufferers, because they paid three-quarters of the taxes. With her eyes fixed firmly on pre-war days as the norm of aristocratic life, the viscountess lamented the forced sale of property at low prices, the closing of the great houses, the impossibility of finding servants, and 'sons and daughters condemned to all but menial tasks, or in the impossibility of even finding such jobs, still dependent on their parents for support, or reduced to penury'. To the viscountess, the little hardship suffered by the aristocracy was equal in sacrifice to the great hardship suffered by the millions of the unemployed, as though there were a qualitative difference in suffering which made small hardships greater for the well-born. At any rate, the viscountess saw 'the passing of a Social Order which by its devotion to their country's welfare and its consideration for the interest of the agricultural classes, proved itself worthy of the proud and honourable position which they had maintained for centuries past'.[11]

Like so many aristocrats with the fixation that the days of Marie Antoinette were just around the corner, the viscountess was crying wolf too soon. The country gentry was, indeed, largely destroyed by the depression, but not the great aristocrats. Yet some among these began to cast longing eyes across the Channel at the rising success of fascism, and to flirt with the possibility of an English Hitler or Mussolini of their own. The fact that a baronet, Sir Oswald Mosley, led the British Union of Fascists, made the party seem quite respectable; many Conservatives, including the press baron Lord Rothermere, applauded Mosley in the early days of the blackshirt movement. Mosley's first wife was one of Lord Curzon's daughters, his second wife was one of Lord Redesdale's, who had been turned into a pro-Nazi himself by the passionate enthusiasm of his two girls, Diana and Unity, and by the flattery lavished on him in Germany by the Nazis, 'who had a completely distorted idea of the amount of influence wielded in English politics by obscure country aristocrats'. But as Mosley's drastic methods of dealing with hereditary wealth and

[11] *Through Eighty Years* (London, 1936) pp. 227-8.

Jewish profiteers began to be known, he lost the support of many wealthy aristocrats and industrialists.

Some, however, of the richest and wealthiest nobles remained on the side of fascism. 'Bendor', the famous and eccentric Duke of Westminster, abused the Jews and praised the Nazis; Hastings, Duke of Bedford, carried appeasement and anti-Semitism to the length of backing the British People's Party. The story that, the moment he became Prime Minister, the greatest Marlborough of them all, Winston Churchill, ordered most of the dukes to be interned because he personally knew how pro-fascist they were, seems merely apocryphal; no peers were interned during the war, not even when Rudolf Hess landed in Scotland and named the aristocrats whom he hoped to see in order to bring about peace between Britain and Germany. Hastings, Duke of Bedford, came nearer the truth when he wrote that Churchill vetoed the 'amiable project' of interning peers like himself, since their imprisonment might have created in America a deep impression of the strength of the anti-war movement.

The appeasers in Britain, however, far outnumbered the pro-Nazis. Particularly notorious was the 'Cliveden Set', which did not have the power of creating mass support for accommodation with the Nazis, but which certainly influenced public opinion in that direction. *The Times* and the *Observer*, both under the control of the Astor brothers, pressed for the policy that Chamberlain followed at Munich; at Cliveden itself, Lady Astor ran week-ends, where the Marquess of Lothian, Sir Samuel Hoare, Sir John Simon and Lord Halifax could all urge the need to live with Hitler and Mussolini, and the wisdom of not scaring the fascist leaders by re-arming. Still, Cliveden was not the hotbed of conspiracy against democracy, Jews and communists that it was later held to be. It only housed political week-ends some of the time; the rest of the time it was just as much a meeting-place of high society as the famous *salons* run by Lady Cunard and Lady Colefax and the American Laura Corrigan, whose 'goal was Royalty, dukes and duchesses, marquesses and marchionesses, and she got them, because she gave them good value for money'.

There was, of course, a small group of men in the Tory party, who were staunchly anti-Hitler and who were accused of war-mongering. A certain aristocratic pre-occupation with honour and courage as well as political intuition was at the back of their lonely stand against the saviour Chamberlain, greeted with national applause when he came back with 'peace for our time' from Munich. The greatest of the protesters, Winston Churchill, listed the reasons for not accepting the destruction of Czecho-slovakia in 1938, and these were both political and aristocratic reasons. 'Not only wise and fair policy,' he wrote, 'but chivalry, honour, and sympathy for a small threatened people made an overwhelming concentration.' A little minority in the Tory Party, including three later Prime Ministers, Churchill and Eden and Macmillan, stood out against their party leader and against dis-approval in the close-knit circles of the Tory aristocracy. 'Among the Conservatives,' Winston Churchill continued, 'families and friends in intimate contact were divided to a degree the like of which I have never seen. Men and women, long bound together by party ties, social amenities and family connections, glared upon one another in scorn and anger.'[12]

It took a brave man or woman to stand out against appeasement in ruling Tory circles; the Duchess of Atholl even lost her seat in parliament for supporting the Republican cause in Spain and firmness against fascism in Europe. There were few aristocrats old-fashioned enough to believe that resistance to bullying was necessary, even at the price of world war. In France, the Comte de Paris was practically alone in opposing the agreement at Munich, and was denounced as a Communist sympathizer by the *Action Française* for his pains.

Despite these divided counsels in the ruling Tory party, and despite the bitterness caused among the poorer parts of the popula-tion because of the slow recovery from the depression, Britain gave an impression of extraordinary stability and traditionalism in the eyes of Europe. The nation had been spared revolution and social turmoil; apparently things went on very much as they

[12] Winston S. Churchill, *The Second World War* (London, 1948) I, pp. 251, 253.

always had done. This misconception of the reactionary ways of Britain, which had less and less to do with its actual industrial strength and social mechanisms, was to deceive the totalitarian powers on the eve of the Second World War. One book, written by a German newspaper correspondent after ten years of residence in England, gave a significant description of the ancient image which the country projected abroad. The very title of the book, *Kings, Lords and Gentlemen: Influence and Power of the English Upper Classes,* showed the backward-looking bias with which its author, Karl Heinz Abshagen, viewed his subject. The fact that the work was first published in 1938 in Nazi Germany showed that Abshagen was saying very much what the Nazi régime wished to believe about the decaying imperial sea-power, ready to fall to the New Order of National Socialism.

Abshagen considered England the only governmental system in Europe that had passed through the social storms of the past forty years without a serious breakdown or modification. The cause of this lay in the feudal origin of its democratic government, which had grown naturally out of the past. Although the Great War and the depression had inflicted savage blows on the social pyramid that rose from the masses up to the throne, ruling Society was basically unaltered. There seemed to be no popular envy of the 'racially different' species of aristocrat, tall and sinewy and slender, speaking in a different accent from the masses. Although the hereditary aristocracy was somewhat exclusive, it still allowed the brilliant upstart to join its ranks; 'in this way the poison fangs of every revolutionary movement are drawn in advance'. The monarchy had consolidated its position, despite the Abdication crisis, by its middle-class behaviour and morality, although these traits were despised by the aristocrats; the ex-King Edward VIII had offended by his association with the divorced American Mrs Simpson and by what Abshagen called his royal sympathies for fascist methods in social policy. George VI, however, with his brother the Duke of Gloucester and his sister the Princess Royal, had married into the British nobility to consolidate the bonds between the German royal family and its adopted country, as

well as to show that the blood royal felt itself no longer set apart
from lesser corpuscles.

Abshagen was particularly struck by the power still retained
by the leading aristocratic families in politics, such as the Cecils
and the Cavendishes. He was also overwhelmed by the riches and
provincial strength of the leading nobles. In 1938, the Marquess
of Bute had sold half of the city of Cardiff, which had belonged
to his family until then; the Duke of Westminster had an income
estimated at some £900,000 a year, twice the King's civil list. The
major nobles lived like the old German princes in their princi-
palities; 'in spite of nominal liberty a relationship similar to
serfdom' made thousands of farmers and labourers on each great
estate 'materially, intellectually, and spiritually dependent on their
ground landlord'. The Earl of Derby's control over 60,000 acres
in Lancashire showed how the old feudal nobility could still
retain power in an industrial area; he had even been invited to
serve as the non-partisan Mayor of Liverpool; 'he rules
Lancashire; that is to say, he rules as far as one may do so by sheer
force of personality, social influence, and a great gift of pulling
strings'. Rival Yorkshire supplied the Foreign Minister, Lord
Halifax, one of seven peers in Neville Chamberlain's cabinet
and a candidate to become Prime Minister should Chamberlain
fall, although he had sincerely declared that he would rather be
Master of Foxhounds in his local hunt than head of the country.
Even if most of the great London houses had been closed down for
lack of money for their upkeep, the great country houses still
ran, with Lord Astor and the Cliveden Set particularly popular
with Abshagen for their apparent policy of conciliation towards
Hitler's Reich.

Abshagen conceded that the aristocracy had lost its political
influence on the large cities, where a sort of 'urban feudalism'
seemed to be growing up based on new families such as the
Chamberlains and the MacDonalds and the Hendersons. Lloyd
George's loss of influence was due in part to his feud with Society,
which he saw as a serpent, if not as the Beast of the Apocalypse,
while Ramsay MacDonald's role as socialist leader of a National

Government was partly the result of his compromise with the peerage, for he was prepared to alienate his own socialist supporters by recommending the creation of Labour peers and by hob-nobbing with Lord Londonderry. The major posts in the diplomatic and civil services, the Anglican Church and the colonial government were held almost to a man by old boys from the eight chief public schools led by Eton and from the two major universities of Oxford and Cambridge; in these places of privileged education, like the exclusive students' corporations of old Germany, young men were 'trained to lordliness'. This caste education had led to the failure of English diplomacy in the twenties and thirties, because the governing powers were unable to comprehend the dynamic new ruling groups of Europe, particularly the fascists. According to Abshagen, the reason the British government was caught by surprise when Austria 'joined' Germany in 1938 was because the British diplomats in Vienna only felt socially at home with old and powerless Austrian nobles, who naturally gave them a false picture of the true popular support of Hitler.

The City of London could not be claimed as an aristocratic preserve, although Abshagen rightly noted that a good many peers of ancient lineage sat on the boards of companies, even when they had no previous business experience. 'The fact that they can do so, and without any great difficulty, is evidence of the high opinion held by the business community of the social influence of the old aristocracy not only on the general public but also, apparently, on the political quarters that control legislation; it is evidence also that the business community is aware that it has not this influence itself in the same measure.' There were City men in Society and members of Society in the City. Curiously enough, unlike trade in commodities, trade in money seemed to have lost its smell at a relatively early date. Many aristocrats went into professions dealing strictly with money, particularly stock-broking and banking, where family dynasties still controlled most of the private banks. Abshagen was particularly struck by the fact that the major English newspapers, outside the liberal

Cadbury group, were all controlled by press lords, the Lords Rothermere and Beaverbrook and Camrose and Kemsley and Iliffe and Riddell and Astor and Southwood. Of course, Abshagen was worried that Jews such as Lord Southwood should become peers, but he consoled himself with the thought that there were few titled Jews, and that 'the dislike of Jewish infiltration is fairly strong in all classes in England'.

In conclusion, Abshagen thought that even this powerful aristocracy might be doomed, because its foreign investments were menaced by the revolutionary forces sweeping the world, and because it was too old-fashioned to come to terms with the dynamic future rulers of Europe such as the Nazis. Perhaps the British aristocracy might once again adapt itself to survival in changing times; but not if it fought another world war against Germany. 'The social structure of England withstood one world war, not without its timbers creaking. A second within a generation would inevitably, whatever its military issue, bring down even this proud building.'[13]

Such was the picture of England on the eve of the Second World War, as seen by an intelligent German in sympathy with the new Germany. Abshagen obviously exaggerated the power of the British aristocrats, because he thought their show of control meant they had real power. Just as the British Empire still seemed to control a fifth of the globe, while in fact it existed only on sufferance because the Americans would not move into the power vacuum created by British financial exhaustion after the Armistice of 1918, so the British aristocracy still seemed to control many of the mechanisms of political and economic power in England, while actually it served only as a patent-leather gloss on the boots of the plutocrats and politicians, who might accept titles, but who did not change their natures by doing so.

Abshagen, indeed, living as he did in the chimera of a Jewish conspiracy, might well have equated the aristocracy with the Jews in Britain, for its actual control was far less than its enemies thought. Like the Jew, the aristocrat was set a little apart from his

[13] K. Abshagen, *Kings, Lords and Gentlemen* (London, 1939) *passim*.

countrymen by his international ties of blood, and thus his positions of power were more noticeable because they were held by somebody who was noticed. Naturally, the vast majority of influential jobs in Britain were filled neither by aristocrats nor Jews; even in Neville Chamberlain's cabinet, fifteen of the twenty-two ministers did not have titles. But the fact that aristocrats and Jews did hold some positions of power, perhaps out of proportion to their numbers in the population, made communists and fascists cry conspiracy when there was little more to condemn than a certain clubbiness and a preference for the society of familiars. If misjudgement of the power of aristocrats and Jews in backward England helped to lead Hitler to despise his future enemy and to provoke a war, all the Führer's spooks and all the Führer's goblins could not put together again the Humpty Dumpty of aristocratic control of Britain, forever broken in pieces by the First World War. Abshagen overestimated the power of the nobility in 1938, thus he overestimated the effect of the coming war upon that power. The struggle against the Nazis would merely hasten the erosion of the British aristocracy that had been slowly wearing out like the wooden crosses on the graves in Flanders.

Few entered the Second World War as elated as those volunteers who had jauntily gone into the First. The ghostly memory of the muddy massacres on the Western Front in the Great War had, indeed, been responsible for much of the policy of appeasement of the 1930's. War had to be avoided at all costs; it was the ultimate evil; now it had to come. Lunching at Blenheim with the Duke of Marlborough in the summer of 1939, Consuelo Vanderbilt, now the wife of Jacques Balsan, felt the same unease that had afflicted her when, surrounded by the glittering splendour of the Tsar's court, she had once sensed disaster; later in Paris, a French cabinet minister whispered to Balsan, 'Nous sommes fichus.' But even more disturbing to the responsible aristocrats than the thought of impending disaster was their sense that they had helped to bring about a Second World War two decades after the end of the First. 'The months of July and August

seemed to be holding their breath, as if in the summer of 1914,'
confessed Baroness Ravensdale. 'I wanted breath to look around
and take stock: where had our foreign policy led us, what had we
done since 1919, as a design for living? It was a patchwork quilt
of shocking taste.'[14]

[14] Baroness Ravensdale, *op. cit.*, p. 216.

Four

ᗧᔕᔕᔕᗧ

THE PURGE OF HONOUR:
1939–45

Preparations for the coming world war in two of the three major totalitarian powers were made by a wholesale purge of the officer corps. In Italy, where Mussolini had failed to get rid of the Crown, the officer corps was backed by the monarch and could not be replaced by good fascists; indeed, the officers led by Marshal Badoglio were later to turn against Mussolini and depose him. In Russia, however, where Stalin held as much of an excessive fear of treason as Hitler, some ten thousand high-ranking officers lost their lives in 1937. This bloody purge against the last anti-Stalinist – miscalled reactionary – attitudes in the Red Army effectively confirmed the control of the Communist Party over the armed forces, at the cost of weakening the efficiency of the high command to an extent that nearly caused total disaster when the Nazis attacked Russia.

Hitler, always ready to follow a ruthless example which worked, decided on a minor purge of his own, which would at least remove the Prussian officers of the old school, who opposed his schemes for the coming European war. He had both the War Minister and the Commander-in-Chief dismissed in 1938, the first for allegedly marrying a whore and the second on a charge of homosexuality faked by the Secret Police; he also used the occasion to retire or transfer most of the aristocratic appointees to high rank brought in by von Seeckt, who had opposed the Nazis at the time of the failed Munich *putsch* of 1923. Again the failure of the remaining generals in the high command to resign *en bloc* allowed Hitler to take over complete official control of the armed forces; he boasted to his Nazi friends later in the day that he now knew every general to be either a coward or a fool.

The fact that the officers could not resign, because the Prussian code and the oath sworn to Hitler in 1934 made this tantamount to mutiny, was merely another instance of aristocratic honour playing into the hands of ruthless politics. Hitler, however, did not dare to go as far as Stalin in his purge, for fear of destroying the efficiency of his own forces, and for fear of losing a counterweight to the powerful Goering and Himmler, whose ruthlessness matched his own. Hitler was perfectly capable, as the Crown Prince of Prussia later testified at the Nuremberg trials, of winning support in the army with the oldest royal method of all, by distributing to friendly generals the baubles they wanted, 'money, gifts, titles and honours'. The Führer could play the aristocrat when it suited him, while hiding a deadly hatred of the aristocracy.

When Hitler did finally open the Second World War in the autumn of 1939, the semi-feudal order in Poland was brought down by the Germans and the Russians in a few weeks. Marshal Rydz-Smigly had only one incomplete tank division; the rest of his shock forces were cavalry regiments. Led by aristocratic officers, these regiments charged with bare sabres in close formation across the dry summer plains. It was neither magnificent nor war, merely massacre. Machine-guns and tanks put an end to the fighting males of the Polish nobility, Warsaw was bombed ruthlessly, Poland partitioned yet again, this time between the Germans and the Russians. An immediate persecution was begun by the SS against the old governing class of Poland and against the Jews who had often been persecuted by that old governing class. For the first time, the Polish aristocrat found himself lumped in with the Jew as an enemy to the state; in the new order for Poland, he was actually worse off than the Jew, for the Russians also decimated the gentry in their area of Poland without touching the ghettos. The German army commanders, still unused to the vileness of Nazi police methods, protested against the atrocities and even condemned some members of the SS to death for murder, arson and rape. The friction between the old regular army and Himmler's special police grew, while Hitler's men complained about the army's 'outmoded conception of chivalry'.

Yet, in the early days of triumph, the German aristocrats were prepared to serve as the rulers of the newly-conquered territories. General von Falkenhorst in Norway and Baron von Falkenhausen in Belgium were perfectly capable of displaying the necessary brutality to contain resistance movements in the occupied countries; it was Falkenhausen who was credited with the device of shooting hostages in reprisal for attacks on Germans. Yet even so, when resistance became too much of a problem such titled administrators as Baron von Neurath, the 'Protector' of the occupied areas of Czechoslovakia, were replaced by SS officials such as Heydrich. Gradually, as Hitler's fears of a *putsch* by aristocratic generals grew, the true Nazis took over the running of the occupied territories more and more.

Sometimes these little men, become great, aped an almost imperial grandeur for themselves. Goering wore black kimonos and varnished his fingernails, had a silver case made for porcelain reproductions of his medals and orders, and insisted that his wife be called 'noble lady'. The racialist philosopher, Dr Alfred Rosenberg, actually claimed that his anti-Semitic and anti-Slavic harangues were delivered from the last Tsar's marble palace of Tsarskoye Selo; in his department for settling the affairs of the conquered territories to the east, he employed the venal and displaced aristocracy of the Baltic and the Ukraine, as if he were running an imperial court. The satrap of the occupied Ukraine itself, Erich Koch, behaved literally as a berserk prince. He took over the vast hunting estate of the Radziwills at Tsuman, famous for its feudal splendour in Tsarist times. The estate had since become a resin-producing area under the Polish and Soviet governments; but Koch had the hundreds of resin-workers deported or shot as partisans, so that he could once again hunt in feudal splendour with his Nazi friends. The Ukrainians had greeted the first German tanks by throwing flowers under their tracks because of Stalin's forced collectivization of the land and elimination of millions of *kulaks*; but Koch's brutal policies towards the 'nigger peoples' of the East soon turned them against the new and worst rulers of all.

Too late, the old German aristocracy also saw its mistake in welcoming Hitler's coming, when all its notions of honour and decency were being outraged by the SS and the concentration camps and the totalitarian ruthlessness of the Nazis. Many of the new industrial barons had followed the example of Gustav Krupp von Bohlen und Halbach, who became in Thyssen's words 'a super Nazi' and the Party's chief raiser of funds; he and his son Alfried were to support Hitler to the bitter end because the Nazis could provide full order books and a docile slave-labour force. The old nobility, however, based on the land and pushed more and more from positions of power by the growing Nazi élite, began to set up the only effective resistance group to Hitler through the aristocrats who remained in the General Staff. In 1938 at the time of the Munich crisis, a conservative army group had been ready to spring a *putsch*; but Hitler's bloodless victory over Czechoslovakia had made the conspirators disband.

During the first years of success of the Second World War, opposition to the all-conquering Führer was impossible; but when the defeats began in Russia and Africa, at Stalingrad and Alamein, a group of high-ranking aristocrats decided to assassinate Hitler and seize power, before his desperate strategy ruined all Germany. They came mostly from extremely wealthy and cosmopolitan families; their travels abroad gave them some idea of the retribution which total defeat under Hitler would bring to Germany at the hands of the vengeful Allies. They themselves were disgusted by the orgies of massacre performed in the name of Nazi racialism by the Security Service. This brutal policy was not only, as General von Senger und Etterlin was to say, an insult to every form of military honour, but in the opinion of one Chief of Operations at General Headquarters, 'a military imbecility that needlessly added to the army's difficulties in fighting the enemy'. The high command may not have found the extermination of many millions of Jews and Slavs morally horrible, but it was certainly bad strategy and bad form.

After some botched attempts on Hitler's life, leadership of the plot fell to the charismatic and mystical Catholic aristocrat from Swabia, Count Claus von Stauffenberg, and he soon made contact with most of the disaffected members of the General Staff, the police and the political opposition. These included Crown Prince Georg of Saxony (now a Jesuit), Prince Louis Ferdinand of Prussia (a possible regent), Count Helmuth von Moltke, the Counts von der Schulenburg and Adam von Trott zu Solz. Gradually the conspirators, under Stauffenberg worked out a plan which embraced a seizure of power on the Home, Western and Eastern Fronts. Many of the great names in Prussian history were found among the conspirators, who also came to include members of the Schwerin and Bismarck and Bernstorff and Brockdorf-Ahlefeldt and Lehndorff families; yet the plotters were perhaps too conservative and honourable by nature to be successful at cloak-and-dagger schemes. Stauffenberg and Moltke, however, looked forward to a new régime, certainly democratic and perhaps socialist, after the fall of Hitler; they wanted to deal with the western democracies and gain their aid in keeping the Eastern Front intact against the advancing Russians, who would certainly destroy the old nobility's Prussian estates if the war were lost by the Germans.

A first attempt by Stauffenberg to kill Hitler failed, but he was not discovered. Meanwhile, Mussolini's fall in Italy at the hands of the King and Badoglio led Hitler to become more and more scared of an aristocratic conspiracy against him because of his obscure origins. He already saw Churchill as part of the world conspiracy of aristocrats and Jews – was he not from the House of Marlborough? Franklin D. Roosevelt was a villain of the same sort, a well-born creature of the Jews, 'from the so-called upper ten thousand', a member of 'the class whose path is smoothed in the democracies'. Now there might be a 'German Badoglio' at home, a plotter in the 'blue international' of the nobility and the old princely families. Most German princes, including all the Hohenzollerns and the Wittelsbachs and the Brunswicks, were dismissed from the army, while Goebbels threatened to expropriate all the princely estates and houses.

Yet before Hitler's rise to power, von Seeckt had made sure that most of the General Staff officers of long experience who had been the architects of the brilliant early German victories were aristocrats or held aristocratic beliefs in the honour and independence of the army. Hitler could not purge all the aristocratic staff officers in the middle of a losing war without disrupting his military machine, even if they might say, like one of Rommel's army commanders, that a National Socialist had no business in a German officers' mess. So Hitler decided to scotch treason by making his comings and goings abrupt and unpredictable. Yet soon after the Allied landing in France, Stauffenberg managed to place a time-bomb under the table of a room where Hitler was holding a conference; the bomb exploded, killing many in the room, but not the Führer.

The revenge taken by Hitler against the aristocratic plotters was sadistic to the point of madness; he used his opportunity finally to crush the independence of the officers and the old nobility. Some 7,000 people were arrested by the Gestapo, of whom nearly 5,000 were executed; all princely and most aristocratic officers were disgraced or put in concentration camps. Some were slowly garotted with piano wires strung on meathooks; the film of this execution was shown to Hitler. Others, including three field marshals and many scores of generals, were put to death quickly or slowly by the Gestapo; even Rommel was ordered to commit suicide. The surviving officers cringed before Hitler's wrath; the old Field-Marshal von Rundstedt agreed to preside over a Court of Honour, or rather dishonour, which dismissed hundred of officers and turned them over to the Gestapo. The Prussian Guderian, the new Chief of Staff, pledged the loyalty of the remaining officer corps to Hitler and made the Nazi salute compulsory in the armed forces instead of the old military salute 'as a sign of the Army's unshakable allegiance to the Führer and of the closest unity between Army and Party'. Guderian invited all officers who were not convinced National Socialists to resign. None did.

In the final year of the Third Reich, with Germany surrounded by its advancing enemies, Hitler at last dared to carry out the purge of the old elements in the army that Stalin had done in 1937 in the Red Army. He filled the higher command with what Ferdinand Prince von der Leyen called 'peasant types', officers who would blindly obey the Führer's strategy, however misconceived. The Nazi Party was dominant over the old aristocracy of Germany just in time to involve the whole nation in a *Götterdämmerung*, the total obliteration of Germany in the event of a defeat. To rub in the Nazis' complete triumph over the old order, Goebbels had the radio commentator Hans Fritzsche denounce the Junkers as the authors of the plot, 'blue-blooded assassins' in league with the reactionary powers of the West. After this radio address, the breach between the Nazis and the old Prussian nobility was complete.

Mussolini had never been able to carry out that vital purge of the armed forces. Once military defeats began, he found himself increasingly deserted by the court and the aristocrats. In October 1940, the Duke of Pistoia had been able to swear by 'the Duce of all the Victories'; yet by the following spring, the titled Marshal Badoglio had already formed a clique of generals against Mussolini and was plotting with Crown Prince Humbert against the Duce. As the hardships and the defeats of the war grew, the Italian people opposed the Fascist régime more and more; once the Allies had landed in Sicily, there was a disgraceful *sauve qui peut* among the governing classes. The Fascist Grand Council dismissed Mussolini and set up another government under the King and Badoglio; the Germans then rescued Mussolini and made him head of a rump government in the North, until he was totally abandoned in 1945 and executed with his mistress by partisans.

In fact, by helping to sabotage Mussolini, the Italian monarchy destroyed itself; it was too implicated with fascism to survive its downfall. Mussolini may have pushed the monarchy into the background, especially after Hitler had 'told him again and again to get rid of all this Royalty'; but the King was probably better off as a ceremonial puppet than as no King at all. In 1946, a plebiscite ended the monarchy in Italy, with the industrial North voting for a republic and the rural South for royalty. The Italian aristocrats, however, managed to hang onto the coat-tails of the Church and the Christian Democratic Party under de Gasperi, who saved their estates by a policy of mild reform which did little to solve the problems of the countryside.

In Eastern Europe, however, there had been no way out for the aristocrats between the grinding stones of fascism and communism. Between 1940 and 1943, co-operation with the Nazi régime was obligatory; during 1944, every expedient for changing sides in order to get the western Allies to stop the advancing Red Army had to be tried. Survival dictated all. Germany's allies, Hungary and Rumania and Bulgaria, could keep a large degree of autonomy until the war was drawing to its end, but it was only a limited hiatus before the final solution.

Fascism did not break up the power of the Magnates in Hungary until 1944, when the Germans could no longer tolerate Horthy's efforts to make a deal with the Allies in the nick of time. Before 1944, a half-hearted pogrom against the Jews had been forced on the Hungarian Premier, Count Teleki; but he had committed suicide when the Nazis invaded Hungary in support of the *putsch* organized by Szálasi and the Arrow Cross. Some members of the House of Magnates, including the leading Hungarian Habsburgs, were enthusiastic supporters of Szálasi as their last hope, especially when he took the traditional oath to the Holy Crown in the Royal Palace; but he, too, tried to steal the communists' thunder by redistributing the large estates of the nobility to the peasants. This desparate effort to win popular support against the advancing Russians was useless, although many of the Hungarian nobles were killed along with the Hungarian Jews for resisting the new fascist régime. Most of the treasures of Hungary were looted and sent to Germany. Although the Szálasi government lasted no more than a few weeks, it began the ruthless emancipation of the Hungarian peasant that the new communist government would continue by methods often as bloody and brutal as the fascist ones. By totalitarian governments of the extreme right and the extreme left, the Hungarian Magnates were obliterated at the end of the Second World War.

Rumania followed a similar pattern. Its independence within the German orbit was more and more circumscribed. The attack on the Jews was stepped up, along with an attack on high society. In 1942, 150 members of the leading social circles were arrested for 'leading a dissolute life of pleasure' while Rumanian armies were fighting on the Russian front; fourteen were sent to concentration camps for their hedonism. In 1944, King Michael decided to copy the King of Italy and switch sides, in order to get the best terms he could from the advancing Russians. He duly deserted the Germans; but he lost his throne all the same. Communist governments were imposed on the pro-German nations of Rumania and Bulgaria, just as they were immediately imposed on the anti-German nation of Poland, and eventually on Czechoslovakia. Behind the final line of advance of the Red Army, the communists took over power. It did not matter whether the nation had fought for the Allies or the Axis, communism was the new rule. And where communism was the new rule, the aristocrats were expropriated as class enemies.

In Western Europe, however, the aristocrats survived behind the line of advance of the Allied armies, whether they had collaborated with the Axis powers or not. In this way, Hitler's belief that he was the victim of an aristocratic conspiracy carried a certain warped conviction. Churchill was certainly an aristocrat, Roosevelt also; de Gaulle came from French gentry and behaved like the blood royal, while even Chiang Kai-shek came from a family of small landowners. In the paranoid world of Hitler, the 'blue international' could be seen as squeezing Germany on one side against the 'red international' on the other, with the universal conspiracy of the Jews as the catalyst between them. The few successes won by Nazi propaganda in places such as Czechoslovakia were promises to the peasants that fascism was a New Order, contrasted to the old feudal order of Bohemia (already eroded by the previous Czech democratic government) and of England Nazi propaganda liked to present England as a tired feudalistic plutocracy without any vitality, only kept going by sucking strength from its empire. Pamphlets printed by the Nazis included such titles as *A Hundred Families Dominate the British Empire* by Giesele Wirsing, and *Hunger in England* by Viscount Lymington. Although the New Order took time to deliver its promises, at least it could not be so bad as the old one.

Like the communists, the Nazis vastly overrated the importance of the monarchy and the aristocracy in the western democracies, because the Junkers were still so powerful in Germany. When Rudolf Hess flew to England on his mad peace mission, he really seemed to think that the Duke of Hamilton was a national figure at the head of a large anti-war party. The Germans considered it a great coup when they persuaded the King of the Belgians to stay in his country, instead of fleeing to exile in England to carry on the struggle like the Dutch and Norwegian royal families. Indeed, the King of the Belgians' decision to stay and his later decision to marry Liliane Baels, forced him to abdicate after the war, especially as his pre-war spokesman, Henri de Man, became an arch-collaborator in occupied Belgium. It was not necessary to lose a royal reputation by staying at home, as the King of Denmark showed when he dared to wear the yellow star himself rather than yield the Danish Jews to Nazi persecution.

The neutral countries, Sweden and Switzerland and Spain and Portugal, offered an asylum for *émigré* aristocrats, some of whom had long prepared for flight by salting fortunes away in numbered accounts in Swiss banks, a practice imitated even by the leading Nazis in case things went wrong. For the aristocrats in neutral countries, the war was a golden epoch with vast profits to be made exporting food or goods or minerals. Sweden waxed fat on selling iron ore to Germany; even Spain began a slow climb back to prosperity after its civil war. Sweden's plenty in the midst of want particularly offended its suffering Scandinavian neighbours. The Finnish aristocracy, fighting desperately against the Russians, considered that their Swedish counterparts had sold out their honour to loll in immoral ease. As soldiering was the original reason for which titles had been granted, neutrality seemed a form of cowardice, a denial of the one duty which the aristocracy still had, the duty of dying nobly.

In occupied France, the aristocracy both compromised and distinguished itself. Hélène, Countess de Portes and Paul Reynaud's mistress, was the villainess of the collapse of the French government and its abdication to Marshal Pétain. She hated the British and forced the French Prime Minister to reject British help; she used to scream in Reynaud's presence, 'I am the mistress here!'– and she was. Most of the ruling families of France behaved with cowardly logic and backed the cause of Vichy after France's military disaster. This made as astute a commentator on French affairs as Sir Denis Brogan declare in 1943 that while the old order could be restored, with minor modifications, in some other countries, it could not be restored in France.

Resistance in France was led by the radical republicans, and also, after 1941, by the communists. Even if de Gaulle himself had been originally reactionary, he soon had to accept the more revolutionary flavour of the opponents of Vichy, supported as Vichy was by the docility of so many distinguished officials and soldiers. As the rich and *les gens bien* were solidly behind Vichy and would not justify their privileges by an unconditional patriotism that would risk all, a sort of Jacobinism was forced on the Gaullist movement.

Of course, there were a few – very few – officers who followed de Gaulle's own choice of individual honour in service of the ideal of free France. Yet it was a difficult decision for an honourable officer to take. On the one side lay the question of obedience to Marshal Pétain, the victor of Verdun and the legitimate leader of homeland France; on the other side lay a duty to serve the cause of undefeated France overseas and an aristocratic general, who asked all French soldiers to put their patriotism and conscience above their military oath. It was a hard choice for an honourable man, and a choice to be presented later by the rebel generals in Algeria, who would see de Gaulle as another Pétain.

Yet as in the other countries of Europe, the French upper classes knew when to trim, particularly as de Gaulle would need their support against his communist allies when the question would be posed, Who was to rule at the end of the war? General Giraud had become the leader of the aristocratic and conservative elements in France, who had wanted to desert Vichy and yet could not bring themselves to join the radical Free French. But when de Gaulle eliminated his rival Giraud in North Africa, he became the heir of Giraud's support. Thus, in Alexander Werth's opinion, the Trojan Horse of the old order was let into the Troy of the new. De Gaulle stopped talking of a revolution in postwar France; his new word was 'renovation'. Once offered the support of the old conservative elements of France, de Gaulle accepted them gratefully; he himself came from royalist and conservative circles and was happy to find himself their leader. Thus his magnanimity towards the aristocratic collaborators with the Vichy régime was also a political act; he needed the support of the old order in order to prevent a social revolution led by the communist elements in the *maquis* after France's liberation. De Gaulle was always a traditionalist, who flirted with a revolutionary solution when it suited him; but unlike other privileged people who played with fire, he did not get burned.

In wartime England, a similar false decline and fall in the position of the aristocracy appeared to be taking place. There was also a similar false hope in a new order after the war. The English upper classes behaved little better than their continental brethren. Some eleven thousand women and children, mainly from rich families, were evacuated to Canada at private expense, until Churchill stopped this demoralizing flight. As England was not invaded by the Nazis, it is impossible to tell whether they would have found as many quislings and collaborators among the privileged classes as they found in all other countries – including the British Channel Islands. Probably they would, although the British aristocracy had no taint of collaboration to live down after the war. Churchill went so far as to nominate a small group of leaders in each community to carry on resistance after a German invasion; perhaps they would have. There is no certainty, except that the aristocracy compromised itself in no way during the war.

Only Sir Oswald Mosley and his wife were interned for some years, while the abdicated Duke of Windsor was hurried off to the West Indies, when he and his Duchess were known to be meeting the German ambassador in Madrid.

As in the war of 1914, the British aristocracy voluntarily relinquished its privileges for the duration, something which the Junkers in Germany were not prepared to do. The nobility forestalled the billeting officers, concerned with finding rooms for bombed families, by offering their country houses to the government; the Percys in Northumberland gave up all their places there; Blenheim was turned into a hospital, although Winston Churchill headed the government. A large section of the *nouveaux riches* did not follow the example of the landowners and had to be compelled by the government. But the expected conscription of property to balance the conscription of all available man- and woman-power, did not take place. Lady Listowel noted how 'monumentally tenacious' were the vested interests of Britain, although all other restrictions on equality went by the board during the war. Society women went to work in factories, including a sister of the Duke of Manchester. The tradition of voluntary service for both sexes when the country was in danger continued among the most traditional group of all.

What voluntary sacrifice could not achieve, conditions did. As early as 1940, the Polish ambassador in London, Count Edward Raczynski, noticed that the distance between the wealthy and the poor had been narrowed extraordinarily. Enormous death duties, supertax to take away all great incomes, strict rationing and the billeting of evacuees had destroyed the old world of privilege. Most of the large London houses were requisitioned by the government or put up for sale, finding no buyers. The *émigré* aristocrats from Europe, who were helping to run the various governments-in-exile or were serving in the Allied armed forces, found life nearly as hard in London as in the wartime capitals which they had evacuated. During the blitz and the blackout, it was hard to imagine that a world of privilege could ever rise again.

In one fringe area, the old aristocracy still had a certain latitude, and that was in the way it fought wars. The Brigade of Guards remained the home of well-born officers, with a penchant for being detached on private expeditions against certain key German generals or positions. The Duke of Atholl still had the privilege of raising his own private army of Highlanders, while Lord Lovat's Scouts switched from horses to armoured cars, in order to raid far behind the enemy lines. Yet the most curious private army of all was led by the Earl of Suffolk, who brought back from the chaos of the collapse of France a cargo of heavy water and scientists and diamonds; Harold Macmillan found him 'a mixture between Sir Francis Drake and the Scarlet Pimpernel'. Later, he formed the first experimental bomb disposal squad, which dealt with the problem of dismantling the dangerous duds dropped on British cities. Eventually, he blew himself to bits on an unexploded bomb. 'With his pointed beard and swaggering clothes,' Baroness Ravensdale wrote, 'he, like Rupert Brooke in 1914, was the one romantic figure of the war.'

There was not much room for romance. A little conscience remained; in one famous case, a Guards officer from a distinguished Scots family preferred court-martial and dishonour to wasting lives in what he thought was an unnecessary attack ordered by the high command. In general, however, the whole nation did not question and worked for long hours on low rations until the war was won. Few had money or good meals: eating well was considered a minor form of treason. And once the war in Europe was over and the nation decisively repudiated its war leader Winston Churchill in favour of Attlee and the Labour Party, the aristocrats really thought that the wartime requisitioning of their property and income would become permanent. They feared total social obliteration at the hands of a government, in which the aristocrats were thought to be 'lower than vermin'.

They feared too easily, while their opposite numbers, the Junkers, did not fear enough. The fate of the Junkers was to be as Wagnerian as the most envious Nazi or communist could have wished. Yet right up to the end, as though centuries of survival would enable them to survive once more, they continued with their normal life in Prussia. One of the prisoners-of-war on a Junker baron's estate acted as a beater for a shooting party in Christmas, 1944; his description ran:

Titled neighbours arrived from miles around, driving up to the *château* in brakes and dogcarts drawn by spirited horses, and accompanied by their green-uniformed foresters bearing extra guns and holding dogs on shining leather leashes. Among the guests were pretty girls in male sporting attire, armed with double-barrelled shotguns. . . . After a barbaric breakfast of hot blood and liver sausages, ersatz coffee and brandy, [began] the butchery, not sport. The doomed game was met by a barrage of shot, fired almost point-blank from which there was no escape. Three hundred and eighty-seven hares were bagged by the Baron and his guests that day. The ragged slave-workers and prisoners looked hungrily at the furry little carcasses stretched out on the snow, but there wasn't any for the beaters. . . .

At a great dinner held in the banqueting hall of the *château* the Baron was proclaimed 'king of the hunt', because he had killed more hares than anyone else. His guests drank his health in bumpers of Mumm and Veuve Clicquot, stolen out of the cellars of Rheims by his youngest brother during the lightning campaign of 1940. Old hunting and student songs were chanted in chorus. Liveried servants moved noiselessly, bearing silver platters heaped with rich food. The girls got tight and bombarded their boy-friends with hothouse flowers, spilling their wine over the damask table-cloth. And there was no magician there to spoil the feast with a dark vision of the tragedy soon to be enacted in that splendid hall. [1]

The Baron von Kirdorff of that particular *château* of Bredow found consolation in the fact that the Junkers had survived the collapse of 1918 and the rise of Hitler in 1933; he was quite unable to conceive that history would not repeat itself and that his patriarchal rule would not continue. 'He, and with a few exceptions all the Junkers of Pomerania and East Prussia, did not want Germany to win the war.' They wanted a draw, which would keep Germany's frontiers and cause the collapse of Hitler, while preserving their estates and privileges. Only when Prussia was

---

[1] B. J. Kospoth, *Red Wins* (London, 1946) pp. 34-5.

actually invaded by the Red Army in 1945 did some of the Junkers begin to flee to the other side of the Elbe. The Prince zu Dohna-Schlobitten set off for the west with a caravan of 200 wagons, 300 men and 4,000 cattle, like a Boer patriarch on the Great Trek or a Mormon prophet making for Utah across the prairies.

Those Junkers who did not flee were doomed, and most stayed, hoping that they could defend their estates from the red terror, as they had done after the First World War. But this time the red terror was backed by the vast Red Army, revenging itself for the millions massacred in Russia in the 'degenerate war' proclaimed by Hitler against the Slavs. It was natural for the Russians to annihilate the Junkers, whom they saw both as the representatives of German militarism and of aristocratic capitalism. 'The evidence of wealth and luxury which the Reds found in the great manor houses, and which to many of these poor devils must have seemed like a dream out of the Arabian Nights, inflamed their fury still more.' Not only the Red Army officers but the Polish commissars revenged themselves on the Junker families, who had survived the fighting and the attempt on Hitler's life. Where they could not escape or were not deported, the Junkers died by bullet, torture, the rope or suicide, sometimes defending their homes to the hopeless last like Baron von Zitzewitz and his few faithful retainers.

One historian calculates that the von Arnim family lost ninety-eight estates and farms; thirty of the family's sons died in the war, one died in a concentration camp, two were shot by the Russians, three were transported, and eight committed suicide. As for the von der Schulenburgs, whose family had spawned three field-marshals and thirty-five generals, they lost twenty-three estates; two of the counts were executed as plotters against Hitler, fourteen more of the family were killed fighting, seven committed suicide, the remainder reached the land left to them in West Germany.[2] The Junkers had made a deal with Hitler and had failed to deal with the West. Thus the peasant vengeance built up over cen-

[2] W. Görlitz, *The German General Staff, Its History and Structure 1657-1945* (London, 1953).

turies of oppression on the Elbe finally destroyed the last estates of the descendants of the old Teutonic Knights, and killed the doomed aristocratic game at point-blank range like hares in a hunt, driven on to the guns by the closing ring of hungry beaters.

If the fate of the Junkers was common across Central Europe, where the Red Army completed the obliteration of the aristocracy which the First World War had begun, the fate of individual aristocrats in the *mêlée* at the end of the Third Reich was as tragic and problematic as that of many a refugee. Even when they died, they could not always find burial. At the worst of the bombing in 1945, coffins were so short in Vienna that the corpse of the most admired beauty of the Habsburg Court before 1914, Princess Nora Fugger de Babenhausen, had to queue for three weeks to get her wooden box – and then she had died on a park bench.

The curious and unreal world of the war's end was nowhere better described than in Céline's mad accounts of the last days of the Vichy government in the castle of Sigmaringen, and nowhere more accurately described from the aristocrat's point of view than in Prince Constantine of Bavaria's anecdotal book, *After the Flood*. Prince Constantine came home in an American convoy to Nymphenburg, his family palace in Bavaria, only to find two looters holding up his grandparents at gun point; the crown jewels, however, turned out to be false. He tells of noble-women making nominal marriages to peasants to get out of Russian-occupied territory, only to fall in love with their uninterested husbands; of a *maquis* arms dump found instead of skeletons in the family vault of the Dukes and Duchesses of Lorraine; of the rough treatment of some Hohenzollerns, 'simply another family of conquered Germans', at the hands of the Allies, unless those Allied officers happened to be aristocrats themselves; of ambitious British officers of obscure origin becoming the darlings of the Italian aristocracy, only to commit suicide when snubbed by that aristocracy come to power again; and even of a Jacobite plot to restore the Wittelsbachs to the throne of Bavaria, with the Duke of Windsor to be appointed as the

Regent of the British Zone of Occupation to teach the Germans the mysteries of constitutional monarchy.

Anything might happen at the end of the war, and usually everything did. As Prince Constantine summed up the chaotic situation of the Europeans, whether liberators or liberated:

We lived the life of the jungle, with neither security nor calm. And the survivors of the flood had to obey the laws of the jungle if they were also to survive the peace: they had to eat or be eaten. The veneer of civilization was gone. What had been hidden was now revealed. Saints turned out to be sinners, and sinners saints. Every banknote might well be forged, every oath a lie. Was the duchess a whore, the minister a gangster? It was all quite possible.[3]

In this cruel and topsy-turvy world, the only important quality was shrewdness, nowhere better seen than in the character of Imperial Count von Coudenhove-Calergi, of half-Austrian and half-Japanese noble descent, whose many languages and imperturbable skill at existence brought him alive out of the holocaust of the German nobility. This holocaust he had forecast when giving a Dance of Death in the Kaiserhof ballroom of Berlin on the eve of the German invasion of Russia. With the Royal Air Force bombing the streets outside the glittering party, he had given the toast, 'Ladies and gentlemen, enjoy yourselves, my dearest dears. *Edite, bibite*, for this is your war: the peace will be appalling for you all.'

[3] Prince Constantine of Bavaria, *After the Flood* (London, 1954) p. 13.

Part Two

EXISTENCE, EROSION, OR EXTINCTION

Five

THE REALITIES OF EXISTENCE

Four countries in Europe show the different ways in which the aristocrats have retained or lost their power. In Spain, the aristocrats have been the most shrewd; while making no publicity for their position of strength, they have held on to most of the good land in the South and they control the banking system of the nation. In no other major European country does the aristocracy keep such a real power. In England, where the peerage has a long tradition of survival through adaptation, it is fighting a losing battle to retain some power, wealth and property. In France, the nobility has kept a little influence by its marriage into the great industrial families, while General de Gaulle has even found some use in the government for splendid anachronisms like himself. In West Germany, however, the aristocracy has lost all of its meaning in a society that seems determined to become the United States of Europe. In the Iberian peninsula, the nobility still lives in the grandeur of the last century; in the Federal Republic of Germany, the nobility is as irrelevant as it will be everywhere in the next century. Between the two extremes, the aristocracy exists or erodes; only in eastern Europe is it nearly extinct.

Without the knowledge of most Spaniards, the nobility controls the six largest banks of the nation, which control nearly four-fifths of the capital of private industry. These banks are the Banco Español de Crédito, the Banco de Bilbao, the Banco Central, the Banco de Biscay, the Banco Urquijo, headed by the

Marquis de Fontalba, and the Banco Hispano-Americano. The boards of all six banks now have on the average one-quarter of titled members, including the Duke de Mama, and the Marquis de la Viesca, de Angnelles and de Pelayo. The other members of the boards of the banks often have family connections with the controlling aristocrats.

It is hard to exaggerate the power of these six main banks, which dominate the country as much as the City dominates England. The six Spanish banks control wholly or in part the electrical industry, the iron industry, the shipyards, chemicals, paper, sugar, and other major industries. The Banco de España, which regulates the private banks for the state in a similar way to the Bank of England, has ten nobles out of the twenty-five members on its board. Thus the financial power of the Spanish aristocracy through the banking system is phenomenal.

On the other hand, General Franco has excluded the nobility from the Falange. In the hierarchy of his party, no aristocrat holds any position within the top 210 party posts. Only one aristocrat, the Marquis Huétor de Santillán, is in the entourage of the Caudillo of Spain. No aristocrat is in the government, and only one, the Marquis de Dávila, among the thirteen members of the Council of the Kingdom. Yet, in the less-known Council of State, there are five aristocrats among its fifty members, the Duke de Almodovar del Rio, the Marquis de Barzanallana and de Valdeiglesias and de Rialp, and the Count de Vallellano. Moreover, in the restricted representative body that passes for parliament, the Cortès, one in seven deputies are from the nobility. Thus the aristocracy is present in the government, although not in the Falange, for fear of its usual monarchist sympathies.

The financial and political power of the Spanish aristocracy is great, yet hidden. Light death duties and low income-tax on large incomes has left the fortunes of the large bankers and land-owners intact. Moreover, since Spain has not known an industrial revolution until the last decade, nearly all economic progress has been initiated through the Spanish banks, which have helped to channel extensive American investment. Capital has bred fortunes in Spain, not backed technological innovation. Rightly fearful since the Civil War that their wealth might be attacked if they flaunted it openly, cleverly, the noble families have learned to make such a virtue of inconspicuous consumption that the actual power of their interests is disguised as a mere lingering of the old ways.

The great estates of the grandees in the south of Spain have not been touched for centuries. Seven grandees still own some 658,000 acres in the south, the family of the Duke de Medinacelli retaining some 235,000 acres alone. In fact, the duke's position is still so feudal that he is reported every year to play a game of chess in which his retainers wear the livery of the chess-pieces and move to the duke's order to play the game. There are still some 10,000 *latifundia* in the South, averaging 1,500 acres each, while the size of the average holding in the whole country amounts to a mere 2.1 acres. Except for the brief effort of the Republican government before the Civil War, agrarian reform has hardly disturbed the doze of the great southern landowners on their hot estates, inherited and neglected from century to century.

Nothing guarantees that this doze shall be a long siesta more than the memory of the Civil War. Few Spaniards are prepared to risk another such carnage, even for the sake of sharing out the land. Other reasons blunt the anger of the southern peasants against the poverty and inequality of their lives. The first is the power of the Catholic Church; some southern landowners *pay* their peasants to go to Mass as a part of their subsistence wages. Moreover, since the days of the *conquistadores* when any Spaniard could carve himself out a fief if he were warrior enough, Spanish rural people have remained partially an aristocracy *manqué*. To a certain extent, they all wish to be aristocrats, and therefore they accept aristocratic values, even if they do not accept the actual terrible maldistribution of wealth. A certain nobility of behaviour and decorum extends right through the manners of the south.

What is peculiar to the southern aristocracy alone is its way of life, which even has its own particular name – *señoritismo*. While some of the grandees are absentee landowners and spend most of their time in Madrid, others lounge about in Granada and Seville and other southern cities, practising the art of *señoritismo*. The art consists of doing as little as possible for as long as possible and as nobly as possible. It is the life of the sons of the prominent, idle and luxurious and melancholy, a lazy stroll between club and bar and casino and evening *paseo*, an effortless effort to be seen doing the correct things with the correct people. Meanwhile, hired factors run the estates and provide the necessary income to be spent in the cities, thus drawing away the hatred of the peasants on to themselves rather than on to the owners of the land.

In this torpid existence, little is done by the owners of capital to put that capital to work, since it might also involve themselves in work. Only five per cent of the capital employed in Spain in a year comes from the south, the rest from the north, where the aristocrats have long since learned to despise *señoritismo* and to work themselves and their money. Southern Spanish landowners with a surplus of capital prefer to invest it abroad or in other regions of Spain, already industrialized. They do not wish to change the rural feudalism of their own territories for the urban dislocation of more advanced regions. The investment of the southern aristocrats in northern industry does, however, give them certain links with the new industrialists, who join in their conspiracy to keep the régime stable, the south backward and the north industrialized. It is curiously similar to the unwritten pact of 1877 in the United States after its Civil War, when the southerners agreed to let the northerners have their industry and their political power as long as the northerners made no more effort to free the rural labourers of the South.

In one way, Franco and the Falange have undercut the political power of the landowners, while leaving them on the land. Before 1931, the local power of the landowners was total; the 'cacique' system sent the proprietors' candidates to office, with or without the voters' support. But now, the Falangists run the political system and they do not take orders from the local aristocrats, who retain more of a social than a political influence.

Franco himself is not above a certain fondness for the privileged.

His daughter Carmen has married Cristóbal, Marquis de Villa-
verde, and the Marquis's father, the banker Count de Argillo,
has become a family intimate. Even so, Franco has had a special
law passed through the Cortès to preserve the name of Franco
in the couple's children, however privileged the father. A Caudillo
has his pride. Yet he has hinted that he will be succeeded by a
constitutional monarchy, in which the aristocracy will have its
place. He has never felt it necessary to proceed against a com-
plaisant nobility, whom he defended in the Civil War and supports
in his régime and ensures in his projected future for Spain.

In 1956, there were 1,693 nobles listed in Spain; these shared
between them 2,184 titles. 368 were listed as Grandees or old
nobles; these were split between the titles of duke and marquis
and count; 249 of these Grandees lived in Madrid. The nobles of
the capital city are exclusively associated in the sixteenth-century
corporation known as the *Real Cuerpo de Hijosdalgo*, which means
'sons of something', that something being landed property. All
Mayors of Madrid are now honorary members of the association
and nobles' wives become *damas*. Women keep their patronym
and pass it on to their children; grandchildren have an equal
claim to inheritance from both parents; women can also pass on
titles not specifically in the male line. The exclusive military
orders from the days of the Paladins still exist, such as the Alcán-
tara, Calatrava, Santiago, Montesa, and the noble order of the
Golden Fleece. So nothing changes for the titled while Spain
changes about them.

The nobility prefers to forget that most of its members tactfully
shed their titles when the Second Republic banned titles, and
merely picked them up again when Franco restored the privilege
of bearing pedigrees in public. The old southern aristocrats and
monarchists, who peer out of the windows of La Peña in the
Gran Vía, are becoming more isolated from the younger aristocrats, who are increasingly marrying wealth and power and who
are carving out an even larger role for themselves in the northern
banks that control the country. The noble family of Luca de Tena
owns *Blanco y Negro*, the largest magazine in the country. In every

field of finance and communications, the aristocracy plays its part.

It is a curious fact that, while the great majority of the Spanish nobility has held itself aloof from business affairs in order to play the lord to the end, a certain proportion – usually from the north – has always used its wealth to achieve economic power. Many a family in Spain and Italy has been ennobled for acting as a banker to the court or the Papacy; that tradition has never died. In the nineteenth century, the Dukes de Alba and de Sevillano, and the Marquesses de Salamanca and de Campo and de Comillas and de Alcanices all associated themselves with foreign capital to build railways and shipyards and to produce armaments. Although the Spanish nobles were never as adaptable as the English peerage, the small proportion of them who kept great wealth and power were sufficient to ensure the survival of their whole group and to keep open places in the banks for the brighter sons of the aristocracy, who could continue to prove that pedigree could still dominate in an industrial age.[1]

Every caste, like every rule, has its exception. In Spain, the exception to the rule of *señoritismo* is given by the notorious Luisa Isabel, Duchess de Medina Sidonia, who is a radical political activist and an admirer of Fidel Castro. It was she who led the protest march of the seven hundred villagers of Palomares, who demanded $2,500,000 of compensation for the traumas caused by the dropping of four unarmed American hydrogen bombs, which landed nearby. The duchess received a sentence of a year in jail for her part in the affair and for her declaration at her arrest: 'We ask only for justice and the people are with me.' The people are hardly with the rest of her caste.

At the time of Napoleon, most of the Spanish nobility sided with the French invader because they thought he could secure their position. In fact, his defeat made their position briefly precarious. In the time of Franco, the Spanish aristocracy with rare exceptions sides with the régime. It has little choice, nor had it much choice in the Civil War, for any radical government must attack its

[1] For details on the position of the Spanish aristocracy, I am much indebted to Jean-Claude Hazera's researches on my behalf.

1 At this house party at Blenheim in 1896, the Prince of Wales, later Edward VII, poses with the shooting party of England's peers and politicians.

2 The Olympic Henley of 1908 is the scene of another formal occasion: Lord Desborough makes a speech before the presentation of trophies.

3 The peers and the poor came to the same end in the Flanders mud.

4 The dead of the First World War were forgotten by the gay young aristocrats of the early 'twenties: Princess Astaficua (with fur) and her pupils at a ball in 1922.

5 The formal occasions
went on: the Duke of
Richmond and the
Duke of Northumberland
at Ascot in 1921.

6 At Eton College Lord
Roderick Pratt (right)
goes to the Fourth of
June in 1929.

7 The preferred sport of the aristocrats was shooting: Prince Henry at a house
party and pheasant shoot held at Water Priory, December 1922.

8 Another preferred sport was polo: Prince Henry in a polo match
at Hurlingham, 1922.

9 The London débutante season began with Queen Charlotte's Ball: the débutantes at the Dorchester, May 1931.

10 The Empire set the stage for the biggest game of them all: the Duke of Sutherland in back of the rhinoceros he had shot in India in 1934.

11 Lady Angela St Clair
Erskine poses with the
Hottentot who saved
her from drowning in
the early 'thirties.

12 Also with her first
trout.

13 After the shoot: Baroness Beck, Lord Kilmarnock and others at Baron Rolf Beck's partridge shoot at Brocket Park, Herts, October 1948.

14 At the Venice Party of September 15, 1951: Lady Diana Duff Cooper (centre back) as Cleopatra, and others in fancy dress.

15 The showman peer: the
Duke of Bedford with
the tourists at Woburn
Abbey, 1958.

16 The photographer peer,
the Earl of Lichfield, as
photographed by himself,
1968.

privileges. Yet times are changing, a middle class is rising in Spain, the workers are becoming richer and more restive, and even the twilight of the old ways in Andalusia darkens into night. Times are changing, and only the brighter of the northern aristocrats have seen that the future of their caste lies in finance, not in land. Even if land is the true basis of an aristocracy, it is a false basis in a nation which must adopt modern technology and urban planning and even agrarian reform. In the end, the estates of the southern aristocrats are doomed, and their blind resistance will only make it worse for them.

Over the border, Portugal under the Salazar government also stayed like southern Spain in the twilight of empire and feudalism, poor and reactionary and hopeless, the home of exiled royalty and faded grandeur. The gap between the rich and the poor is wider there than anywhere else in Europe. Even the *nouveaux riches* ape the ways of the aristocrats and measure their status by the number of relations they can support in idleness and servants in penury. Because there is nc law of primogeniture, all the sons of a noble or wealthy father must receive a share of the estate; so the male children sit about at home to wait, like sleek dogs lounging in expectation of their master's death so that they can chew his bones. But the partition of estates has led to poverty among the old families as well as among the peasants of the north. The countryside is littered with shabby houses, where only a peeling coat-of-arms over the door reminds the stranger of glories, now past and lost.

What is genteel poverty for a Portuguese aristocrat is slow starvation for a peasant. No agrarian reform has disturbed the feudal countryside. In the north, subdivided peasant plots have made each individual small-holding so minimal that they cannot even be counted by the tax authorities. Yet in the South, the smaller holdings average some 7,000 acres each. The four greater landowners in Portugal, including the Duke de Cadaval and the Duke de Palmella, own 235,000 acres – the same area of land that is held by 50,400 small farmers. The peasant working his own or his master's land can hope for little more than subsistence at the best and beggary at the worst. Even Salazar's occasional show of building a dam has not resulted in the construction of a workable irrigation system.

This whole rickety régime of privilege is kept going by Salazar's secret police, the official police, the armed forces and their imperial wars. These wars in Africa to keep the last vestiges of Portugal's overseas conquests prevent the nation from reforming itself to enter modern Europe. The shade of the ill-fated King Sebastian who died with the whole of the ancient Portuguese chivalry in Africa still haunts Portugal into costly follies for the sake of old glories. Army officers are still forbidden to marry outside the educated or wealthy or noble classes; divorce among the aristocracy is severely discouraged as if it would undermine the morality and puritanism of the régime. Salazar governed Portugal by an illusion; but that illusion is still believed, despite the recent proof of Salazar's mortality. His successor cannot continue the illusion indefinitely. Reform will come soon. Then the aristocracy of Portugal will have to bestir itself to survive after its long rural sleep into an age which has almost forgotten feudalism.

In Britain, however, the relics of feudalism keep a certain cherished place in the industrial social order, a place which even reforming politicians have accepted because of their party's wish to grant titles to its own. The very ease with which the holders of old titles have accepted to rub shoulders with the holders of new ones in the House of Lords, and the refusal of the public to distinguish in the news items between ancient aristocrats and recent ones, has led to a general feeling that a title can still be the reward of a well-spent – or a well-spending – life. With trade union leaders in the Lords and football players as baronets and pop singers imperially decorated in the Honours List, a certain democracy of titles has made titles certain in a democracy.

The camouflage of inclusiveness is still real enough at the level of wealth. There, the old families who have inherited money are usually eager to marry money, entertain money, control money, make money, and even collect their old age pensions or their expenses of four and a half guineas daily for attending the House of Lords. A sample was recently taken of the occupations of one hundred peers. The impression of the sampler was that one-third of the thousand peers of England still possessed a large estate. Just under a quarter of the peers were landowners alone, just under a fifth were landowners and company directors, just over a quarter were company directors alone. Of the company directors, the majority were in industry and commerce, then in banking and insurance, and then in the newspaper or communications world.

The peers with directorships in the leading hundred big businesses of the country were predominantly of recent creation. Wealth is soon blessed by a title in Britain. Ninety peers have seats on the boards of the leading hundred companies. Only thirty-one of these are even second-generation peers, while only three actually hold titles that date from more than ninety years ago, and another three come from families of gentry with a long lineage. Big business has spawned its own aristocracy which the Crown and the political parties have blessed. The *parvenus* have rarely accepted the inheritors of prestige in the area of industrial decision. Although most of the big banks and insurance companies tend to have a couple of peers on their boards to reassure their investors, they pick and choose the clever ones and make them work a little for their salaries.[2]

With such an easy access to titles among industrialists, the peerage of Britain has expanded while the British Empire has contracted. The need to staff far dominions with possessors of pomp and pedigree has diminished sharply, while the urge to acquire social distinctions at home has increased. The patronage secretary of the Prime Minister has hinted that three-quarters of those who think that they have deserved a title by services to their country or their party are turned down. What is important is that the industrialists have learned to accept the old aristocrats as part and parcel of the social structure, just as the old aristocrats have learned to accept the industrialists by a politic and public refusal to

[2] See R. Perrott, *The Aristocrats* (London, 1968).

account pedigree as worth a damn in the modern state. 'After all,' Lord Montagu of Beaulieu says, 'we were all *nouveaux riches* once.'

The real power of the ancient peers lies in their inherited property rather than in big business. The Duke of Westminster still owns 270 acres of choice London property in the Grosvenor estate, while Viscount Portman and Lord Howard de Walden and the Earl of Cadogan possess some hundred acres of London property apiece. The recent law of leasehold reform, which allowed leaseholders to buy their freeholds at a reasonable rate or to extend their leaseholds, has not greatly affected the large London estates because of the inertia or poverty of the leaseholders. When the law was mooted, the Labour Minister responsible was called an 'ill-intentioned Marxist Robin Hood', while the dire prediction was made, 'The estates will preside over their own dissolution.' But they have not dissolved, and their dissolution seems postponed to a slow erosion until a law attacks family trusts or a war incinerates all London without distinction of title to the land.

Yet the great estates do slowly diminish in size, due to high taxation or to a wealthy family caught mourning the untimely death of an heir, to whom the estates have just been bequeathed to avoid the duties payable on his father's or his mother's death. The father could say with Philippus:

> Old Nico laid, upon the earth
> Over young Melité, a wreath.
> Where is the righteousness of death?[3]

But the state does not bother with righteousness any more than death does; it takes all it can from young or old.

A measure of the slow decline in aristocratic incomes lies in one statistic of residence. In the most expensive area of London, the postal district marked W1, 34 peers now live compared to the 109 who inhabited the district a little over thirty years ago. Noble families can no longer afford to keep up a town house or apartment as well as a country estate. The conservation of ancestral and rural acres comes before an urban existence, which never

[3] This Greek epigram comes from my own translation of *Selections from the Greek Anthology* (London, 1967).

attracted a great proportion of the British peers even in their heyday. Their homes have usually been set among their farms or shoots, while London has merely been a place to sow the wild oats of youth.

The noble families of the land have conserved their property to a remarkable degree, even after the slaughter of the world wars and the surtax and death duties of more democratic times. The fact that they can no longer coast along from generation to generation has forced them to learn the arts of land management, investment and showmanship. A fourfold increase in the value of land since the last world war and a doubling of the productivity of the soil has helped – but only at the cost of selling off parts of the land and of learning how to develop the soil.

England has never been a country where statistics were as important as discretion. Only two surveys of landownership have ever been made, Domesday Book and the Land Survey of 1873, in which landowners often misrepresented the size of their estates to gain prestige by exaggeration or to conceal wealth by diminution – or merely from ignorance. Even today, many of the great Scots landowners barely know how big their estates are. 'At a very rough guess ... about 130,000 acres,' says Sir Donald Cameron of Lochiel; but he does not exactly know, nor choose to know.

The changes in the British system of landowning since 1873 can be suggested, but not accurately charted. Of the 56,000,000 acres of Britain, 6,000,000 now belong to public bodies, chiefly the Forestry Commission, the armed forces, the National Trust (once called by its chairman Lord Antrim 'a self-perpetuating oligarchy'), the National Coal Board, British Railways, and the airport authorities. The Crown, still the apex of aristocracy, owns some 275,000 acres, the Church of England some 170,000 acres, and the Universities of Oxford and Cambridge some 275,000 acres – thus leaving the Queen and her Church and her older universities very rich.

This does not prevent some noble landowners from owning sizeable areas of Britain. The most recent calculation gives 56 large aristocratic landowners in England and Wales some 900,000 acres between them, and 23 Scots landowners some 1,500,000 acres; the author estimates that his sample represents about one-seventh of the land held by the 'landed classes'. In this case, the owners of large estates would still possess between a quarter and a third of the whole area of England, Scotland and Wales, with land values ranging from £240 an acre for good English arable land down to £3 an acre for poor Scots moorland or mountain.[4] If these figures are accurate, it would leave the owners of the large estates almost balancing the yeomen farmers as the proprietors of the soil of their country. A slow transfer of ownership is taking place, for the large landowners have lost more than half of their land since the survey of 1873, while the farmers and the banks and the insurance companies have taken up that land. More than one-fifth of Britain is already owned by companies and trusts, some of which may in turn cloak effective ownership by a single family. But another century of slow change is more than likely to bring about the end of the old private estate. As the Marquess of Bath says, it is a matter of three more generations.

For the moment, however, there is a lot of life left in the great estates. 'Down to our last 150,000 acres,' as the Countess of Sutherland blithely says, thinking of the family estate which was

[4] R. Perrott, *op. cit.*, pp. 151-5. As Mr Perrott has quoted his estimate of the areas of most of the large estates owned by the peerage in his sample, he seems to have overestimated the proportion of the whole country owned by the 'landed classes', when he says that his sample represents about one-seventh of their total holding. Taking into account the amount of land held by public bodies, companies and trusts, and farmers in England and Scotland and Wales, not to mention the remnants of common land, I do not think the great private estates can possibly occupy more than one-fifth of the land area of the island. Yet accurate figures are impossible to come by. Mr Perrott quotes the extent of the Duke of Buccleuch's estate as 220,000 acres, while one of the sources on which he relies for his information, the article on 'Who Really Owns Britain?' in the *Weekend Telegraph* of 2 December 1966, gives the acreage held by the Duke of Buccleuch as 336,000 acres. Since the peerage refuses to calculate its holdings correctly, since the Land Registry does not contain information upon their holdings, since the dividing line between the peerage and the gentry is always changing because of the creation of new titles, figures of aristocratic landholding in England remain as rough and ready as a Saxon warlord.

nine times as large less than a century ago. Some two hundred titled families in England and Wales are paper millionaires by the value of their land alone, even though this brings in a small return on its capital value. Only in the Scots Highlands does possession of acres rarely mean some wealth; as one of the Duke of Buccleuch's agents says of the local landowners, 'People with ten to twenty thousand acres make less out of them than a man with a small tobacconist's shop in London.'

This may be true – or it may be a case of conspicuous camouflage. Certainly, the more successful landowners such as the Duke of Hamilton with two industrial towns on his property believe in the slogan of his estate manager, 'Don't just let – develop.' There, factory rents can bring in £3,000 per acre, while the Hamilton Estates Commission runs eighteen businesses, ranging from hotels to sawmills. The Countess of Seafield has found it highly profitable to allow some of her 180,000 acres on Speyside to become a winter tourist resort; the local saying has altered, 'God gave the land, the sea and the sky to man but the Spey to the Countess of Seafield – and the skiers.'

The tenacity of the British landowners in clinging on to their land is partly the result of seeing the land as a trust, not as a possession. As the Earl of Leicester says of his inheritance, 'I am a tenant for life; I am very happy here making some contribution to the careful running of the estate.' But the preservation of the estate can lead to some ruthless decisions about the destruction of parts of it. The present descendant of the sporting and extravagant Yellow Earl of Lonsdale, the friend of the Kaiser and Warden of the Borders, has left the ancestral home to archaeology. 'The castle was costing me £2,000 a year to keep the rain out. So I tore off the roof and let the rain in.' With some judicious sales of land and careful investment, he has managed to pay off two lots of death duties and to preserve much of the Lowther inheritance, now a profitable concern.[5]

[5] I am also indebted for my information to the articles written by Nicholas Wollaston and Macdonald Hastings in the *Weekend Telegraph*, 2 December 1966, and to the articles by Mervyn Jones in the *Observer*, March 21 and 28, 1965.

In fact, the abandoning of the great country houses to save the estate has been exceeded only by the exploitation of those houses as tourist attractions. Between 1952 and 1964, some four hundred houses of architectural interest were abandoned or demolished, leaving only two-thirds of the peerage owning a country mansion. Yet eight hundred stately homes are now open to the public, which pays for their preservation by the state or by their owners. The National Trust often allows members of the families, which have bequeathed their property to the nation, to stay on in a wing of their former home. And if these families have been reduced to the status of elegant caretakers, few have elected to join the ranks of the noble showmen and aristocratic mountebanks who run their stately homes for pleasure, profit and publicity as if they had inherited a circus rather than a showpiece.

The most notorious of these showmen is John, Duke of Bedford. As the peer who seems to get more success and publicity than any other, he creates envy among his competitors in the tourist trade, an envy which his behaviour does nothing to allay. Recently, Countess Manvers opened Thoresby Park to the public although she considered it 'a bit *infra dig*' and only did so to keep the roof on; yet she would not alter her behaviour, remarking, 'I don't believe in standing on my head to drag people in – not like the Bedfords at Woburn Abbey.' But the Duke of Bedford, who once let out the park to a nudist gathering as well as continually running a zoo and rushing towards every nearby spotlight, is happy to shrug off such criticism with a realism that has nothing to do with manners:

We are in a competitive business and like any other commercial undertaking, half the battle is publicity. Unless you draw attention to yourself and your wares, people will take no notice of you. In order to make sure that people do not forget that they are welcome at Woburn, I have thrust myself quite unashamedly in the public eye. I have been accused of being undignified. That is quite true, I am. If you take your dignity to a pawnbroker he won't give you much for it. My relatives think I am crazy, but I intend to keep up with the times. I don't think there is any point in being toffee-nosed or sticking your nose in the air and pretending you're something you are not. Being a showman is much more fun than sitting about in dignity or potting pheasants. In show business I have made infinitely more friends than I would ever have made trailing across a grouse moor.[6]

The most professional of the stately home managers, Lord Montagu of Beaulieu, claims to draw in more people to see his operation – half a million each year – than the Duke of Bedford does. Yet stately home attendances, like battle casualties inflicted on the enemy, are often inflated for public consumption. While the Duke of Bedford thinks that Beaulieu is a big gimmick and little more than a garage, Lord Montagu thinks the Duke of Bedford lives his own gimmickry and calls Woburn little more than a zoo. What is certain is that Lord Montagu, in the absence of Van Dycks and Canalettos, has used his considerable talent for public relations and management to give the man in the street 'a good day out', if not a cultural one.

The estate of Beaulieu caters for every tourist taste, from folk music to a motor museum to a yacht marina. And Lord Montagu shares with his chief competitor the fierce belief that the peerage must adapt or perish, although that adaptation need not throw away all discretion. The noble warriors of old must turn into ignoble showmen of modern times in the fight to preserve their estates. The mace of yesteryear is the admass of today. Lord Montagu has even written a text-book for his fellows bearing the subtitle: *How to live in a stately home and make money*. The final words of the book are trenchant:

We must abandon the pretence that the world still owes us a living. We must adopt the attitude and methods of the Impresario. We can all do this with discretion sometimes reinforced with a degree of ruthlessness. If at times we appear over mercenary, too publicity-conscious, even shameless, then this is being forced upon us. We have a difficult but important role to fulfil. I believe that the end will always justify the means. To some that end may appear a little whimsy, a little sentimental. But the more emotional the end the more rational the means.

[6] John, Duke of Bedford: *A Silver-Plated Spoon* (London, 1959) p. 219.

Our ideals can be amateur but our methods must be professional. Unless we adapt ourselves to the times and conditions in which we live we shall suffer a fate as final, if less dramatic, as the French feudal aristocracy at the end of the eighteenth century. If this happens our great country houses will become as empty and lifeless as many of the Châteaux of the Loire.[7]

Yet Lord Montagu is a radical among stately home owners as well as among aristocrats in his revolutionary call to drop the manners inculcated over the centuries. The times may force the aristocrats to adapt or die, but not every eagle can become a peacock just because his eyrie is changed into a tourist trap. Most of those who open up their homes to the public do not open up themselves. For every peer who is an extrovert like Lord Hertford and likes tourists taking his picture and staring at him, a dozen would agree with the Duke of Marlborough who keeps to his own part of Blenheim Palace with the remark, 'No, I certainly don't consider myself part of the show.' But the Duke certainly does consider himself a part of Blenheim, which he refuses to leave to the nation with the telling comment, 'That's the point – an Englishman's home is his castle' . . . or his palace.

From the lions of Longleat that have become part of the national folklore to the discretion of Blenheim, the owners of the landed estates have learned to adapt their ways a lot or a little, certainly enough to improvise for a few generations more. They have a claim, indeed, to be nearer the British people than they have ever been. For they have partially become the caretakers of the national rural heritage. By conserving so much for themselves, they have preserved a great deal of unspoilt land for the present and future enjoyment of the nation.

Lady Diana Cooper noted that her grandfather, the Duke of Rutland, used to open Belvoir to tourists even before the First World War. These used to wait for him at the entrance to the house, and he would take off his hat and bow very slightly to them, smiling. 'He loved his tourists,' she wrote, as if the Duke were

[7] Lord Montagu of Beaulieu, *The Gilt and Gingerbread* (London, 1967) pp. 204-5.

the possessor even of his visitors. 'They represented to him England and liberty and the feudal system, and were a link between the nobility and the people.' Now tourists represent survival and repair-money and the communications system, and they are still a link between the nobility and the people.

A stately home makes its master into its slave. Those aristocrats who possess large houses can never join in the democratic industrial society of the day, however much they may wish. Birth has made them guardians and managers of their inheritance in difficult times for those who have had their education. As the owner of the second oldest name in England and of Berkeley Castle says, 'People like us have been punished all the way through. It's all we can do to keep going in any shape or form.' Yet, he 'wouldn't want to hand over to the National Trust the way some others have done. You wouldn't like to feel you were living at their grace and favour, so to speak.'

Yet, of course, there can be little sympathy for the rich man or the last-ditch fighter who chooses to try and preserve a dying way of life. Whatever Lord Montagu writes, the means do not always justify the end, when the end is selfish and the means questionable. The maintenance of an estate is a *chosen* slavery, for aristocrats can deny or dissipate their birthright, like the famous Earls of Breadalbane, who have managed to get rid of more than 438,000 acres in less than a century, so that the present poor Earl has not one acre to call his own or his family's. As the explorer Anquetil, the freest of free men, said to Sebastian, the heir of the house of Chevron, in Vita Sackville-West's remarkable novel, *The Edwardians*:

'You don't want to escape from Chevron. You think that you love it, that you give it glad and happy service, but you are really its victim. A place like Chevron is really a despot of the most sinister sort: it disguises its tyranny under the mask of love.... You are not allowed to be a free agent. Your life has been ordained for you from the beginning. ... It is the weight of the past. Not only will you esteem material objects because they are old – but, more banefully, you will venerate ideas and institutions because they have remained for a long time in force; for so long a time as to appear to you absolute and unalterable. That is real atrophy of the soul. You inherit your code ready-made.'[8]

Although the old French nobility had a few commercial interests, particularly royalties from mining and insurance and property development and vineyards, the bulk of the *noblesse* preferred marriage as the short cut to riches. The task of keeping a wealthy wife happy seemed more gentlemanly than running a big business. Even if the Orleanist nobility was inseparable from banking and industry with such families as the Rothschilds and the Laffittes and the Duchâtels, it was still a recent and *bourgeois* nobility, ennobled like the great English beer and press lords for reasons of policy rather than pedigree. The drive for status by the *grands bourgeois* led to many families regilding a coat-of-arms which the family did not know it possessed until it needed it.

Among the old nobility, more traditional ways of making money prevailed. The culture of good wine seemed a happy way of confusing vintage with peerage. The board of Clicquot in 1951 had the best part of the Almanach de Gotha sitting on it. But the marriage of riches was the particular talent of the French noble families, and through marriage some of them remain near the levers of industrial power.

'Two hundred families are masters of the French economy and, in fact, of French politics,' Daladier declared in 1934. 'They are forces which a democratic state should not tolerate, which Richelieu would not have tolerated in the Kingdom of France.' The phrase 'two hundred families', which dated from Napoleon's decision to put the Bank of France under the control of its two hundred larger shareholders, became notorious and helped to put into power Léon Blum's Popular Front government, which put through a programme of social reform and nationalization before the war. In fact, there never were two hundred great industrial families which controlled the economy of the country ; there were fewer. Some of the richer families took the important decisions, which the flock of the other great families followed.

[8] V. Sackville-West, *The Edwardians* (London, 1930) pp. 68-9.

A small number of the *grands bourgeois* kept to themselves, even in the marriage of their children. The Michelin dynasty has monotonously married its cousins 'to keep the dowry in the family'. Only one aristocrat has managed to join its inbred ranks, the Count de Auber de Peyrelongue. Other *grands bourgeois*, like the steel and engineering family of the Schneiders, have regularly married into the nobility since the late nineteenth century, so that by 1960 Pierre de Cossé, Duke de Brissac, who had married May Schneider, was head of a complex of engineering and electrical and steel companies, while the great Schneider company itself recently had on its board the Marquis de Rafélis Saint-Sauveur and the Duchess de Brissac, with the de Ganay and de Brantes families prominently listed among its shareholders. Similarly, the great armaments family of Wendel has been open to aristocratic penetration. Since its huge social success in the nineteenth century when one of the daughters of Charles de Wendel married the Duke de Maillé and the other the Marquis de Montaigu, the Wendels and the French nobility have been very much part and parcel of each other. Of course, little need be said of the famous French Rothschild family, which has become more aristocratic than the aristocrats. A genius for banking allied to a taste for picking pretty girls and horses has given to the Rothschilds a firm place in French high society.

Among such great financial families, lesser aristocratic families have risen through marriage. The Vogués, who have interests in banks and transport and chemicals and steel as well as in agriculture, have managed to strike up family connections with the Rothschilds, the Cossé-Brissacs, and the Arenbergs; these alliances in turn unite them to the Schneiders and the Wendels. Although the title of *noblesse* of the Vogués dates from 1303 and the title of Marquis in the family from 1723, they have usually preferred to marry real power rather than old blood.

Even the family of Charles de Gaulle did not choose to marry entirely into its fellow gentry. On his mother's side, General de Gaulle is allied to some of the great northern industrial families, the Kolb-Bernards and the Maillot-Droulers and the Gustave de Corbies. Through his wife, he is connected to the wealthy pencil-makers, Baignol et Farjon. His son has married into the Wendel family by choosing as a wife Henriette de Montalembert, and his daughter has married into the Schneider family by choosing as a husband Alain de Boissieu de Luigné, a cavalry colonel. Even de Gaulle's brother Pierre sits on the board of a Schneider bank.[9]

And so on *ad infinitum*. The obsession of some French writers with the abracadabra of family alliances and the conspiracy of powerful marriages can be taken to absurdity. Ever since the days of the *Action Française*, a morbid fascination for discovering how the 'pure blood' of the French nobility has been mixed up with the Jews and the lesser-born has given out many details and little light. Marriage into a family hardly ensures power within that family. A rich wife may be a positive inducement to a titled husband to do nothing at all. Indubitably, French aristocrats do marry outside their ranks and, indubitably, wealthy families do try to pick noble or rich spouses for their children. In France, the custom of the *dot* has turned many a famous marriage into more of a merger. But with the gradual decline of the dowry system, choices are becoming freer for the sons and daughters of the powerful or noble – especially as the government of Charles de Gaulle is currently offering more opportunities for the aristocrat than have been offered since the days of Louis Napoleon.

Without seeming to consider the advanced age of General de Gaulle and the republican tradition of France, the Duke de Broglie can confidently assert that 'the new generation of the nobility since the war is extremely interested in politics and is getting into it'. As far as he is concerned, politics is one of the inherited skills of his family, and he is glad to be able to exercise it. 'Nobility has a great part to play,' he says as dogmatically as his leader. 'We shall survive, we *do* survive.' Temporarily, France seems to have lost enough of its anti-aristocratic feelings to accept a well-born leader, who is aristocratic enough to see that two or

---

[9] I am particularly indebted for these details to *Crapouillot*, April 1961; also to the works of Raymond Dior, Augustin Hamon, and Henry Coston.

three of the French dukes are present at most large formal functions in the Fifth Republic. Another public servant, the Count de Chambrun, considers that de Gaulle has a deep respect for the aristocracy and sees that it has something to give the country, even though the revolution in French thought has meant a refusal to dwell on past glories.

Yet perhaps de Gaulle's use of the French aristocracy is hardly surprising; an aristocrat himself, he has never been backward in putting himself forward to serve his country. His attitude does not stimulate all well-born Frenchmen. Against him stand the old guard of the French aristocracy, who see him and his vision of the future of France just as the rich American reactionaries saw Franklin D. Roosevelt and his New Deals. To the conservative French nobles who have refused to back de Gaulle, the General is nearly a communist and certainly 'a class enemy'. They consider themselves disgracefully betrayed by one of their own kind; his flirtation with Russia and his support of the welfare state seem little short of treason. His chief noble backer, the Duke de Broglie, is dismissed as an opportunist of foreign extraction; the de Broglies had, after all, left Italy for France only a few centuries before and 'blood always tells'.

The aristocrat in politics provokes a far more violent reaction from the aristocrats outside politics than any middle-class or proletarian politician, who is expected to behave as badly as his class. Over and over again, as an excuse for not trying to keep their hands on some political power at the expense of their sense of righteousness and pedigree, the aristocrats call politics 'a dirty business'. That the intrigues of the courtiers at Versailles under the *ancien régime* were just as dirty a business seems to have escaped the memory of the retired aristocrats; at least in the old days the mass of the people respected the courtiers, even if court life made them intriguing and corrupt. What they do not like now is the need to pander to the mob in order to get elected. When a recent aristocrat like Couve de Murville can find the whole process of running for a seat in parliament quite so blatantly distasteful, how can a duke of ancient blood be expected to accommodate himself better to the electorate? The fact that de Gaulle does play the vote-getting game with such skill while yet retaining an air of grandeur annoys the conservatives even more. He seems to demonstrate the possiblity of great men from old families still carving a place for themselves in the modern world, while at the same time he makes a mockery of those who pretend to stay out of politics and hug their sense of blamelessness and breeding at home.

West Germany had much to rebuild after the end of the Nazi régime, since the Allies had destroyed more in Hitler's nation than he had managed to destroy in theirs. In their huge post-war reconstruction, the West Germans have changed not only the face of their country, but also the structure of their society. The Nazis had already destroyed many of the aristocratic power groups which had survived the Weimar Republic; but the partition of Germany and the technological triumph of the western part has created a new aristocracy of managers and a mobile concept of society, which judges the rank of people against a shifting standard of status, and which wholly denies the set hierarchies of the Kaiser's world.

The result of the Second World War was unsettling for the old families of Germany. The Americans, according to Ferdinand Prince von der Leyen, thought most titled people had been Nazis, and tried to dispossess them of their land. Between 1939 and 1955, only one-half of fathers in the wealthier families saw their sons remain in the same economic situation. Vast population movements, the devastation and rebuilding of whole cities in which one-third of the inhabitants were newcomers, and the inclusion in West Germany of one-quarter of its population from outside its frontiers led to what the sociologist Helmut Schelsky called 'a far advanced breakdown of social distinctions'. Even the Crown Prince of Prussia allowed his daughter to marry Clyde Harris, an interior decorator from Texas. Concepts like 'morganatic', 'not appropriate to one's rank', seemed out of date to the Crown Prince, although the marriage took place in Hohenzollernburg, his last great family castle.

A similar acceptance of the new American ways gathered speed everywhere. All the new German élites outside the trade unions and the Social Democratic Party were predominantly middle class in outlook as in the United States, which had done so much to destroy the old Germany and to rebuild the new one in its own mobile image. As Friedrich Sieburg noted regretfully in 1958, there was no more Society nor good company left in Germany. Catastrophe had done less to abolish social differences than post-war reconstruction.

A careful study of West German élites in 1959 showed that only eight per cent of members of those élites bore aristocratic names, while ten per cent came from proletarian backgrounds and the vast majority came from the bourgeoisie. Of course, the aristocracy and the gentry were still over-represented in the élites, since they numbered less than one-half of one per cent of the nation; but their power was eroding even in their more sacred preserves. Less than one-fifth of the new German military élite bore aristocratic or Junker names, one-sixth of the diplomatic corps, one-eighth of the Cabinet in 1956, one-eleventh of the Civil Service, and only one-fiftieth of the industrial leaders of the nation.[10]

West Germany's post-war economic miracle meant that the actual rulers of the new Germany were and are the industrialists and the technocrats. Sociologists see the present élites of Germany as split between the big businessmen, the politicians, the university leaders and professors, the churchmen, the stars of the mass media and of sport, the military top brass, and the chief members of the legal profession. These élites hardly mix with each other and may contain a few of the old aristocrats; but the aristocrats as a coherent élite through inheritance have been totally supplanted.

In the gay life of the new Germany, the less cautious aristocrats are sometimes seen, brought in at a price by some industrialist or seeker after the printed gossip which possession of a title can still conjure from the press. But since this 'aristocracy of mere money'

[10] Karl Deutsch and Lewis Edinger, *Germany Rejoins the Powers* (Stanford, California, 1959) *passim*.

has largely taken over the gossip columns by its extravagance and appetite for reading about itself, the old aristocracy has been allowed to slip gracefully back into a proud obscurity, while its sons and daughters may now enter professions once denied to them by their class's obsession with what was seemly for it to do.

Only in Southern Germany, never quite as exclusive and stiff-necked as Prussia, has there been a successful mingling between the older aristocrats and the new ones of wealth and technocracy. In Munich, the *Prominenz* include all the rich and some of the noble. Yet, although the most fashionable dance of the year is the *Damen Ball*, the *Adel Ball* still continues exclusively for the high aristocracy. The one reporter clandestinely present in recent years noted the tattered finery of the guests at the *Adel Ball*; they would allow only each other to be a witness of their shabbiness. These *Standesherren*, the members of the eighty ancient families owing allegiance only to the Emperor in the old Holy Roman Empire that has been defunct since 1806, still tend to keep very much to themselves; but even they are learning to bow to the winds of change and the rods of the newly rich and powerful. What is forever gone except as a nostalgic dream is an aristocratic conspiracy to bring back the monarchy or to upset the republican state, which has brought about the economic miracle and has spread riches to every group prepared to lend a hand.

In his interesting work, *Nobility in Transition*, Joachim von Dissow stressed the ambivalent nature of the aristocrat's legacy to Germany. The aristocrat's dedicated service to court and state was both selfish and selfless. He knew that the old order would protect his class and his family because of the principle of hierarchy. His service to the Kaiser and the Church was, in a sense, service to himself. For if the aristocracy served God and the monarch, God and the monarch served the aristocracy. Thus the dedication of the aristocracy to honour rather than profit was not entirely disinterested.

Contrary to the myth of feudal extravagance, von Dissow noted that thrift and economy were more common aristocratic habits than wastefulness. Agriculture had to be practised carefully to maintain the family property and to bring in a reasonable income; no risks were to be taken to increase the family fortune, which should be handed on much as it was. Prosperity could be enjoyed, but wealth was hardly worth the dangerous effort. As the aristocracy did not earn wealth, it had to inherit money or marry money or receive the low stipend paid to army or government officials. This dislike of the material outlook was so great that it permeated every detail of the education of the aristocrat. When he was a child, von Dissow himself was told he was materialistic if he showed pleasure at being given chocolate or sweets.

Von Dissow noticed, however, that the failure of the German aristocracy lay in its inability or unwillingness to accustom itself to changed conditions, as the English aristocracy had. Whatever was outside the realm of kingdom and army and state and church was only dimly perceived and instantly dismissed – economics, science, intellectual life, and, in particular, democratic politics and social realities. This ostrich mentality led to the German aristocracy appearing anachronistic in the eyes of its contemporaries and perishing as a ruling class in the turbulence of the times. Yet this very same blinkered outlook also gave the aristocratic caste the clear outlines and firm stance which distinguished it from its victorious rival – the salaried bourgeoisie.

The legacy of the aristocratic mentality seemed to von Dissow something indirect, even subterranean. Although a technocratic and industrial society had little use for elaborate codes of behaviour, yet a certain belief in integrity and honour had blunted the worst excesses of American capitalism as adopted by Germany. Perhaps the most dangerous legacy of the aristocracy was its exaltation of the strong leader. Von Dissow did not disguise the fact that the German aristocracy of officers and industrialists and bankers and landowners idealized Hitler until he began to lose the Second World War. Their emotional commitment to the myth of the Kaiser made Hitler's airs of grandeur very attractive to them after the weaker personalities of the Weimar Republic.[11]

The same danger of a new Nazi Germany, while the ideal of

[11] Joachim von Dissow, *Adel Im Übergang* (Stuttgart, 1961).

the Leader is still a strong element in the German mentality, also worries Ferdinand Prince von der Leyen in his own work on his country. He wishes it had been longer before Germany was allowed another professional army, because of his country's inherited militarism. Although National Socialism is no longer much of a danger, human nature remains the same and, therefore, the same weaknesses could engender the same crimes. Yet Prince von der Leyen suggests a curious reason why the Germans should have felt so compelled to forget their aristocracy. It is because there is a national need to obliterate the past and the walking representatives of that past by a people tired of the role of repentant sinners for the crimes committed against the Jews more than twenty years ago.[12] Again the equation between the aristocrat and the Jew appears, each shouldered aside like a bad memory of the past in the forward-looking Germany of today. Ironically enough, the Jews of Central Europe often still bear the names of the old princely houses of the Holy Roman Empire such as Loewenstein and Lobkowicz, since once they identified themselves as far as possible with their princely protectors.

The neo-Nazi party in modern Germany, the NPD, recently successful in winning representation in provincial and state elections, was put together by a man who came from the Prussian nobility of Pomerania, and who began his political career as a monarchist. Adolf von Thadden has a talent for organization and, above all, for concealing dark appeals to bigotry and racialism under sweet and reasonable propaganda. Hitler's aged Youth Leader and aristocratic friend, Baldur von Schirach, recognized the NPD for what it is, when he declared on television : 'There is always a difference in a radical party between what it says it is and what it is . . . I know the undertone only too well.'

The particular propaganda of the NPD aims at whitewashing the Nazi past by refusing to recognize the crimes of the National Socialists. Its spokesmen claim that, as the British invented concentration camps in the Boer War, the Germans should not have been punished for the idea after the Second World War. Anyway,

[12] Ferdinand, Prinz von der Leyen, *op. cit.*

surely the Allied crimes at Nuremberg against the Nazi leaders were far greater than the crimes that the Nazis committed against the Jews. This logic of distortion and these statistics of fantasy appeal to a mass wish to forget that the defeat of 1945 ever happened, and to regain the frontiers of the Kaiser's Germany, so much larger and more stable.

Yet there is no question that the neo-Nazi tendency in the new Germany is a minor phenomenon up till now. Its danger lies in its influence over powerful men and in the slow infiltration of ex-Nazis back into positions of authority, men such as Lübke, the President of the Federal Republic, Kiesinger, the Chancellor, and General Count Johann Adolf von Kielmansegg, the leader of the NATO land forces in the centre of Europe. While there is little evidence that Lübke or Kiesinger joined the Nazi Party for other reasons than opportunism, Kielmansegg was unwise enough to publish a book in 1941 about his experiences as an officer on the General Staff in the heady days of the early victories. Then, he stimulated a tank division before Leningrad with the order, 'To do the utmost for Führer and fatherland until the final decision has been won and Germany's future made secure,' while he considered Poland a filthy country because of the many Jews living there and France a stagnating country with a general atmosphere 'of degeneration and depravity'.[13]

Still, time forgives the past of the fanatic or of the mere server of time. Opportunism makes opportunity knock more than once. A 'clean' record of co-operation with the Nazis is no longer prejudicial in the Federal Republic; in fact, it has some merit in seeming to offer a reconciliation between the old beliefs and the new ones. And if certain neo-Nazi tendencies and ex-Nazi men in power give cause for concern, other developments give cause for democratic hope. The incredible return of the pro-Nazi Alfried von Krupp von Bohlen und Halbach to his family's business empire after his sentencing at Nuremberg for war crimes, since the Americans thought he would be of use to them at the

[13] Count Johann Adolf von Kielmansegg, '*Panzer zwischen Warschau und Atlantik*', *Die Wahrmacht* (Berlin, 1941).

time of the Korean War, finally ended in the economic backwardness of the Krupp business after 156 years of family control through
Alfried Krupp's final refusal to adapt to modern technology.

Economics proved more ruthless than Allied revenge in
breaking up the power of the Ruhr industrial barons. The Krupp
family has espoused philanthropy and has lost much of its force,
the Thyssens have diversified their £80,000,000 investment in
steel into many other industries under the guidance of Fritz von
Thyssen's widow and her daughter, Countess Anita de Zichy.
The rich industrial families who backed Hitler have made a
remarkable recovery with the assistance of American capital;
but the very extent of the German boom has weakened the old
oligopolies by conjuring up a host of millionaires in the new
currency – some 3,500 within twelve years after the end of the
war. Yet there were more than 15,000 gold-mark millionaires
in the Kaiser's Germany, which shows that the muck of wealth
is far better spread than it used to be.

Here the new Germany has most successfully imitated the
United States. Prosperity has always solved the worse problems
of the United States, not reform. The American way has never
been to correct an abuse nor to share a cake fairly, but to bake
another cake and to sugar over its cracks. In the Federal Republic
general prosperity has removed the condition of mass misery
which had provided the original cause of the rise of the Nazis.
And the development of new industries and millionaires has
broken up the oligopoly of the old ones. As the aristocracy of
pre-war big business superseded the old titled aristocracy of the
Kaiser's Germany, so the state and the new industries and millionaires are pushing aside the great old family firms of the industrial
barons. Aristocracy, by its very nature, is not good at fierce competition nor new methods. Thus it is bound to be displaced or to be
renewed or to resist and perish. In Germany, the America of
Europe, titles are now irrelevant, old money gives way to new
fortunes, and competition rules all.

The other countries of Europe have adopted to a greater or less degree the patterns of survival, erosion or near extinction shown by the aristocracies of Spain and Portugal, England, France, and West Germany. In Italy, the aristocracy survived the fall of Mussolini and even of the monarchy by clinging to the coat-tails of the Christian Democratic Party, which hardly wanted to preserve the privileges of some of its backers. Since little was done about land reform in the post-war years, communism made giant strides in northern rural areas because of the continuing land hunger of the peasants. This time the democratic government managed to check the forcible occupation of the land of absentee landlords in Calabria in 1949 and in parts of the Po Valley a year later. There was no crisis as in 1919 and no second Mussolini. Yet not until the 'Green Plan' of December 1961, did the peasants consider that they were as well treated as under Mussolini, for they were given free issues of farm clothing, guaranteed prices and markets, large subsidies, and finally hope – the hope that the government would really handle the problem of absentee and in-different landlords, who were concerned with their vast southern estates as the basis of their family titles, not as soil for the feeding of the people.

Very slowly, the government is moving to dispossess even the southern princes of their unnecessary acres, very slowly these princes are giving way in order to have a larger income to spend in the *dolce vita* of Rome and the resorts of international society, very slowly the peasants are becoming educated through schools and temporary emigration to factory jobs in the north. Meanwhile, the government wins few votes in the reform areas, where peasant ignorance is still exploitable by reactionary appeals. The great landowners, now alienated from the 'socialism' of their saviours the Christian Democrats, have thrown their support to the reviving monarchists and neo-fascists. A Bourbon nostalgia, particularly near Naples and particularly fed by those magazines devoted to gossip about the titled of past and present, has led to a small revival of the right wing among those who would benefit most from a left-wing solution to the problem of their poverty and unemployment.

Among the Italian aristocracy itself, it is noticeable that some of the men work, while many of the women do. Italy, long a covert matriarchy, has become an overt one in certain noble circles. 'It is no longer thought to be *pas comme il faut* for women from our milieu to work,' says the Countess Franca Pecari Giraldi. Her Florentine feminine friends are very much concerned with the world of fashion and art and leather goods. In Rome, the whole world of the galleries is in the hands of women art dealers, often sprung from the aristocracy. A rich woman, indeed, who brings property to her husband, now insists on a marriage contract which leaves her affairs in her own hands. Although the business situation is not yet as matriarchal as in Thailand, among the Italian aristocracy the women are both earning the money and spending it.

Yet the Italian nobility remains generally selfish and short-sighted, therefore vulnerable to any sudden social change in Italy, where the Communist Party remains very powerful. A particular case is that of Mimi Valguarrera, Princess di Niscemi, and first cousin to the Duke di Lampedusa, who wrote *The Leopard*. The Princess runs an artificial jewellery business and a dress shop on Seventh Avenue in New York. She claims that her feeling for the traditional makes her goods successful even in the United States. 'We Italians were born with a sense of the sumptuous. From an early age, we were brought up to see the costumes of the nobles through the ages and splendours of church dress.' Yet her sense of the modern age does not persuade her to dispossess herself of her vast estates in Sicily and Spain, where the peasants live in poverty and where the absentee Princess rarely goes.

No major European aristocracy, except perhaps the British aristocracy, has voluntarily relinquished power without a social revolution, whether violent and bloody and brief, or commercial and casual and slow. The sufferers from the violent revolution that has overtaken eastern Europe have had to shift as they can. The better of them have decided to stay in their own countries behind the Iron Curtain, working for a new society within the socialist system adopted by their home countries. Ilya Ilyich

Tolstoy, who would have been the eighth count of the line, returned to Russia after the 'magnificent sacrifice and glory' of his people during the Second World War. He is now a professor at Moscow State University and says that nothing would terrify him more than owning the Tolstoy estate again. 'Twice recently I dreamed it was mine – and woke up in a cold sweat. Leaky roofs, repairs, bickering over servants – what nightmares! Who's insane enough to wish that misery on himself?' The house is now an orphanage, and its heir likes it that way. Indeed, he says that the modern Russian state embodies more of his grandfather's godly ideals than the Tsar's Russia ever did.

Other aristocrats who stayed in eastern Europe have not fared so well. Ernst Trost, who recently made a tour in search of them, found the widow of the famous Count Károlyi still living in a part of the family palace in Budapest. The government allowed her to lecture about her dead husband and treated her well, because he had been almost alone among the Hungarian aristocrats in being a social reformer. The past tells in the present treatment of the aristocratic. In Prague, the names Czernin and Lobkowicz and Schönborn were now borne by manual labourers, porters and salesmen. They kept to themselves for fear of denunciation and met each other only at funerals. They chose to remain where their families had always remained. 'I wouldn't know where to go,' one ex-count said. 'We have been in Bohemia for centuries and we belong here.'

Sometimes the aristocrats have become the literal caretakers of their old properties, not the wealthy overseers maintained by the English National Trust. The aged Count Mensdorff still lives in three rooms of his castle in Boskovice, and his wife knits pullovers for money. In Krakau, Prince Puslowski still has one room, crammed with his furniture, where he receives visitors and apologizes for being 'forced into a rather cramped way of life'. He took the precaution of giving his home in Krakau to the university before it was confiscated, and thus has been allowed to retain a single room until fit for a single coffin.[14]

[14] Ernst Trost, *Das blieb vom Doppeladler* (Vienna, 1966).

Thus the old aristocracy still exists, sometimes joyfully, in eastern Europe. In western Europe, the *émigré* aristocrats often live materially better, regretting their lost homelands bitterly. They mostly had a time of great adventure at the end of the Second World War and emerged from it rather more educated in the ways of the people than they had been before. Ludwig Prince Windischgrätz became a docker in the Argentine for a short period, able to adapt and survive even in his sixties. Prince Krzysykof Wironiecki, now the owner of a restaurant in the King's Road in Chelsea, remembers escaping from the Germans down the hot summer lanes with literally nothing except the clothes on his back. 'There I was with nothing, no country, no worries of ownership, not a care in the world – I don't remember ever being so happy.' He joined the Free Polish army for the war, then worked his way in England from the position of barman through house-painting into restaurant-owning. Poland and his estate is a past, lost dream.

The *émigré* aristocrats have had to adapt to the total loss of their estates and a new life in western Europe, for they know that they will never be able to return to any possessions they left behind them. As Sir Lewis Namier so brilliantly summed up their situation in his *Vanished Supremacies* :

All past social superiorities have been wiped out behind the Iron Curtain, and most of the cultural values which the educated classes had created. Anti-Socialist, clerical peasant communities may yet arise in States now satellites of Russia. But a reinstatement of the dispossessed upper and middle classes is impossible. And it is even more idle to think of a reconquest of territories once held on the basis of those vanished supremacies. Now territories in Europe can only be regained with 'vacant possession': that is, radically cleared of their present inhabitants. [15]

In Scandinavia the aristocracy is irrelevant and manages as well as anybody else. The Scandinavians have a long tradition of personal and political freedom, even though Norway was ruled for so long by Sweden and Denmark, and Finland was controlled

[15] L. Namier, *Vanished Supremacies* (London, 1958) pp. 214-15.

by Sweden and Russia. 'The average man felt himself to be a free man, not a creature at the disposal of an aristocracy. He was not ridden with a sense of inferiority.' In agricultural Denmark, nineteen out of twenty farms are owned by their operators, and only one farm in a hundred is large enough to be called an estate. Co-operatives dominate the rural economy, as they do elsewhere in Scandinavia. In Sweden, where less than one-tenth of the land is cultivable, old castles and medieval manor houses fill the fertile areas of southern Sweden, but they do not dominate the farm life. Without any forced land reform, the 25,000 nobles who still exist in Sweden have lost their power over the agricultural economy and retain only 150 manorial estates. This power was never even possessed by the aristocrats in Norway, which is hardly cultivable at all.

The Finnish miracle of post-war reconstruction was achieved by brutal work, the use of trees, and severe land reform to resettle the 425,000 refugees from the areas of Finland confiscated by the Russians. A draconian land reform gave 2,700,000 acres – owned by the state, the townships, noble families and land speculators – to the refugee farm families. The result is a nation of 285,000 small farmers and no estates.[16] The Finnish aristocracy has little else to cling onto except its pedigree, carefully recorded in a small red Book of Knights.

In Holland and Belgium, the nobility is neither quite as irrelevant as in Scandinavia nor quite as important as in England across the North Sea. The monarchy in both countries is far less popular than the English monarchy, due to unfortunate marriages with princelings from hated Germany and to behaviour which seemed both short-sighted and selfish to the people of the Low Countries. In Belgium, the French-speaking aristocrats are particularly threatened by the rise of Flemish separatism, which hates these lordly remnants of former conquerors. Yet a group of Belgian nobles, Baron Leon Lambert and the Baron Snoy et d'Oppuers and the Baron Boels, exert great financial influence through their banking power. In Holland, the aristocrats exist obscurely and as

[16] See D. Connery, *The Scandinavians* (London, 1966).

far from the unpopular court as possible; they have a shrewd idea that the future of their titles should not be bound too closely to the future of the throne.

In only one European country has the aristocracy positively benefited by a change of régime in recent years. That country is Greece, where the generals may have ousted the monarchy temporarily, but have certainly confirmed the rule of the privileged. Of course, in a certain sense, there is no aristocracy still in Greece, except an *émigré* one. The old families who ruled the Christian provinces when the Turks controlled Greece were granted the hereditary title of Prince; but these titles were withdrawn from them and may only be used abroad. Venice's rule of the Ionian Islands resulted in Italian titles being as common as pebbles on the beach; but these titles may only be used on the islands, where half the families have them anyway. Athenian society has its social distinctions; but, as for pedigree, the most distinguished claim is to be descended from one of the heroes of the War of Independence – particularly under the present régime.

In Vienna, where Austrian titles are banned, a club has been formed called the St Johanns-Club to serve as a meeting place for the old nobility of Europe and as an incentive for their mutual aid in becoming once again a conservative power in the modern world. Its membership includes sixteen princes and about ninety other aristocrats from Austria, West Germany, France, Italy, Belgium, Sweden and Finland. Interestingly enough, the majority of the Austrian members are employed in various professions as are many of the German aristocrats, while the nobility of the other countries is usually out of work. This would seem to suggest a rule: where an aristocrat is least appreciated and least wealthy, he will find a job. The Austrian founders of the club have even written the virtue of their necessities into the club's credo with the words: 'The aristocracy should practise professions as this will increase their influence and benefit society as a whole.'

One of the club's members, Dr Johann Christoph Freiherr von Allmayer-Beck, has written in the club's brochure an able case for the continuing role of the nobility. To him, appearances suggest that the 'slandered and tattered aristocracy' is regaining power, but in fact it is only appealing to 'the tremendous growth of a practically international snobbery'. The truth is that the nobility has fallen from its high estate, and had even fallen by the time of the First World War.

At this point the author quotes a letter from Alexander von Villers to Baron Warsberg, dated 1879; the letter states that 'aristocracy was once a station, it is not any more, it has ceased to be a station and is now only a memory.' Villers was correct that the feudal system had already given way nearly everywhere to *bourgeois* industrial democracy. Aristocrats could manage to be powerful in the politics and even in the commerce of the modern state; but their feudal rights and position were gone, and the progress of democracy was bound to curtail any power which they retained. From the point of view of social standing, nobility was already redundant.

Yet Dr Allmayer-Beck finds the modern age hungry for élites and tired of anonymity and the sea of uniformity. It chooses inferior élites from film-stars and football players and the like. Authority is no longer in the hands of the old-style 'legitimate' leaders; it rests with political parties and the mass media – a comparatively fickle and inconstant basis as these public organizations depend for their existence on the whim of public opinion. 'Is it not a matter of extreme seriousness that the future of our continent is entrusted to a class of leaders which is extremely unhomogeneous in its composition, disparate in its objectives, and anything but attractive in its overall political conception?'

Dr Allmayer-Beck suggests an answer to his problem. It is, of course, the new emergence of the aristocracy as national leaders, after a spiritual and ascetic regeneration in its own ranks. The old aristocracy must become again the *best* of men and Christians, and it must struggle again for its lost authority. Otherwise, it will lose even the remnants it still has, as progress passes it by. 'To a certain extent, this has happened already, for it would otherwise be hard to explain the curious state of affairs which has resulted in the aristocracy being sought out as a social attraction, loved as an organizer of festivities and scandals, admired and secretly envied, often still determining matters of external form, but, as a caste, totally without influence in decisive matters of political and social life.'

Dr Allmayer-Beck's view of the loss of real power by the aristocracy is too Austrian a view; as has been noted, the aristocracy still retains a real power in Spain and Portugal, and to a certain extent in England and France. But even in northern and central Europe, Dr Allmayer-Beck exhorts the nobility to rise again from its ashes.

The real question at the present time is the extent to which the former aristocracy may belong to the new class of leaders. Unless clarity is reached on this point, the old nobility will lose all scope for influence and become mere social decoration. The aristocracy does not have the right, any more than any other section of society, to withdraw from public affairs and mourn the passing of a better age. This passivity is harmful, not only to aristocracy itself, but also to the rest of society, the state and the supra-national community . . . because the old aristocracy in its substance, its upbringing and its centuries-old tradition and culture, has received a heritage, the renunciation of which would be a great loss to the new class of leaders.[17]

Yet that loss is inevitable. The old aristocracy may, here and there, throw up a Charles de Gaulle; but this nod to the past can only become a total democratic shaking of the head in denial of the old aristocratic values. In only one European state, infinitely small and infinitely lucky to survive, does the old feudal world and the new commercial world combine in a harmony of self-interest that is the *summum bonum* of all who hope in vain for an aristocratic revival. That state is, of course, the princely state of Liechtenstein, where Franz Josef II, Prince zu Liechtenstein, reigns from his thirteenth-century castle above the town and the principality like a benevolent godfather of the world of tax evasion through company law.

[17] Dr J. C. von Allmayer-Beck 'Adel und Moderne Gesellschaft', *Tagung Konservativer Europäer* (Vienna, June, 1960).

The prince himself is one of the dozen richest men in Europe, recently richer by some $6,000,000 from the sale of the last Leonardo da Vinci in private hands to an American museum. His family's collection of paintings, removed from Austrian galleries for safety during the war and never returned because the prince does not honour agreements made with Nazi governments, is worth at least $50,000,000. The prince also has a majority shareholding in a Liechtenstein bank and large land-holdings in the principality. He carefully refrains from buying up the whole area's business, for fear of becoming unpopular. He is already considered something of a foreigner by his 19,000 subjects, since his family chiefly resided in the old Austrian Empire before its fall, and took its wealth from grateful Emperors.

Yet the anachronism of this principality with its easy company laws and secretive banks, which have learned the lessons of discretion from the Swiss financiers who own Liechtenstein's industries, has allowed the name of Liechtenstein to become famous in the shadowy world of concealed company profits, mutual funds, unexplained capital, and tax avoidance. The legal existence of Liechtenstein and the shrewdness of its prince has made it the most perfect feudal commercial state in Europe, a model of the success of the wily old ways in outwitting the power of the industrial modern nations.

Six

THE SHADOWS OF SURVIVAL

There is a Darwinian law for the modern European aristocracy. It is concerned not so much with the survival of the fittest or the best, as with the survival of the well-born. The methods advocated for that survival vary. What is certain is that, the more an aristocrat works in modern life, the less he believes in the virtues of ancient birth. We all make virtues out of our inherited talents and our choices; aristocrats particularly do so, as each one of them is accustomed to thinking that his example is good for all his class, if not all the world. Thus those who have turned themselves into industrialists or bankers tend to preach their self-made image and denigrate their lineage, while those who have largely opted out of modern life and who are fighting for survival on the decreasing returns of agriculture do the opposite. The golden past attracts in the lean present. In the definition of what aristocracy means to a modern European aristocrat, the job he has – or the job he chooses not to have – is all-important.

To an active Florentine marquis such as Dino Frescobaldi, aristocracy means power and wealth; without the opportunity to rule, an aristocracy does not exist.

The nobles who take tea on the Via Veneto or in their houses and do nothing are nothing. The aristocracy which is now poor and tries somehow to keep up appearances is nothing. To be an aristocrat, you must be rich and be a leader – otherwise it is meaningless. To be a leader is what counts. The Fiat people, the big industrial families of Milan and Turin, are the aristocrats of today with just a few old rich remaining families.

The Belgian banker, Jean Prince d'Arenberg, is slightly less out-spoken, but takes much the same position.

The aristocracy must not be frozen, it must work or die. If you look back in history, the aristocracy had functions. The counts looked after their villages, the dukes headed the armies, the aristocracy was active and had some duties to do, and today, if the aristocracy does not want to die, it must work.

Of course, in terms of real power and wealth in a modern industrial state, work naturally means an involvement in business. And here the aristocrats have had to overcome a psychological handicap, a certain inbred distaste for having anything to do with industry outside the more gentlemanly areas of banking. In the case of the nobles of eastern Europe, finally dispossessed after the Second World War, necessity made them turn more easily to business as a method of acquiring the new capital which would buy them an estate in western Europe. In Munich and Vienna, much of the old aristocracy from Hungary and Czechoslovakia and Yugoslavia has found jobs in industry and publishing. Even without losing the family lands, industry can seem the best way to maintain power and keep up an inherited position, since a noble pedigree can even be a disadvantage in other fields. The Austrian Georg Prince zu Fürstenberg found his distinguished name a handicap for a political career in post-war socialist Austria.

In spite of my ambition and love of politics, in 1947 I had realized I had come to a cross-roads. There were two paths for me to choose. One was the path of political power, which seemed pretty impossible after careful consideration, although my heart was in it. The other was wealth, economics and security. The latter was, in fact, the most appropriate for me to take under the circumstances. But of course it will always be my destiny to work as well in public duties. . . .

Prince zu Fürstenberg is now managing large interests in paper, chemicals and patents. To the more active spirits among the aristocrats, the shift of the base of power from land to factories and finance has meant their own shift in order to keep their hands on the levers of power. For what did aristocracy mean originally except the *rule* of the best? Yet each aristocrat who has made some effort to keep real power in the new industrial world is outnumbered by at least ten times as many aristocrats who are fighting a rear-guard action against the modern world, and losing. Does this loss of actual control make a nonsense of the concept of a hereditary nobility? It does in the opinion of the brilliant Austrian architect, the Count von Wickenbourg, who has even married outside the charmed circle of the aristocracy in pursuit of mere happiness. For him, 'the aristocracy meant something years ago, the ruling classes. But they aren't the ruling classes today, are they? They are no more stupid or intelligent than any other kind of person. They are the same, only a bit out of perspective.' Better to build well for future democracy than to harp on past differences.

Yet such apostles of the role of the aristocracy in industry or apologists for the present unreality of the whole class are in the minority. Most of the aristocrats make a virtue out of their detachment from the grossness of modern life through the independence given by consciousness of good breeding. Ferdinand Prince von der Leyen puts this point of view very nicely from his isolated castle, where servants draw the visitor up to see the master on a chair-lift, suspended on ropes and worked by hand. The Prince still thinks the ancient nobles of the Holy Roman Empire have a part to play in the modern world. 'They are not trying to keep up, as the English say, with the Smiths and the Joneses. They are what they are. Therefore they can say what they really feel. Too few do so today. There cannot be enough to do this.' The aristocrat has a duty to be independent in thought and action, as modern times force conformity on the rest of mankind.

For the more conservative of the well-born, the word aristocracy defines a more narrow code of duty. Even if the *rule* of the best is no longer possible, the duty and the example of the better-born is. For Prince Antoine de Ligne, 'the word aristocrat means duty. We are privileged to be given a chance to help other people in a less fortunate position.' To the Marquis de Villoutreys, 'the aristocrat is usually among a certain number of grand families not necessarily even known, but families who have remained with their traditions and true family life'. At its most extreme, this position is held by Valdimaro Marquis di Furavanti.

If you are born an aristocrat, it is not your fault, but it is God's will. Therefore you must have responsibilities. You must learn to lead people in reading the gospels and teaching the less fortunate the right way to live by example. . . . If one is born, one has to be who one is. So one has to lead as pure a life as possible like the Knights of Malta in ancient times.

As an ideal of *noblesse oblige*, the Marquis di Furavanti's definition of the aristocrat's way is exemplary. But in fact, Angélique Countess d'Oultremont's view of the aristocracy comes closer to its general belief in its exclusiveness. A passionate supporter of an international society of the European nobility, she coldly defines the one dominant creed of the true aristocrat. 'The word aristocracy to me means only one thing, *a chosen few*.' This few is not chosen by the people, but by God; their duty is to be themselves and to concentrate on their own innate qualities. Such narcissism is politically dangerous in isolating a class of people from national life; but it also has the advantage of making the aristocrats withdraw to a position of inconspicuous self-satisfaction, where their failure to interfere with others may lead to others not interfering with them.

The last and most appealing definition of aristocracy by the aristocrats themselves comes from the recognition that some are aristocrats by nature and without title. For evidently men are born unequal and only by organization can they make themselves more equal. To the Baroness Kervyn, the word aristocrat simply means 'better than others, not some one who is necessarily "born" as my mother would say. Aristocracy implies a whole attitude to responsibilities, a sense of looking after the public.' The Duke de Maillé agrees for the record. 'The word aristocrat for me means a way of thinking. It no longer has any rights.' An aristocrat is as an aristocrat does. By this definition, any man who behaves well with a sense of duty towards others is an aristocrat, whatever his background. In the place of the rule of the well-born, these last defenders of the aristocracy seem to desire the true Greek ideal of the rule of the better or the best, recognizing that goodness is hardly a hereditary quality, as any student of the history of the kings of Europe knows.

So much for how the European nobility sees its present role, with a few preaching the dictum of adapt or die, and the many answering with the defiance of trying to be different and better. The same divergence of opinion is found when the aristocrats are asked about the future of their class. Here of course, the positions are rather topsy-turvy. Those who have most successfully changed their ways to suit modern times often see a long future for old titles; those who have resisted changes often see a slow extinction of noble names and ways. Given the irredeemable snobbery of most of the human race, titles may well seem to have a long run ahead of them; but given the finite ruthlessness of history with all things useless and decorative, the prophets of hereditary doom must be correct in the end.

To many powerful people of the new industrial aristocracy, titles are already worthless. Madame Jacques Solvay, the wife of the richest man in Belgium and perhaps the leading hostess of the country, says a little contemptuously, 'Here in Belgium, if you consider you deserve a title, you can always ask for it.' If the Solvays asked for a title, they would certainly get one, being on the best of terms with the Belgian royal family. Yet it is difficult to see what advantage it would be to them. Nobility has its own precedence, in which the most ancient titles and families come first. Once the holder of a new title joins the nobility, he has to accept the order of precedence already laid down by the past. As long as he remains outside that nobility, however, he does not have to accept the superiority of anybody else. Thus it is hardly in the interest of the leading industrialist in a country to become a minor noble. In the modern terms of capitalism and democracy, he is already what the grand duke was in the days of feudalism. After defeating the power of the landed aristocrats, the prouder of the industrialists may well find it strange to accept the antiquated rules of protocol and precedence of the losers.

Yet the old nobility sees its own chances of survival in just such an alliance with the new grandees of the industrial world. The barriers of aristocratic exclusion have been almost dropped to include the *nouveaux riches*. It is considered the civilizing mission of the old nobility to educate the raw possessors of mere wealth in how to spend it well. Prince Antoine de Ligne considers that the aristocracy still has a large role to play, 'with or without money'. But 'money is, after all, synonymous with power'. Thus the *nouveaux riches* must have the chance of becoming *vieux riches* and thus eventually aristocrats. Even the dedicated Countess d'Oultremont, who believes that 'there is no need to change the Belgian aristocracy as it is excellent in all ways,' supports the admission of the rich and the qualified to the lower ranks of that aristocracy. The proper sort of new blood, in her opinion, is healthy in the veins of the old families, who continue to serve the world by being themselves. 'No matter what happens,' the countess declares, 'there will always be aristocrats to be looked up to, and there will always be aristocrats who are important to life – not for what they do but for the way they think and behave in life.'

Such a belief in an indefinite future for the nobility is not contagious among the aristocrats, who have the example of eastern Europe to consider. Those who have personally fled and begun a new life, such as Johanna Baroness Hertzogenberg, find the future of the aristocracy lies in 'what it can do – mostly intellectually. After all, we have had advantages in the past and even today. Money is not everything. Education, the way to behave, and the way to arrange things, this is vastly important.'

The very fact that the style of the *ancienne noblesse* has vanished can be a help towards the future of its surviving children. 'Most of the young aristocrats have never known the grandeur of the past,' the Prince von der Leyen says, 'and thus they work extremely well and successfully.' The need for camouflage, indeed, in such an anti-aristocratic city as Vienna makes noble parents see

that their children are brought up in a manner superficially similar
to the rest. 'In Austria,' Karl Count Draskovich says, 'there is
not so much difference between the noble and another young
person. Both have an equal start. It is not a social problem. Anyone
who thinks it is, is a fool.'

If some think adaptation to the modern world is the way to
guarantee a future for the aristocracy, others choose obscurity.
What is not noticed may well be ignored. Most European obser-
vers would consider Switzerland one of the more democratic and
egalitarian of countries, almost without a hereditary aristocracy;
yet, in the opinion of the acute Vigo Count Collenberg, Switzerland is the most aristocratic country in Europe. It was part of the
Holy Roman Empire; but when that Empire split apart, only
the imperial nobles in Switzerland kept their castles and positions
and much of their power, while aristocracies of leading burgher
families ruled in Berne and Lucerne. Ancient families such as
the Wattenwyls and the Graffenrieds remained influential in every
way. An aristocrat recently headed the Swiss police, another the
largest Swiss bank.

In Count Collenberg's opinion, half of the hundred leading
people in Switzerland come from old feudal families. Their very
lack of large estates has ensured their future in business and
banking, in the army and the civil service. The head of nearly
every Canton comes from the same feudal families. And yet,
sensing the democratic and egalitarian temper of the age, the
Swiss nobility keeps its real power hidden through its obsession
with obscurity. It seems to fear, like the heads of the Mafia, that
publicity alone will bring about its downfall. For the true aristocrat, discretion is the better part of vanity.

Adaptation or obscurity do not seem sufficiently attractive as
methods of survival to all the aristocracy. For conservatives such
as the Count de Maître, who divides the world into 'us' and
'them', the possession of a title is only a passing advantage; he is
afraid that 'the aristocracy will finally disappear'. Its disappearance
may be partially a form of chosen *hara-kiri* for the genuine
aristocrat. 'France is the last country in the world to under-

stand the *grande noblesse*,' Louise de Vilmorin says. 'Many of the women prefer to remain old maids rather than marry below their status.' Better that the class die out than to opt out of the class.

Yet such a form of suicide through fastidiousness is rather different from the radical solution proposed by the Baron Allard, almost unique among the aristocrats in being a supporter of Mao Tse-tung. He confesses cheerfully that he would like to overthrow the Belgian government by his writing, that the administration is so weak that it does not even dare to put him in jail, and that 'force is a virtue – only if badly used does it become violence'. For him, the future of the aristocracy lies in joining the social revolution of the Maoists by any means whatsoever. 'Aristocrats should go into government positions,' the Baron advises cryptically, 'if they know what they are doing.'[1]

In de Gaulle's France, which uses the ancient nobility more openly than any other European state, the aristocrats do feel that they know what they are doing in accepting positions in the government. Yet the General is too much the splendid anachronism to present a model for the aristocrats of the future. The basis of the power of the old nobility was feudalism; the ownership of land and titles involved service to the supreme feudal lord and the Church and the people. The old nobles have lost many of their acres, and the possession of acres has lost much of its power and privileges.

The landed aristocracy may still stress its duty in the villages to act as Burgomasters or heads of charitable organisations; but the state has long taken away the rights of taxing the people or of judging them or of enrolling them in an army to fight. As long as

---

[1] Whenever he wished to see the world, Baron Allard used to sign on as a stoker and disappear into unknown seas. Once on a return journey from the Congo, the baron tells of looking up from the lower deck to find King Albert of the Belgians looking down on him.

'What are you doing there, baron?' the King called.

'The same as you, Your Majesty,' Baron Allard replied. 'Going back to Antwerp.'

the old nobility sticks to its memories of a past way of life, it is doomed to a slow erosion like the walls of its castles under the wind and rain. But if it uses the respect which certain names and titles still secure in most of the capitalist democracies, and if it uses its inherited capital to invest in the industrial state, it can retain an influence in the modern nation quite out of proportion to its numbers.

The future of the aristocracy in Europe lies in exploiting an old inheritance to carve out a new province in industry and finance. Yet such a switch requires a spirit of competition that may be lacking and the tacit acceptance of a small place in a wealthy society that does not necessarily bow to a long pedigree. It is certainly easier to luxuriate in the superiority of birth and position in rural isolation, where a noble family and local peasant families may have been linked in a condescending embrace from century to century.

Not only the perceptive aristocrats see the need to adapt; so does one of their chief supporters, the Roman Catholic Church. Just as the aristocracy has often tried to disengage itself from the royal family in a country where the royal family was doomed, so the Vatican has largely disengaged itself from the Italian aristocracy, whose future is uncertain. Members of the papal secular aristocracy of Rome, headed by the Colonna and Orsini and Torlonia families, have had the duties of wearing black and standing still in a position of honour as Prince Assistant during solemn ceremonies in the Vatican. The Italian noble families had provided the Pope from their ranks for three hundred years before 1903; but in the twentieth century, the Roman Catholic hierarchy has slowly become more international and less aristocratic.

The Pope has seen fit to discipline the Roman nobility when it has failed in its political or personal behaviour. Pius XII deprived a Chigi of his post in the papal court for running for the wrong political party in a local election in Rome, while Prince Filippo Corsini lost his post as Prince Assistant for being involved in unfavourable publicity with the British film star, the late Belinda

Lee. In 1964, Paul VI told the Roman nobles that he could no longer provide them with their places for secular service at the Vatican; times had changed, he said, and were changing even more.[2]

At the beginning of 1968, the extinction of the papal nobility was finally announced. A commission of four Cardinals, including the Cardinals de Fürstenberg and dell'Acqua, recommended the abolition of hereditary Vatican titles, while the Pope himself refused to receive the five hundred members of the 'black aristocracy' at his January audience. At the end of March, the Pope dealt the final blow. All the ancient titles of the 'black aristocracy', such as Honoured Servant in Purple Robes and Mace Bearer and Custodian of the Papal Crown, were swept away, along with privileges including tax-exempt car licences, cigarettes, petrol, liquor and imported food. Reportedly, the 'black aristocracy' fought harder to preserve its material privileges than its medieval appendages. But there was no place for either in the new Vatican.

So the Catholic Church, with its expanding congregation, cuts itself off from its traditional ties with the local Roman nobility, whose power shrinks and whose conduct becomes more scandalous as Rome becomes the centre of a film industry as well as a religion. As in other countries in Europe, those aristocrats with an eye to the future have moved into business. Despite initial aristocratic horror at his desire to make 'funny hats and shirts', Emilio Pucci from the old Florentine family has made a fortune and bought back the family estates with the profits of designing clothes. His success has spurred on many imitators, so that the Italian rag trade has become a question of sorting out the counts

[2] The Barberini family tell the story of an old vendetta between the Roman nobility and the Papacy. Mussolini confiscated one of the Barberini palaces and presented it to the Pope. When Mussolini was dead and Italy had lost the Second World War, the Barberinis expected the Pope to return the palace. They waited in vain. The palace was not returned. Then one day the Pope went out on the balcony of the disputed palace and was attacked and badly stung by a swarm of horse-flies. As the Barberini coat-of-arms represents a small insect, the Barberinis could go about Rome exulting in the divine vengeance of their family against the Pope.

from the marquesas. Publicity has a great deal to do with it. However bad a collection of clothes, a title will always bring in the press, and a very grand title will usually be flattered.[3]

So the aristocrats of Europe see themselves in their struggle towards existence, erosion or extinction. Their psychology in their present situation is variable; but on one thing they are agreed. None renounces his or her titles legally – except to run for the House of Commons in England. A title is a fact of birth, by accident or design. It must be carried until one is buried. Whatever adaptation may be made to modern times in a style of living, there must be no alteration to the inheritance, if possible.

Yet it is hard to pretend that aristocracy means much when a large amount of property is not attached to the title. Alexis de Tocqueville was right; land is the basis of all titles – the very word 'title' is used in English law to give an owner the right of possessing a piece of property. And the psychology of aristocracy has a great deal to do with the psychology of possession – and the successful disguising of it. Few things reveal more about the aristocratic attitude than its views on property, something to be retained devoutly and excused casually.

Noblesse oblige compels possessors of large amounts of property to be natural, even off-hand, about their domains, as though anyone could own and enjoy as much territory if the luck of birth had been on his side. It is rare to find anyone as frank as Hastings, Duke of Bedford, who confessed, 'It may sound most immoral, but I never found the slightest difficulty in becoming passionately attached, not merely to *one* very big house and estate, but to two others as well.' Although many other landed peers may feel the same passion for private areas rather too large to excuse or defend, their code and modesty forbids them to declare their passion openly – but then, the late Duke of Bedford was always considered an eccentric by his contemporaries and was forbidden to enter the House of Lords for part of the Second World War.

Yet there is a hidden passion in owners of ancestral property

[3] For all the quotations contained in this chapter, I am indebted to interviews kindly granted to Jacquemine Charrott-Lodwidge.

that is revealed unconsciously in their obsession about thieves and burglars. In aristocratic memoirs, two stories endlessly recur. The first story represents a wish fulfilment. A thief steals a valuable trinket from a noble lord or lady without knowing the source of his loot; but the moment that the thief recognizes that his swag comes from that particular noble lord or lady, he returns the trinket apologetically with the words, 'If I'd known it was your lordship (or ladyship) I wouldn't have done such a thing for all the world!' The wish fulfilment in such a repeated story is obvious; the guilt of possessing too much is assuaged by the thought that even thieves really *want* one to possess that much. There is also the comforting dream that the kindly people, who love lords and ladies in their innermost hearts, will restore anything lost by hazard or to government.

The second favourite story of the aristocratic memoir is the comic burglar story, which may end with the same thief's apology after a frightening introduction about childish fears of noises in the night. Yet usually the second story is more honest and involves a confession by the teller that he is more frightened by burglars than by anyone else. The owner of a title as well as property feels doubly threatened by the intruder in the night. When Lady Susan Anson thought that a burglar was under her bed, she ran to the door and shouted, 'There is nothing of any value in this room except me, and I am about to leave.'

Lord Athlumney, a war hero in Kitchener's Egyptian campaign, was terrified that burglars might stamp on his bare feet if he left his bed to chase them, and he bitterly resented his mother for making him get up one night to protect her house from robbery. 'And you are the woman who cried when I went to the war,' he declared to her, 'yet you send me down to my certain death without a twinge of conscience.' Of course, he made so much deliberate noise approaching the burglars that they were gone before he arrived. Yet his cowardice hardly approached that of the notorious Antoine de Noailles, the Duke de Mouchy, who gave up all his wife's jewels to burglars on their promise not to hurt him and was then delighted to find out what good-looking fellows they were when they dropped their masks to drink his health.

After the communist, the burglar remains the ultimate bogey of the rich nobility. Look how often in his plays George Bernard Shaw cleverly introduced the thief into the aristocratic household, in order to act as the mock judge and judged of those present; the thief is naturally always comic, so as not to alarm the fantasies of the propertied audience. The comic thief gives the robbed the chance to philosophize over the heady freedom of the criminal, as the Patient does in *Too True to be Good* to the pair of villains about to steal her pearl necklace: 'It's all very well for you two criminals: you can do what you like. If you were ladies and gentlemen, you'd know how hard it is not to do what everybody else does.' But the attractive freedom of the criminal is also a dangerous freedom, at which the good theatre audiences would never laugh. For, alone in the depth of the night, the burglar is the one man who can creep in and remove both life and property without giving a damn. He is the one man whom pomp and pedigree cannot influence – except in the comfortable exorcism of the after-dinner story or comedy.

Part Three

THE DIFFERENCE

Seven

Seven

AN EARLY SENSE
OF DIFFERENCE

If heredity sets many of the aristocrats apart from their fellow men, their upbringing can mitigate or exaggerate the discrimination of their genes. Certain differences creep into the education of most aristocratic children, which may or may not warp them permanently from the common thread. Usually, aristocrats are brought up by one or more nannies rather than a mother. These surrogate mothers may be better or worse than mothers by umbilical cord; but at any rate they are not of the same flesh and blood, and they give their charges the curious sense of being ruled by people who may be masters to children, but who are servants to the children's parents.

There are other problems for the aristocratic child. He or she may have to cope with a distant relationship with mother and father. Equally well, the large houses of the aristocracy work on the psychology of the small child within them, although the normally large families of the well-born tend to allay these fears. In the private education of aristocratic children by governess and tutor, a sense of difference from other children may be instilled, increased by the chosen private school or convent where most children of good family are sent for a few years to finish their education. Only if the child is clever enough to reach a university does he or she come into contact with a world less restricted by the preferences of parents. Such is the environment of difference usual to the aristocratic child.

Of course, there are exceptions to this rule of childhood. Only when an aristocracy is stable and wealthy can it impose its settled patterns of education on its heirs. The members of the nobility caught in the world wars in Europe or fleeing from their consequences have had to bring up their children as best they could. Some modern aristocrats have had their schooling in labour camps or in the front line, while others were glad to be able to study in the local school rather than get no education at all. But generally, and especially in the peace of the last twenty years, the aristocrats of Europe have continued to bring up their children to be a little different from the rest and to know that they are. As Schopenhauer wrote when considering the effect of its training on the nobility, 'There is no absurdity so palpable but that it may be planted firmly in the human head if you only begin to inculcate it before the age of five, by constantly repeating it with an air of great solemnity.'

Britain's greatest gift to the ruling classes of the world and her most influential invisible export has been the English nanny. She was dominant in the wealthy nursery at home and a symbol of international status abroad. She strides along now in memory, if less often in fact, just as she always was, wearing her uniform and her flat shoes, knowing her own place and keeping her charges in theirs, hard to please and hard in pleats, starched and starved of motherhood, decorous and sometimes decorated, prim, proper, practical, self-sacrificial, not modern but maiden, immutable until sacked, mistress of the nursery, dispenser of infant lore and laws, sometimes living with a child to become his housekeeper in his manhood and nanny to his children. The only intimate knowledge of the thought and behaviour of other kinds of people came to many an aristocratic child from this dedicated family dependant, wasting her own years in bringing up the children of others.

Some nannies were loved and stayed, some nannies were loved and went, and some nannies were hated. Nanny Sibley gave up her own marriage to bring up Lord Curzon's three daughters on the death of their mother in 1906 and became 'the real prop and backbone' of their lives. Even without such obvious self-sacrifice, many nannies became sternly devoted to their infant charges, who returned the devotion uncritically. In the childhood of Lady Diana Manners, her nanny was 'all and everything', even if she looked like a 'dried-up monkey' with long teeth and broken veins in her cheeks.

Nanny always wore black, winter and summer – a bodice and skirt made of 'stuff'. On her head she wore for the Park a minute black bonnet that just covered the top of her dear head, moored down with strong black velvet ribbons tied beneath her chin. I loved her dearly, because I was an affectionate, incurious, uninquiring child, so that it seemed only natural that I should not be allowed to take a toy in my perambulator to the Park, or my doll to the garden, and that Nanny would never cuddle or comfort me. Nor did she ever play with me.[1]

Even if a nanny might provide such cold comfort for a loving child, at least the nanny was always there, unlike parents. In his memoirs, Harold Macmillan tells of his nanny, who served his family for three generations, managing him both as a child and as a married man 'with a strict rigidity and relentless economy . . . unchanging in appearance or in dress, tiny but domineering, affectionate but firm'. Macmillan confirmed that the centre of the normal upper-class household in Britain was the nanny who stayed with a family until her death. A curious sort of ambivalent affection usually kept the old nanny living in a cottage near the family who had hired her, to serve as a proof of their gratitude for her long sacrifice; every child and grandchild on a visit had the duty of calling on the family's old nanny before visiting their own flesh and blood.

Not all nannies stayed. Some preferred their private lives or other employers to a life-long dependence on one family. The loss of his first nurse induced in the late Duke of Bedford 'a permanent fear-complex' that other people who had gained his affection might also be snatched away from him. When Lady Angela St Clair Erskine's nanny went to another family, she was found at the age of five battering on the door of the other family's house in Curzon Street, demanding that her nanny should leave

[1] Diana Duff Cooper; *The Rainbow Comes and Goes* (London, 1961) pp. 11-12.

the new baby and return to her; her reward for this declaration of love was a drubbing with a slipper by her new governess. One young and noble Etonian remembered bursting into tears on his first day at school because he was being parted from his old nurse for the first time in his life. The trouble with substitute mothers was that they could be taken away with the approval of society, which does not easily allow a natural mother the right to abandon her child.

On the continent, the English nanny also seems an impermanent part of the childhood of many modern aristocrats, whose memories of her vary according to character. On the whole, the nanny seems to have played a smaller part in the upbringing of young children, who were seen more often by their parents than in England. For each Prince Antoine de Ligne, who had a 'pretty negative relationship with his parents in the diplomatic corps' and thus depended on a succession of kind nannies, there were ten aristocrats who saw their parents frequently throughout their childhood and depended on their English nannies for little more than supervision at play and instruction in the English language. Perhaps the English nannies felt their position was more precarious abroad, or perhaps they were forbidden to strike their charges, for they certainly seem to have been kinder overseas than at home. Most continental aristocrats developed an early affection for England from the good behaviour of their nannies, who could even unbend enough, as in the case of the Duke de Maillé, to allow the children 'a very free life' in the family castle.

Loathsome nannies were also one of the occupational risks of aristocratic birth. In old-fashioned families, where a little torture was considered good for the souls of children, any latent sadism in a nanny was given a free rein in the name of discipline. Lady Cynthia Colville, daughter of the Marquess of Crewe, remembers being shaken, whipped, and made to stand for hours in a corner, as well as having her head held in a basin of cold water until 'drowning seemed to loom on the horizon'. The Count de Maître had an 'extremely unkind and dirty English nanny, clean on top and unspeakable underneath', who made his life a misery when out of his parents' sight. Although ill-treatment by a nanny could get the nanny dismissed, what of ill-treatment suffered in the name of virtue? When Renald Count de Simony visited his grandparents, he was allowed to see them only for two minutes each morning and each night; otherwise he could be put into a hair-shirt for the good of his soul. The rigours of an extreme Protestant or Catholic upbringing could be particularly hard on a child, when born to a family which believed in the duty of the nobility to set an example of goodness and purity.

The relationship of a child to its nanny depended on the amount of time spared by its mother and father to its upbringing. Here factors of time and geography are important. At the beginning of the century, small children in the nobility saw little of their parents; now they see much more of their parents, because of the change in the theories of raising children. Also the British were notorious in spending more time caring for their animals than their children, while the continental aristocracy took rather more pride in being considered good parents. Even such a young peer as Lord Dynevor can confess that he 'knew his nanny better than his parents,' a thing which no modern continental aristocrat will admit. Yet the opposite can be true. Few mothers would have the extreme devotion of the wealthy Oonagh, Lady Oranmore and Browne, who even sleeps in the same room as her five young grandchildren or adopted children.

Of course, the sheer logistics of aristocratic life in a large house create a physical gap between children and parents most of the time – the first are always looking for the second down an endless corridor. In the country house or estate where the children are usually brought up, the father is often away, either making money in the neighbouring city or supervising the land or shooting. The mother, too, has her social calls to pay. Therefore, meals are the only regular times of contact between parents and offspring. In fact, some English fathers still forbid their children to eat out of the nursery until puberty, but these cases are increasingly rare. The child of good family has crept down to breakfast and lunch and tea and even to an occasional dinner. Only on formal occasions are most children now excluded from the table of their parents.

Perhaps the most common fear of the aristocratic child is the fear of the dark and enormous house. In many memoirs and interviews, the sole spot of poetry and gothic horror is the memory of trying to reach safety and bed down a night corridor. Before electricity, the old castles and country houses were gloomy labyrinths by evening with occasional log fires and oil lamps making patches of flickering light in the general murk. At Woburn Abbey, oil lamps were still being used into the nineteen-thirties; electricity was a long time coming into the ancient monuments. The result was a fine crop of fears and traumas induced in the children lost in the ancestral piles. As Sir Edward Cadogan described his youthful stays at Babraham:

The ordeal of 'going up to bed', if undergone alone, was certainly the most disconcerting of my emotional experiences. There was something sinister about the ill-lit passages and staircases and recesses that had to be negotiated before the haven of the nursery was attained. When young I had an uncontrollable aversion to darkness, a prejudice I doubtless shared with many other children of an imaginative disposition but which in my case recurs on occasion even to this day. [2]

The Earl of Pembroke had worse terrors at Wilton:

I was frightened of the dark when I was small. In the cloisters, there were dim oil lamps with statuary all round making weird shadows. Another fear was fire. I was very frightened when I was about six. The staircase caught fire and I've never forgotten it to this day. I have a terror of fire.

Instances of childish fears of the gloom and the spooks of a huge house can be repeated *ad nauseam*, from the experience of the Marquess of Bath who lived as a child 'miles away at the top of Longleat and we crept about with candles making shadows and the slightest wind would blow them out' to the testimony of Sir Jeremy Mostyn, who 'lived during the War in two large houses and slept in a large bed, terrified of the dark and of ghosts.' This terror could even be exaggerated by gothic family fancies.

[2] Sir Edward Cadogan, *Before the Deluge* (London, 1961) p. 30.

The present Earl of Halifax had a grandfather who brought him up on the supernatural.

In winter, after chapel, grandfather thought it was good for the imagination to take us children up to the attic. He would dress up as the witch Gargoor reading King Solomon. He would come up behind us and we would look in a mirror and run like mad. He terrified my father before us. We would run like mad, only to find as my father had done, that grandfather had reached the bedroom, while we leapt on the bed waiting for the witch.

But perhaps no aristocratic child had quite the imaginative horror of Lady Clodagh Anson as a child in Badminton:

A thing that always filled me with fear in the evening was a huge stag's head that was over the door in the night nursery. I used to be positive that its body was outside, and that it was struggling to get into the room. I would lay awake for ages with my eyes fixed on it, and be sure I could see it moving farther and farther in. The funny part about these childish terrors is that one never tells anybody about them at the time; I don't think I have ever mentioned my horror of that deer's head to any living soul to this day, nor did I ever think of it in the daytime, or look outside the door to see if its body was really there.

How much these early fears marked each aristocratic child depended on his sensitivity; but certainly the coldness and loneliness and darkness of the great houses, with parents often far away down the corridors or absent in society, and with nannies often strict over any sign of fear, forced most of the children into a form of self-reliance. Courage was deliberately taught to Angélique Countess d'Oultremont, whose parents used to pretend they had lost something in some distant and dark corner of the *château* and sent off their children to look for it. In Lady Clodagh Anson's case, a positive virtue was made out of the neglect of the children. 'Mother always said that if we were such fools as to feel cold or hungry and do nothing about it we deserved to get chills and starve, and it made us nippy at looking after ourselves, so I passed the same views on to my children.'[3]

[3] Lady Clodagh Anson, *Book* (London, 1932) pp. 68, 82.

Yet if his parents' preoccupation with the family past inflicted large and uncomfortable dwellings on the aristocratic child, their preoccupation with the family future usually gave the child a host of brothers and sisters. The answer to large houses usually lay in large families to fill them and ward off their terrors. Over and over again, the modern European nobles explain away their early lack of terror in their *châteaux* by referring to the company of their brothers and sisters. The Marquis de Villoutreys says, 'As a child it never entered my head to be frightened in our large house – there were so many of us, I suppose.' In his case, as in the case of many other settled aristocratic families, a sense of complete security as a child was engendered by an extreme parochialism. 'As most aristocrats,' he says, ignoring the possibility of many nobles being on the wrong side in the Reformation, 'we had a very Catholic upbringing, and the only journey I undertook was at the age of fifteen when I went to a Catholic Congress in Vienna.'

Short of war or social revolution, the young aristocrat stayed put on his family estate, sure of his proper place in God's order and man's. He was also sure of his place in the immediate hierarchy of his family. 'All children are snobs,' as Lord Norwich justly observed, 'and the aristocracy of childhood is age.' An elder brother due to inherit the estate was probably the best schooling in rights and privileges that any aristocratic child could ever have, and a younger sister the best receiver of grants of charity and condescension. A feeling of position could be a very early development, as the New York postman discovered when he left a letter for Viscount Mandeville and expressed a wish to see a real live lord. At that moment, a tiny figure in a sailor suit pirouetted and said, 'Then look at me.'

With various factors separating the average aristocratic child from his contemporaries, such as a nanny and a large house and a deference shown by certain adults who happened to be servants, an early sense of difference to other children could result. Sometimes this feeling of apartness was deliberately encouraged. 'Certainly we were made to feel different as children from others,' the Baroness Kervyn says bluntly; 'my parents were great snobs.' Sometimes the choice of suitable playmates could disguise a careful quarantine of aristocratic children. 'I suppose we were different from other children,' the Countess d'Oultremont says, 'but as we only had friends of our own kind to play with we didn't notice anything different.' Where such social barriers did not exist, young nobles could live in that blissful state of ignorance called childhood. 'We played with the peasants,' the Duke de Maillé says, 'and I can honestly say we didn't in the least bit feel different from them, except that we lived in a large house and they in a cottage.'

Still, the Duke de Maillé was lucky. Even if aristocratic parents wished their children to feel just as any other country child, nannies did not always share the same opinion. With her parents away most of the time, the daughter of the first Viscount Cowdray was brought up by her nanny to be class-conscious with reminders such as 'little ladies don't sit down on doorsteps but wait for the front door to be opened by the butler'. In Sonia Keppel's charming memoirs about being an Edwardian daughter, the realization of class distinction came with a sudden shock when she wrote to the absent butler in London, after he had become one of the main-stays of her isolated country life.

Invariably beginning: 'Darling Mr Rolfe' and ending: 'Your loving Sonia', after one or two of these epistles, rather abruptly, he put me in my place. 'Dear Miss Sonia,' he wrote, 'You are getting a big girl now, and you must call me Rolfe. And you must stop signing yourself "Your loving Sonia". It does not do. Yours respectfully, W. Rolfe.' ... 'Rolfe' immediately became an impersonal distant figure, handing me messages on a silver salver, and taking my umbrella from me as I came indoors. With alarming suddenness now, deliberately he with-drew into the background, leaving me irresolute and unbalanced, having to stand alone. [4]

Such a long-lasting innocence and ignorance about the role of servants and other people in society could only be preserved in the country. In the city, the arithmetic of class-distinction could

[4] Sonia Keppel, *Edwardian Daughter* (London, 1958) p. 110.

be added up more easily. As Cynthia Asquith justly remembered, life in London was a great destroyer of rural illusion.

Hard, straitened and meagre though life in country cottages might be, at least it was not dingy, but from those town tenements there seeped a sense of sordid poverty that poisoned the very air. The East and West Ends of London were too closely juxtaposed, the contrast between them too violent to fail to penetrate even the trance of happy childhood, deep though that was.[5]

It is not so much that the city child is a wise child, but that the city child cannot be screened from strange sights and sounds and smells. The great delight and terror of the city is that it provides the daily stage of the differences and indifferences of men. Inequality cannot be disguised. The aristocratic child in the city must become conscious of the gulf between his life and that of other children, if the family has real wealth. But of course, if the family is a refugee one as so many noble families were after the social changes of the twentieth century, a well-born child could merge into a more normal pattern of existence almost in the manner born.

The experience of Count von Wickenbourg was never one of apartness. His father lived poorly off his painting, while he himself was educated at an ordinary high school in Vienna. 'Yes,' he admits, 'it was considered a bit odd by the rest of the family.' After that, the Nazi take-over of Austria put him into a Labour Force in Poland and then into the army on the Western Front. After the war, he studied architecture at the University of Graz and went on a Fulbright scholarship to America. He might have been any intelligent young Austrian caught up in the war. A similar case is that of the young Count von Coudenhove-Calergi, whose uncle gave a Dance of Death in Berlin under the Allied bombs; he lived before and during the war in Prague, where his father taught Japanese. At sixteen, the family fled to Vienna, where he went to high school. He began his business career by selling plastic bags.

In both of these two cases, the adjustment of the aristocratic

[5] Cynthia Asquith, *op. cit.*, p. 140.

child to modern life was made easy. It was more difficult for those who had to change their way of life in the middle of their education. Georg Prince zu Fürstenberg was originally brought up in private schools, the last one founded by the Empress Maria Theresa to train aristocrats for public service. But the Nazi invasion of Austria closed the school and Prince Fürstenberg found himself in a labour camp doing para-military training. Afterwards, he worked in a road-building gang and then found himself fighting on the Russian front, until he was invalided out of the army in 1943. Recovered by 1944, he joined the Austrian resistance after the Allied invasion of Italy. He received a dishonourable discharge from the army and had to report daily to the Gestapo; but he could begin studying again, eventually receiving his university degree three years later. For Prince Fürstenberg, the war was a forcible baptism into mass misery.

The experience of other refugees from a different generation or sex was less hard, but required an equal adjustment. Karl Prince zu Schwarzenberg was brought up by tutors in the Czechoslovakia of the 1940's, because his parents were afraid he would be indoctrinated with the wrong ideas at school. 'Not only that, it was very difficult to be a Schwarzenberg in Czechoslovakia under the Nazi or communist governments. One had to be very quiet about everything.' In 1948, however, the Czech Schwarzenbergs fled to Vienna, where the Prince went to school and university to study law. His family had lost all their lands in Czechoslovakia for the fourth time, once confiscated by Charles the Fifth, once by order of Gustavus Adolphus, once expropriated by the First Czech Republic and once by the Second Czech Republic. But the irony of inheritance gave the young Prince Schwarzenberg the estate of the Austrian Schwarzenbergs on the right side of the Iron Curtain, so that he now possesses some 60,000 acres, about a sixth of the property lost in Czechoslovakia. The more international an aristocratic family was, the more chance its refugee sons had of falling into a second inheritance.

For another refugee from old Bohemia, Johanna Baroness Hertzogenberg, 'the saying that the nobility is one great family

was a real fact'. She had been given governesses and a convent
education until she went to Prague University; then she fled to
the West in 1946, where the Austrian and Bavarian nobility
received her and her aged parents with open arms. 'In spite of the
shortage of everything,' she says, 'noble families took in dozens
of children and old people in the old castles. These were terribly
primitive, so you can imagine what it was like, with the rooms
filled to capacity and little food available to share around.' In
Baroness Hertzogenberg's opinion, the nobility treated its own
in distress far better than the professors and the priests treated
their own. The right pedigree was of more importance than a
temporary poverty, and even if the aged Hertzogenbergs had to
paint toys and do domestic work to survive, their daughter is
now a respected art historian.

The necessities imposed by war and revolution gave the remnants of the Central European aristocrats enough of a taste of
hardship to break them out of their cocoon and fit them for
survival in the modern world. Very occasionally, as in the case of
the Wittelsbach princess, Irmgard Princess von Bayern, a good
angel seems to have protected her life and innocence in the middle
of horror, so that she can settle down to seclusion and breeding
horses in Bavaria as if the war had been a nightmare forever gone,
in which her mother died in Buchenwald by Hitler's orders and
only her youth saved her own life. Brought up in convents in
Florence and London and caught at school in Brussels in 1940, she
and her sisters were saved from the German attack by a special
train sent by the King of Italy. In peacetime, the family seems
to have recaptured something of their idyllic life of the thirties,
when as small children, in the Princess's words, 'we moved from
one castle to another according to the season. Our summer palace
was Berchtesgarden – I was born there.'

The case-histories of the displaced European aristocrats show
a sporadic education by nurse or high school, tragedy or war.
Nothing general can be said of the effects of upbringing on such
a refugee nobility; in the case of Irmgard Princess von Bayern,
the war has left her withdrawn and shy; in the case of Karl

Prince zu Schwarzenberg, the war has left him with a fierce determination to succeed. But the very instability of the educational background of the displaced aristocrats makes each of their stories highly individual. At least, one thing can be said about most of the nobility of Central Europe – it has a shrewd knowledge of the precariousness of wealth and existence. No wrapper of silver paper has obscured its vision of the harsher facts of living.

Where countries were less involved in the direct consequences of the rise and fall of the Nazi régime, young aristocrats received a far more stable and traditional further education. The boys were given tutors or governesses from a foreign country to learn another language, usually French if the children were English, or English if the children were not; the fashion for learning German had rather faded since the First World War. Then the boys proceeded to some private school of the right exclusiveness or religion; no private school was more famous or more used than Eton College. Then, if the boy was intelligent or there was money enough, on to university or farming college. A little learning in the classics or agriculture was not thought a dangerous thing.

Of the twenty-seven British dukes, eighteen went to Eton, and more would have gone if they had been able to pass the minimal requirements of the entrance examination. Eton has remained what Sir Edward Cadogan called it:

. . . quite frankly the training ground of boys who were the inheritors of influence and wealth. The population of the school was not, as some might imagine, either then or since exclusively of aristocratic origin. Far from it, only the minority of its members belonged to the old landowning classes or to a patrician caste already impoverished by the political turn of events. The majority could be said to be more representative of the plutocracy, but in any case we must admit that it was a training more for those who were likely to have some description of greatness thrust upon them, rather than for those who might acquire it exclusively by merit. [6]

The training consisted until recently of an emphasis on daily sport, early rising, self-discipline and discipline by the rod, the

[6] Sir Edward Cadogan, *op. cit.*, p. 62.

acquisition of manners and a style in the writing of English and Latin and Greek, and the pleasant consciousness of being at the most superior school in the world. The masters at Eton, more highly paid than any others teaching at their level of education, frequently found their lessons wasted on boys who had been selected by the various house-masters for their names rather than their brains. It is rare in history that such a good school has had such an idle *clientèle* outside a few notable exceptions; perhaps its belated change to sterner entrance examinations and more teaching of the sciences will make it more efficacious. Otherwise it will doubtless return to the original purpose of its founder, Henry vi of England, who meant it as a foundation for poor scholars; it has, after all, as the socialist Member of Parliament Jack Jones once observed so accurately, been stolen from the working classes.

Only one leading English aristocrat has been known in recent years not to go to a private school, miscalled public school. Eton or Winchester or their less successful imitators have tried to educate nearly all of the English aristocrats, with Gordonstoun always ready to provide a brawny curriculum on the progressive German pattern. Most aristocrats have been happy at these schools and have begun many of their life-long friendships among people of their own sort. The noose of the old school tie in England is strung young and hangs long. Most Etonians are very good at recognizing each other in a friendly fashion.

The one exception to the rule, the present Duke of Bedford, was educated privately because his father had been so bullied at Eton. He bitterly resented this forced seclusion 'from the unseemly outside world'. As he wrote of his upbringing:

Instead of having some commonsense knocked into me as a boy, life did not start administering its kicks until I was nearly grown up, a painful experience I am determined none of my sons shall share. Mine was a world of nurses and tutors, bereft of parental affection, and with no stimulus to learn anything, not even the facts concerning my family background. [7]

[7] John, Duke of Bedford, *op. cit.*, p. 3.

He has since reacted from his education by becoming the most extrovert showman of all the dukes, which is merely another proof of the continuing failure of parents to mould children after their wishes.

Because of laws requiring state schools and because of the lack of good private schools outside the expensive and permissive Swiss alpine schools for wealthy drop-outs, other European aristocrats with a settled youth tend to have been educated far longer by tutors and governesses at home and to have reached university more often. The exception of the Duke of Bedford's education in England is often the rule in France and Spain. As Renald Count de Simony says, he was eighteen years old before he realized that not everyone from his *milieu* lived in a castle; until that age, he had always just moved from castle to castle and picked up his education between them.

More and more, younger male aristocrats in Europe are allowed by their parents to attend the local school, especially when the law cannot be deceived. But their education is still very much at home and in languages. It is not unusual in Northern Italy to find a boy of good family speaking four languages well at the age of ten, the product of a succession of tutors and strategic boarding abroad. As Consuelo Duchess of Marlborough once noticed of the Austrian aristocrats, they could at least speak many languages, even if they had little to say in any of them.

Although the boys are gradually escaping from the reign of tutors, the girls of good family in Europe are rarely allowed outside the range of governesses, unless they are locked inside the walls of a convent. An obsessive fear for the virtue of its young daughters still seems to grip the continental nobility, as if virginity was still as great a prize now as in the Middle Ages. At any rate, the education in all except the speaking of languages that is available to most well-born girls remains inferior. If they are not lucky enough to be accepted by a university, or if their parents forbid their higher education, they can have less educational opportunity than many *bourgeois* girls. As for the more snobbish of the girls' private schools in England, the failure of their methods of education is notorious.

England is unique in possessing a system of private schools, particularly for boys, where any early education in the social differences can be exaggerated throughout adolescence. Within Eton itself, there is a self-electing aristocracy called 'Pop' which is allowed all the privileges of lording it in peacock dress over the rest. In Europe, such an official education in the virtues of hierarchy is obtainable only by private tuition on a great estate. It is doubtful whether much sense of aristocratic superiority can survive the battle-ground of the *lycée*. Compulsory public education may well be coming to Britain under the Labour government; as Lady Gaitskell said recently in the House of Lords, she looks forward to the time when 'great names like Eton and Winchester will survive with the label *comprehensive* attached to them'. If it does, then only emigration or extraordinary exertions will allow even the British aristocracy to educate its sons apart from the rest of the nation.

Eight

⸎

A DIFFERENT DESCENT

All men have obsessions, some have inspirations, and a few have pedigree. While most men and women love their country and their family, aristocrats love their genealogy. A certain sense of distinction keeps a man warm when the wind blows. This sense of superiority is provided to the mass by nationalism or racism, to the district by local products or football teams, to the group by comradeship and exclusiveness, and to the aristocrat by contemplating the generations that begat him. Perhaps the Baron in Jean Renoir's version of *The Lower Depths* most succinctly summed up what a feeling for the past means to a man of noble birth, even in the flop-house : 'To be noble is like having clap, something of it always stays in you.'

The preoccupation with the past has much to do with the drive for status in the present. There is a small palace industry in the production of genuine genealogies for those who wish to trace their descent back to the Kings of Europe. Of course, as one of the specialists in this field charmingly admitted in his introduction to a work of genealogy privately produced for a high price for those American families mentioned in it:

Mathematicians tell us that by the law of geometrical progression the whole English people must be descended from William the Conqueror, or all the people of Western Europe from the great Charlemagne, since any person now living would have in the time of the Conqueror a greater number of ancestors than there were people in all England, or a larger number of ancestors than there were in all the lands ruled by Charlemagne. They argue, therefore, that royal descent is of no special value or interest.[1]

[1] Professor Arthur Adams, *Royal Descent*.

Of course the intermarriage and selective breeding of human beings as well as dogs and horses can produce some interesting strains. The mental illnesses and haemophilia of the monarchs of Europe were notorious at one time, with 'royal bleeders' doomed to die young everywhere. A preference for marrying one's own kind and for increasing the size of the family estate also led to an enormous amount of consanguinity with its advantages and disadvantages among the European aristocracy. As Princess Catherine Radziwill reported of the old Austrian aristocracy, all the Lobkowiczs, Auerspergs, Liechtensteins, Trauttmansdorffs and Schwarzenbergs were so closely allied that they could be said 'to constitute one large family'. This did not prevent Consuelo, Duchess of Marlborough, from observing their aimless resemblance and noting that breeding could be too much of a good thing.

What is noticeable about the aristocrats is that generations of inbreeding and the ability to choose and get the prettier women of their time have generally made them rather taller, lankier, and better-looking than the average. Alas, unlike the Jews, the aristocrats have never thought intelligence was worth a wedding. Land and titles were always marriageable, money sometimes was, beauty could be, but brains hardly ever. Ugliness, however, could be just as transmissible as beauty through the generations. As a previous Duchess de La Rochefoucauld once remarked to a French aristocrat, when observing that the most prominent feature of an unknown girl bore a striking similarity to his own: 'God forgives, and the world forgets; but the nose remains.'

In a century that has seen Hitler and suffers from the vileness of racism, eugenics has become a tainted science. Before the disasters implicit in theories of breeding and natural selection were too apparent, curious works such as Anthony Ludovici's *A Defence of Aristocracy* could appear, in which inbreeding to the point of incest could be defended, on the grounds that inbreeding was disastrous only 'if the ingredients of disaster are already in the stock'. Thus inbreeding would turn the worse into the worst until it was extinct, but the better into the best until it was dominant. Ludovici, writing in 1915, was complaining that the aristocracy had already married far too much outside its own group, and that its loss of power was due to its incompetence in inbreeding.

Such theories seem repugnant now. Although few would deny the importance of heredity, fewer still would claim that heredity ensured anything much in the children of given parents. In the age of democracy and anti-imperialism, environment and education seem more profitable lines of study than blood and kin. It is perhaps because of this that most aristocrats, at least in public, play down their pedigree and prefer to define themselves in terms of character and function rather than ancestry. Of course, marriage remains the all-important touchstone by which a noble proves whether he still does care about pedigree or not. And the fact that sixteen of the twenty-six English dukes at one time married noble wives, while the Duke of Northumberland is closely related by marriage to a quarter of the other dukes, still shows a certain preference in the peerage for good breeding.

Yet in interviews, the British peers prefer to understate any genetic reason for their titles. Very few will say bluntly like Earl Waldegrave, 'I'm a biologist and it's a question of pedigree.' Those who do agree with him, prefer gloomily to predict that even if once pedigree mattered, modern history and the peers' own bad behaviour has made pedigree no longer a consideration in deciding who is an aristocrat. 'When I was young,' the Earl of Westmeath says, 'aristocrats were aristocrats; they had a position . . . but now, they have destroyed themselves. Look at Bedford and Co., they have brought aristocracy down to the fish-and-chip level.' The Marquess of Bath is even more blunt. 'Of course, now everyone is equal. In my father's day, we were one thing and the rest, well, scum. . . . In the old days, a title counted for everything – money one didn't talk about. Today, that's all that counts.'

If, then, an aristocrat is not determined by pedigree any longer, what are his inherited characteristics? Many of the British peers treat the whole thing as a historical joke. To Lord Devlin, an aristocrat conjures up 'the seventeenth century, lace collars, beating servants, and the French guillotine' – in fact, the very picture that the Duke de Maillé feels is unfairly instilled into French schoolchildren to make them think modern aristocrats are a terrible lot. An aristocrat makes the Earl of Halifax think of an 'old grandfather with a beard looking very grand in an old picture'. But the greatest irony is that the peer with the longest proven pedigree in all Europe, Lord O'Neill, descended from the kings of Ireland in direct line for sixteen hundred years, thinks that 'an aristocrat conjures up a "Spy" cartoon figure, rather lanky and out of control.' Nothing more serious than that.

Yet jokes hide a certain worry that things are not quite as they once were, in Tara's halls and elsewhere. Pedigree and titles must still be found a meaning, although some genealogists prefer to spend their time proving that the Queen of England is related to George Washington and is the fourth cousin twice removed of Alice in Wonderland. Otherwise, titles should be renounced, and few peers will do that. Thus the British peerage tends to make its accommodation with democracy in democracy's terms, in claiming that aristocracy is not limited to noble birth and that it still has a function to play.

You don't have to have a title to be an aristocrat.

(Hon. Hanning Phillips)

It means a gentleman rather than one who has a long pedigree.

(Sir Jeremy Mostyn)

It has nothing to do with being a peer. After all, one of my work-men could be what we call one of nature's gentlemen and behave more like a gentleman than some peers.   (Lord Montagu of Beaulieu)

It is a responsibility for people.   (Earl of Leicester)

An aristocrat is a gentleman in the old sense. Just at ease with everybody.   (Lord Howard de Walden)

It doesn't mean anything. It's always connected with land. Aristo-crats owned more land than other people, and soon they won't.

(Lord Dynevor)

Really, there's little difference in buying a title and getting a title for being the bastard son of a king. It's what you make of it when you've got it.   (Earl of Pembroke)

Of course, this British underplaying of the role of pedigree in the question of what makes up an aristocracy delivers them into the hands of the European nobility, which claims that the English nobility does not exist. Just as children try to prove their own superiority in the school playgrounds by boasting of what their fathers have done, so aristocrats like to prove their superiority in the international playgrounds by boasting of the deeds of their great-great-great-great-grandfathers – and farther than that. To any aristocrat bearing a name that used to rule in the Holy Roman Empire, all other non-imperial nobles are highly suspicious. As Britain was never in the Holy Roman Empire and as most British titles are so recent as to appear indecent, obviously the British peerage *needs* to find a reason for itself in everything except noble birth.

Yet the pedigree game extends to Europe as well. Vigo Count Collenberg says dogmatically that there are fewer than ten noble families in Holland, while Renald Count de Simony allows only five aristocrats in the whole of Belgium. Such an assertion is arrant nonsense to Angélique Countess d'Oultremont, who thinks that the Belgian aristocracy is the only living aristocracy in Europe today and therefore the most important. She, naturally, will not allow any British members in her Belgium-based society for the international aristocracy, because of their recent origin. An English Garter King of Arms agrees with her, stating that, 'nobility, in the sense that the word bears on the Continent ... has not existed since the Norman Conquest.'

In France, where matters of pedigree are only less important than matters of vintage, Baron Barclay estimates that there are a mere thirty or forty true aristocrats, who bear titles officially recognized by the State. Fewer than half of the hundred French dukes of 1790 now exist, and eleven of these have usurped the rank; only four of the whole number have pure noble blood extending for four generations. About 3,600 other families have acquired patents of nobility from some domestic or foreign source and can fairly lay claim to some sort of title in all except official and republican circles. But the baron throws up his pen in despair at the sight of some half million Frenchmen who have falsely ennobled themselves in their own republic, once the scourge of the aristocracy.[2] As Jules de Noailles says:

Faking honours is a great pastime in France. The French love titles and will go to any lengths to have them. As this is a republic, they can't be arrested or fined for doing it as titles in fact do not exist! To cook up a really good title costs about half a million francs.

Perhaps Philippe Jullian had the last word on this national failing for grandeur at any price when he observed that it was evident that the French revered Queen Elizabeth the Second far more than the English appeared to do.

In Italy, the prevalence of titles is also something of a joke. Apart from papal titles, now abolished, the old titles originate in the more ancient city republics, such as Genoa, Milan, Venice, Florence, and also Naples. As the irreverent Florentine marquis, Dino Frescobaldi, comments on these, the question of the grade of title depended on whether one joined the winning or the losing side in the various invasions of Italy. When the Spaniards, for instance, demanded help from the counts of Naples and Sicily, the counts would fight for the Spaniards only on the condition that they all laid down their coats of arms to become dukes and princes. Venice, which remained independent rather longer than the rest, kept its lesser titles, so that a Venetian count is now worth a Genoese marquis. 'Fighting,' the Marquis Frescobaldi observes, 'we lost power and gained titles. You might say, we had the frame without the picture. We still kept our lands – and wine.'

As for the more recent nobility of Italy, few stories can be crueller than those about aristocrats ennobled by the Piedmontese Kings of Italy in their brief tenure of the throne from the Risorgimento until the close of the Second World War. The old aristo-

[2] See Baron Barclay, *Paradoxe de la Noblesse Française* (Paris, 1967).

crats tell two tales about their new associates. One refers to the poor count who bears the name of an airport outside Rome. The King is reputed to have conferred this title on a bystander who helped him flee the airport hurriedly during the war. The second story tells of the same king shouting to his secretary to give all the accounts to the people waiting outside; his secretary misheard his words and made all the waiting people counts. As for the present Pope, who has abolished papal titles, the Marquis Frescobaldi reports that the old aristocrats think of him as worse than the Grand Wizard of the Ku Klux Klan – or Karl Marx.

Even among the grander aristocrats, the true princes of the Holy Roman Empire, the stories of how they put each other down over questions of status and pedigree are fondly conserved and repeated. The higher you stand, the harder you fall. Karl Prince zu Schwarzenberg likes to tell a story against the Lobkowicz family, apparently as distinguished as his own. The cream of the cream of the European nobility are, undoubtedly, the *Standesherren* of Germany. Unfortunately, the princes of the Austrian Empire could not claim to be in that category without owning an hereditary estate in Germany. So Karl Prince zu Schwarzenberg, whose family has always straddled the frontiers with a strong German base, likes to tell of a Lobkowicz, a mere duke, who bought a supposed village called Sternstein, consisting of little more than two trees and a rock, in order to be ennobled by the last Austrian Emperor as Prince Sternstein and a genuine *Standesherr*. If England once had its rotten borough electoral system, Austria certainly had its rotten title imperial system.

Yet Karl Prince zu Schwarzenberg prefers those distinguished Hungarian and Austrian families like the Esterházys, who did not bother to become *Standesherren* artificially, and thus lost all legal claim to their titles when the Republic of Austria abolished titles after the fall of the Habsburg Empire. Not even a Scots duke, whose lineage was moderately distant and whose state was fairly great, could match up to the true splendour of the old Habsburg aristocrats. Once, apparently, the Duke of Buccleuch met an

Esterházy prince at the Court of St James's and boasted that he had five thousand sheep on his Scots estate. 'How odd!' the Esterházy prince replied. 'That is exactly the number of shepherds I have.' The story is still told by the Schwarzenbergs to prove that their past imperial superiority lingers on today.

If a pedigree is really important, the families of the old Holy Roman Empire do have a better claim to a better pedigree than the rest. The titles of the Holy Roman Empire have long survived its dissolution in 1806, and even Voltaire's famous remark about that Empire: 'In what is it Holy? In what is it Roman? In what is it an Empire?' An anachronism well before its demise, the Empire's paper princes still claim a precise prestige from its almost mystical acres. In this practice, they are admittedly following the habit of the last Habsburg Emperor, who could never give up a title even if the territory had been lost long before. The Emperor Franz Josef still asserted that he was King of Jerusalem, Grand Duke of Tuscany and Krakau, Duke of Lorraine and Parma and Modena and Ragusa, and Grand Voivode of the Voivodina Serbia, when not an Austrian policeman was within leagues of any of these places.

The actual *Standesherren* of 'high' German aristocracy consist of families who were dignitaries and princes of the Imperial Diet of the Holy Roman Empire before its end. In other words, they were sovereign in their own areas and subject only to the Emperor, not to any other local German ruler. There were very mixed families in this class, Hohenlohe, Castell, Oettingen, and many others. Their number was about eighty in 1806 and they nominally ruled just over a million subjects. The technically 'low' German aristocracy consists of the medieval serving aristocracy of princes and counts, not represented at the Imperial Diet, and of untitled gentry. Sometimes, a rich or powerful 'low' aristocrat was accepted as a 'high' one, particularly from powerful families such as the Hohenzollerns and particularly when they married a 'high' wife. The Habsburg government was naturally fond of the 'high' German aristocrats and the Prussian government of the 'low'. For the first had titles that transcended Germany's later national frontiers, while the second always owed allegiance within Germany's limits.

Curiously enough, among the 'low' aristocracy are found many of the 'original' nobles, whose titles date from before AD 1400. The proven source of these families often antedates those of the 'high' families despite claims to origins in the time of Charlemagne. In terms of the length of a family tree, the distinctions between 'high' and 'low' aristocracy are now almost meaningless, as are so many artificial distinctions of race and colour and creed. But each society, however rarefied, must have its petty differences to serve as conversation. Otherwise, men and women would hardly find enough use for their tongues. Perhaps within the old Habsburg Empire, only Hungary managed to devalue titles to an extent where they became futile, and nearly everybody who was not a peasant nor a proletarian was addressed as 'Your Excellency' or 'Your Dignity' or 'Your Greatness' or 'Your Authority'. As soon as swans become as common as sparrows, there is a sudden end to their apparent claim to distinction.

Tacitus reported that even in the time of the Romans, the German tribes had an aristocracy. Luckily, however, they left no written records, as they did not know how to write. Otherwise, the genealogies of the 'high' aristocracy would stretch back even farther into the backwoods. The sterility of such a pre-occupation with pedigree was nowhere better exposed than in Ludwig Prince Windischgrätz's account of accompanying the Hohenzollern Prince Leopold around China before the First World War. Wherever he went, the Prince travelled with three hundred pairs of male and female shoes; whenever he opened his mouth, it was to enlighten his hosts and guests about the several hundred years of importance of the Hohenzollern family. At Hei-Hung, Prince Leopold met the Chinese Prince Pun-Lun and told him of the Hohenzollerns for the whole of the long evening. Finally, the Chinese Prince opened his mouth and said:

Your Royal Highness will perhaps be aware that the Chinese have always been adherents of ancestor worship. As far as I am concerned,

I am hardly in a position to speak on the subject because the records in my family archives do not go back farther than three thousand eight hundred years. But I beg of you to talk to my Ming dynasty cousins. They can tell you about matters of six thousand years ago. [3]

The trouble with pedigree is that it no longer bears much relation to human excellence. Even if it is more interesting, though less useful, a study than marine zoology, it can rarely establish the births and marriages and deaths of a family for more than a few generations before plunging into hypothesis. Any human being can properly state that his ancestry through the ape as far as protozoic ooze and primeval slime makes the longest family tree seem like a twig on the forest growth of the human race. Even if one considers the likely length of the existence of mankind, studies of genealogy seem the most petty scratching for status on the most enormous flesh of our kind. No hereditary aristocrat has even answered properly the question that John Ball posed at the time of the Peasant Revolt in England:

> When Adam delved and Eve span
> Who was then the gentleman?

Despair at the fond illusions of the benefits of their own pedigrees turns many aristocrats to the more immediate satisfactions of breeding horses and dogs. Incontestably, the mating of a good race-horse with another good race-horse can produce a faster race-horse, though not a better one. It is no accident that the aristocrats find themselves at their happiest at Ascot and Longchamps, watching in front of applauding crowds the triumphant proof that good breeding tells and that pedigree pays off at the post. Sometimes, an aristocrat even seems to rate his horse above himself. When interviewed, the shy Wittelsbach princess, Irmgard von Bayern, refused to be photographed; but she wished for photographs to be taken of the horses which she bred. In modern times, the dream of aristocratic excellence has been transferred from the human to the beast.

Yet if a horse can be bred for size and speed, it can also be bred

[3] Ludwig Prince Windischgrätz, *My Adventures and Misadventures* (London, 1966) p. 22.

for retrogression. Count Draskovich has succeeded in breeding horses back to the state which they had reached at the first millenium. The auroch has again been recreated out of common cattle. Selective breeding need not ensure progress – unless progress in a certain direction is the aim of that selective breeding. When Prince Philip of Edinburgh recently fell off his polo pony, he declared that when God saw fit to make the most stupid of creatures, He made the horse. Man has not improved the horse's wisdom.

Naturally, the aristocrats could have become more intelligent than other people through selective breeding, like such English families as the Huxleys and the Russells. They preferred, however, to choose birth and wealth and good looks in their wives. Thus they failed to follow the example of the most socially successful people in human history, the Jews, whose regular pursuit of intelligence in marriage has raised them extraordinarily and quickly to the highest standard of their former peers. As Henry Shaw put so well in his acute analysis of the class structure of his own community, which reflected so many other communities of European Jewry:

In terms of social mobility, Anglo-Jewry has a record which is quite amazing in a community which is young in years. Its half million Jews, generally affluent, have within its ranks more than a dozen Peers of the Realm, a handful of Privy Councillors and a goodly contingent of Baronets and Knights which is almost an *embarras de richesse*. It is likely that the Anglo-Jewish community will continue to develop in this vein.

What, however, is very significant is that in this process of social movement one attitude still remains as a Jewish characteristic. Even the Jewish 'aristocrat' or the new kind of leader does not object to taking into his family as a son-in-law someone of great intellectual brilliance irrespective of his family origin, be it ever so humble. Thus, is Jewish social mobility made rapid. [4]

Such a pursuit of mental excellence might well have kept the old aristocracy extremely powerful in the age of modern

[4] Henry Shaw, 'Jewish Social Classes', *Twentieth Century* (Spring, 1965).

technology. Those who will not adapt must perish. Jean Prince d'Arenberg's accusation against the older generations of his class here has its truth. He accuses them of allowing their strong position to be frittered away without bequeathing to their children another strong position in a changing world.

The aristocrats have been let down by their fathers and grandfathers. I would say that the downfall came at the Belle Epoque. They all went down, down hill, sleeping with their friends' wives, not giving a damn about their responsibilities. From Deauville to Monte Carlo to Baden Baden, a bit of shooting, a lot of promiscuity, and too much drink and gambling. This was the failure of the aristocrats. It is now up to them. They must find their true function for themselves, which they lost at the end of the nineteenth century. They became and have become *dead*.

In fact, until the shock of lost lands and fortunes drove many of the aristocrats back to work at the end of the Second World War, the nobility of Europe was largely squandering its inherited assets and talents. Now the reverse is increasingly the case. An inherited title proves something which can be exploited in every career save politics in a socialist country. For instance, in Austria, 'the great black bogey of the aristocracy' is a handicap in the government career of Count Max von Thurn. But elsewhere, a title helps. Although most aristocrats pass off the use of a title as little more than an advantage in getting a table at a crowded restaurant, some are far more blunt about its value. Although the Marquess of Bath does not think that the aristocrats have anything special to contribute, 'they can get to the top more easily'. And Georg Prince zu Fürstenberg finds that his title, although officially abolished in Austria, makes dealings with businessmen simple. 'Knowing the name and the reputation of the family, they have thought, "Ah well, he must be a decent enough fellow."'

At any rate, the use of pedigree in business and showmanship has come to seem a more rational way of treating the luck of birth than hoarding a sense of nobility to display only in the company of other nobles. After all, if good breeding can be the chief asset in a show dog, why not in an aristocrat? In his hilarious dictionary of snobbism, Philippe Jullian made this point wickedly and shrewdly by including only one exquisite family tree in the whole book, that of a poodle called Attila. It was the last word on the virtues of pedigree.

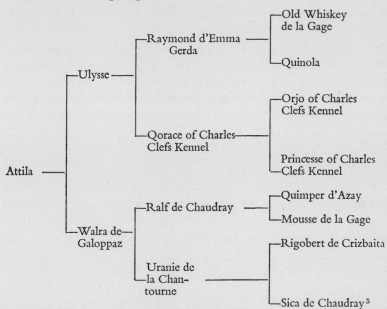

As La Bruyère so rightly observed in his time, certain people bear three names for fear of being without one.

[5] Philippe Jullian, *Dictionnaire du Snobisme* (Paris, 1958) p. 48.

Nine

THE PUBLICITY OF DIFFERENCE

The actual exploitation of a hereditary title demands certain factors. Firstly, the willingness of the holder to exploit it and his cleverness in doing so. And secondly, the willingness of the public to be exploited. Hustlers depend on suckers just as honours depend on respect of them. In the age of mass communications, the peer's privacy has been invaded just as much as the people's. And those peers are doing best for themselves who have learned to use mass communications to bring them private profits or sometimes to project themselves into the public eye.

The aristocrat who exploits his advantages contends that the general public likes to admire somebody who is different. In fact, the mass media do feed on the unusual and the out-of-the-way. With the function of the warrior gone, the function of the entertainer has come. To the extrovert peer or the impoverished one, this is no bad thing.

Great or noble men have never enjoyed much privacy. Witnesses had to be present at the birth and death of kings and queens. When Carlos II of Spain was dying, the courtiers watched with interest his doctors trying out the warm entrails of a pigeon on his belly. When Queen Caroline of England was screaming in her last throes, wishing her eldest son at the bottom-most pit of hell, a throng of the important was around to take note of her husband complaining that she looked like a dying cow. Memoirs of the gossip of courts and their corridors have always been plentiful, while the scandals of the aristocracy have always titillated the masses. What is new is that the aristocrats themselves are now prepared to profit directly from self-advertisement and even from selling their own intimate secrets. The exhibitionist in the stately home seems now to flaunt his notoriety rather than skulk in his anonymity.

Memoirs have charted the change, as the mechanisms of publicity have triumphed even over aristocratic diffidence. In 1902, Louisa de Tuscany, Crown Princess of Saxony, was in the middle of having her marriage publicly and humiliatingly repudiated by her husband. Bribery had put her private letters into her enemies' hands, and relative penury was near. Nine years later she was to write her memoirs to clear her reputation, but at the time she suffered in silence 'a positive persecution from newspaper reporters'. Always refusing to be interviewed, she even ignored a direct approach from an American reporter who declared to her as she came out of her hotel room: 'Say, Princess, I've the power to cover this stairway with banknotes for you to walk on if you will just let me have a few words with you. Is it a deal?'

Deals came after the First World War, when some of the aristocrats had to shift for a living. In the London of the 1920's Lady Angela St Clair Erskine found herself billed in the *Daily Graphic* as the 'First Lady of Title to Edit a Woman's Page', and then resigned when she found that somebody else wrote the page under her title. She watched a phenomenon that was to become quite frequent, the hosts beginning to feed on the parasites.

The New Poor have made journalism a means of livelihood. . . . The influx into Fleet Street from the West End has not been altogether popular, for in Fleet Street there is a definite Trade Union spirit. . . . It is surely not for anyone else to decide who has need to work, and who not. The Press have made so much copy out of the Idle Rich, that they should be the last to complain when one of these actually gets down to work.

Lady Angela, always a pioneer in the techniques of the New Poor, then turned to opening a boutique, which was successful until the depression. Thus she was a bridge figure between the old days of discretion and the new ones of advertisement. From the straddle of 1932, she could praise the ancient ways without condemning the modern ones.

The real difference between then and now is that *our* one endeavour was to keep our deeds, whether good or bad, from the public. Young people call us hypocrites. We merely had no advertising sense, and what we did we did because we wanted to do it, and not to attract attention or to bring us notoriety. Today publicity has been brought to a fine art, and to be recognized by Sasha or Schwabe is a modern accolade.[1]

Sasha and Schwabe have passed, Ponds has remained. In a series of famous advertisements after the First World War, English titled ladies including Diana, Duchess of Newcastle, appeared for money and glory, advertising the virtues of a brand of cold cream for keeping their complexions soft and lady-like. The aristocrat had at last joined the actress in the promotion of branded goods. That tendency has now gone a long way. Aristocratic men have joined their women in the act. The world now knows from photograph and caption how to:

LIVE LIKE A BARON,
LOOK LIKE A PRINCE.
DO IT WITH A CUSTOM ROYAL SUIT.

Baron George Wrangell, noted collector of antique art, does it up royally with a Custom Royal Suit. He knows that Daroff gives him fabrics that are scissored and sewn like cloth of gold. The kind royalty deserves. Lively, true, flattering. . . .

Equally, the Marquess of Bath appears in a drawing by Felix Topolski commissioned by a notable brand of Scotch distillers. In the background is a distant view of Longleat. In the foreground, the advertisement declares that the Marquess of Bath knows something when he drinks a particular brand of whisky. This special knowledge comes from his being a noble lord and descendant of one of Europe's grand families. It is the whisky, however, which is the aristocrat.[2] The language of advertising has long debased the

---

[1] Lady Angela Erskine, *Fore and Aft* (London, 1932) pp. 19, 30-31.
[2] These advertisements appeared in *Newsweek* during 1967 and 1968.

true meaning of words such as aristocrat, but not until recently did the true aristocrats themselves join in the mass attack on the values of themselves.

Yet there is advertising and advertising. The Duke of Bedford goes round advertising himself in order to keep the tourists flocking to Woburn Abbey and paying for its upkeep. He will go so far as to pose with a nylon stocking over his face in a magazine supplement on crime. The stocking distorts his face enough to make him appear a hairless bruiser, with his nose flattened and his ears mere stumps. It proves its point, that nobody can tell whether the criminal in the nylon mask is a duke or not. But the question remains, why should the duke get into the mask at all, and just what is he proving? Of course, Henry the Fifth as Prince of Wales was known to enjoy posing as a footpad with Sir John Falstaff, but that was a time ago, and the king repented of it.

Other aristocrats live deliberately off advertising, manipulating that curious field of sinecure and cynosure that is called public relations. Perhaps the most notorious of these is Prince Serge Obolensky, who is ready for a large fee to promote any luxurious object or wealthy cause. His most recent paid junket was his advertisement of the new Paradise Island Hotel at Nassau, built at the cost of fifty-five million dollars and the cost of the promotional week-end. To the more frivolous of the aristocrats, the offer of free trips to the sun can prove almost irresistible. Thus the prince was able to gather together such international lights as the Maharajah and Maharani of Jaipur, Lady Astor, Lord Lichfield, the Count and Countess de Romanones-Quintanilla, the Princess Pignatelli and the Marquis Pucci and the Countess Crespi, the Princess d'Arenberg, and a host of American aristocrats without titles. Even Richard Nixon was there. So the hotel was consecrated with the sleep and pleasure of three hundred and sixty-two of the international set, listening to the siren song of the Prince Obolensky, doing his duty by his clients.

Perhaps the most notorious of those who have used their titles to advance their public careers are the titled ladies who have gone on the stage. In the old Edwardian days, peers married actresses, who then left the stage to enjoy their new fortune. Lady Diana Manners, the most famous beauty of her time and a duke's daughter, reversed the fashion by making her name in the gossip columns, then making a fortune for her new marriage by using her fame to start a career in the cinema and on the stage. After starring in a couple of silent films about Good King Charles's golden days and Queen Elizabeth the First's glorious ones, she went off to New York to play in Max Reinhardt's wordless spectacle *The Miracle*, competing for the lead with Maria Carmi, who had married well and called herself Princess Matchabelli. The two titled ladies jockeyed for first place, and the quieter Lady Diana Manners won, because the princess 'behaved very *grande dame*, stretched out a left hand to all the principals' mouths and put all their backs up'.

Although Lady Diana Manners was highly praised for her performance, there was little question about why she got the part. Her impresario, as she knew, had read the *Tatler* and the *Sketch*, and he was impressed by ducal daughters. Reinhardt merely wanted a dumb and beautiful picture of aristocratic elegance, who could stand still for one hour before breaking her pose, as on ceremony at a royal occasion. This is exactly what he got. 'I never had the potter's thumb to shape me to this part,' Lady Diana confessed. 'I came out cast from a mould and saved them all a lot of trouble.' And she also got exactly what she wanted – a nest-egg, aided by journalism and the profitable Pond's advertisement.[3]

Different times, different ways. Two titled ladies, Soraya, once Queen of Iran, and Lee Bouvier, the sister of Jacqueline Onassis and the wife of Prince Radziwill, have tried their luck on screen and stage; but a certain noble propriety in an age of talking abandon has prevented their careers from being more than blocked out in wood. They could have played *The Miracle* superbly, but they cannot play *Laura* warmly. The only one who appears able to plunge into the sensual world of the modern

[3] See Diana Duff Cooper, *The Light of Common Day* (London, 1959) pp. 13-25.

screen goddesses without the least hesitation is the remarkable
Princess Ira zu Fürstenberg.

Already a friend of Clark Gable while still at finishing school,
the princess's beauty and first marriage to Prince Alfonso zu
Hohenlohe-Langenburg at the age of fifteen and separation from
her second playboy husband, the wealthy Brazilian Pignatari,
left her with one asset, the continued attention of the world's
gossip columns. She kept it by well-publicized appearances
everywhere. The inevitable Prince Obolensky arranged one, a
showing of fashions by her and Baroness Fiona Thyssen in New
York. 'She is the most modern aristocrat I have ever met,' said the
dress designer Paco Rabanne. 'She moves with a freedom which
is in complete contrast to the rigidity of the British Royal
Family.' Princess Ira also turned to the normal way of rising
starlets, cheese-cake photographs and *risqué* interviews. The
identification of the mass media and the aristocracy could not be
more complete.

In the French man's magazine called *Lui*, Princess Ira appeared
naked in a series of photographs, her hands clasped over her
breasts in the pose of Susannah pleasantly surprised by the Elders.
She was advertising her latest film, *Rasputin*, a film about a man
who had also done something to destroy the aristocratic principle.
In her interview with *Lui*, which accompanied the photographs,
the princess showed that she had moved on from the world of
formal introductions.

LUI: When a man accosts you in the street, a man whom you do
not know, how do you react?
IRA: I am always very flattered, I am always very nice. I am always
curious . . . in fact, I always like it.
LUI: Then all the world has his chance with you?
IRA: Well, yes! Nearly all the world, but, sometimes I am not
very nice, that depends on the day, if I'm in a very good mood,
if I'm in a bad one, and when I'm in a bad one I am not very nice.
But, in general, I am pretty pleasant, especially if the man who
accosts me is witty!

LUI: Do you ever happen to accost a man?

IRA: No, that's not my way of going about it, I prefer to let myself be attacked, of course if there's a very handsome man I like, but that happens very rarely, from time to time I try. But I don't attack them directly. Because I don't think it's a good tactic.

LUI: What are the arguments which make you fall for a man?

IRA: It's very difficult to say. That depends on moments, the instants when you meet me. If it happens to be a moment when I'm sad, disillusioned, the moment when I'm alone, lost, then yes, you can seduce me. It's a question of timing. I think that's really primordial. . . . Each of us to our own time.[4]

Each of us to our own time. No other aristocrat has yet accommodated himself or herself as well to their own time as Princess Ira zu Fürstenberg. She has the total courage of her modernity. And certainly, her behaviour is far better than those aristocrats who are prepared to sell to the public the gossip about their own lives. After his recent and notorious divorce case, the Duke of Argyll had to be restrained by the English courts from printing details of his wife's past conduct and misconduct in a Sunday newspaper, the *People*, which was prepared to pay him largely for these confidences. In giving injunctions to prevent the publication of these details, the Judge had to rebuke the duke. As *The Times* reported the case, the verdict stated:

The immorality of the Duchess undermined the confidences of the future but did not betray the confidences of the past. The policy of the law was to preserve mutual trust between husband and wife. Accordingly, her adultery did not license the Duke to publish unchecked the most intimate confidences of earlier and happier days because the mutual trust might be impaired.[5]

Yet if some members of the aristocracy can be venal, they are merely imitating the majority of the human race. Money is a democratic concern. And for every aristocrat who cashes in directly from his title, there are a dozen who shun publicity or

[4] *Lui*, June 1967.
[5] *The Times*, 10 December 1964.

become its victims without any thought of payment for their services. Without a diet of royal and noble marriages and scandals, many of the world's illustrated magazines for women would close their presses. No follower of aristocratic romance could complain of the free copy provided by the recent wedding of Count Henri de Laborde de Montpezat to Crown Princess Margarethe of Denmark and by the wedding of Isabella of France to an Austrian noble from the Schönborn-Buccheim family. Journalists successfully turned both these occasions into vicarious mass romances.

Very rarely is any money taken to help defray the costs of these expensive alliances. Yet the stepfather of the present Princess Jutta of Prussia, a businessman from the Ruhr, caused a public scandal by selling to a West German magazine the exclusive rights to photograph his daughter's wedding to Prince Michael of Prussia. The excluded photographers stormed the wedding party and got whatever satisfaction they could from photographing the royal pair dancing. Normally, however, the titled wish the world to watch and read freely about their public displays of morality, however much they may seek to hide their major scandals, such as the Profumo or Montesi affairs. For all the world loves a great wedding – and a great undoing.

Yet those aristocrats who seek publicity can legitimately claim that they are satisfying a popular demand. For the basis of modern nobility is mass snobbery. If the attitudes of eastern Europe suddenly became those of western Europe, and a man who bore a title was looked on as lower than a man who bore a load of dung, there would be few aristocrats brave enough to risk public derision. But unquestionably, mass snobbery has both a social and a political importance. In Italy, the gossip columns about the lives of the aristocrats have allowed a limited revival of the monarchists in the South, where the princes have such a long tradition of oppressing the people. In Gaullist France, to bear a noble name is scarcely a political handicap, and in England it was a positive advantage. The decline in the radicalism of the European proletariat and the emancipation of their wives in terms of leisure and voting has led to a lessening of the bias against the remnants of feudalism, also to a romantic attachment to memories of a golden age of lords and ladies that never was.

A random sample of opinion on the aristocracy across Europe gives little evidence of bias. For example:

Nobility for me is something romantic. I wish we had a King and nobles here. . . . There's something in the way they walk and their manners. . . .
(French Hotel Maid)

The nobility is lucky. They are always gentlemen. They are always taught languages and how to behave. Even if they haven't got a lot of brains, they have a sort of confidence. (French Chemist)

They are what they are. You can't change them. Put them into any old clothes, mix them up with anyone ordinary, you can still tell them. Funny thing, it has something to do with the way they talk, it makes you feel like nothing. (German Hall Porter)

Just like the film stars, that's what they are. Without the good shapes.
(German Café Owner)

I should like to be one of them, the upper caste, I mean. I should like to have a father who was a Lord who had been to Oxford . . . I'm not anything. (English Clerk)

Even when one of those sampled publicly expressed hostility to the aristocrats, he was always opposed or shouted down. One French dustman stated that he loathed aristocrats and that they would behave just as badly as they had before the French Revolution, if they were given another chance; but he admitted that his wife liked them, particularly the Queen of England. Another Frenchman caused a minor riot in a Strasbourg café by saying that he wished Hitler had left the Jews alone and had exterminated the aristocracy, every man and woman and child who bore a *de* or a *von* in front of their name. He was howled down by the whole café and could only retreat into a paraphrase of Montaigne's observation on Kings, that, like any man, every one of them sat on his own bum. 'The aristocrats are and always have been an insult to the creation of man. They have arms and legs and a head

229 The Publicity of Difference 229

just as you and I have, and they eat and drink and relieve themselves just as you and I do.'

Anti-feudalism, however, like anti-clericalism is less and less significant as the nobility and the churches grow less and less powerful. Unless helped by government propaganda, it is difficult to hate a bogeyman without teeth. In most rural districts of Europe, there is a definite affection for those aristocrats who still live on the land. For they now have a common cause with the peasants they once oppressed – the preservation of the landscape and the conservation of the old ways.

As the countryside becomes depopulated and less important in the affairs of the nation, those who remain there to fight for its dying patterns become the genuine leaders of their communities. It is odd that certain decent aristocrats have once again found their old lost function in the battle to preserve their local villages against pylons and suburbs and motorways. For once again they are fighting to protect their domain against the mailed fist of a distant government and the wandering armies of tourists and the plague of communications.

This actual correspondence of interests between many of the rural aristocrats and gentry on one side, and many of the farmers and rural labourers on the other side, perpetuates the myth that the genuine 'people' still love the old nobles. It is rare to find an aristocrat who does not say that he gets on very well with country people and even urban workers, but he cannot stand the middle class. In fact, the aristocrats' concern with pedigree sometimes makes them rate the peasants very high on the scale of blood, due to the inbreeding of so many village communities. 'The aristocrats for me are the peasants,' the Count de Chambrun declares bluntly. 'They are the pure bloods. They never mix except among themselves, whereas the aristocrats marry industrialists, Jews, film stars and anyone.'

The ultimate sophistication in an aristocrat is to declare his real simplicity. 'I come from a good peasant family,' the literary Count Antonini of Venice says, 'and I like good peasant food.' This simplicity is often genuine. When the Count and Countess de Murade state that they lead a very simple life 'almost like peasants', the man who runs the village garage agrees. 'They work so hard. Everybody loves them and the village would be nothing without them. Sometimes I don't think they eat as well as I do.' Where a genuine sense of *noblesse oblige* exists on a declining rural income, the behaviour of the aristocracy can be highly aristocratic.

The greatest irony of all is when a whole people thinks itself aristocratic, because their sense of identification with the ways of the aristocracy is so great. This is true of parts of Spain and Scotland and Wales and Norway, and even of Poland. In the random sample of public attitudes, one Welsh couple was asked about the aristocracy and made the reply that all Welsh people were aristocrats. 'It's in the blood, you know – not mixed like the English.' According to one acute commentator on the life and culture of Poland, even communism is a mere red tinge on the noble traits of the Polish peasant.

Poland changes its social and demographic character; the most numerous class in the nation, that which, according to legend, gave her her first kings, after long centuries of mute existence in the shadow and in oblivion, now returns to power. . . . And yet, the general aspect of life does not much change, for during the centuries of very close and intimate existence with the numerous Polish gentry, after many and frequent ennoblements in the past, as a result of education and of the political role that the peasant has already begun to play now, he is stamped with the customs, usages, and manners of the gentry.

This is a fact: the modern Polish peasant is a very well-brought-up man, often better than his neighbours still living in the castle. He is distinguished and physically handsome. He is aristocratic. While disappearing, the nobility has not left it without heritage. There is nothing for it; Poland *is* an aristocratic country; but it is not, as Lamartine said, 'an aristocracy without people', it is an aristocratic nation without an aristocracy. [6]

In the cities of Europe, however, there is little sense of identifica-

[6] Waclaw Lednicki, *Life and Culture of Poland as Reflected in Polish Literature* (New York, 1944) p. 157.

tion with the aristocracy. By tradition, the city burghers helped the kings against the feudal nobles, and the urban proletariat opposed the landed classes. Moreover, in the cities, the aristocrats are rarely seen except enjoying a gilded leisure, while the popular press is far less interested in their good works than in their conpicuous misdeeds. Few of the urban aristocrats can be fully distinguished from the other members of that group of the very rich and the notorious and the beautiful who pass under the name of Café Society – or Nescafé Society, as an English duchess calls it.

The hotch-potch of bankers, industrialists, film stars, playboys, models and aristocrats, who recognize each other blatantly in the chosen spots of the world at the right season, performs its envied and despised function daily in the newspapers. Its excuse is that it provides an escapism for the masses, its crime is that it sets an example of triviality and squandering that is abominable in a world where tens of millions starve. Even its charities provide more waste to the fortunate than aid to the unfortunate. The famous Masked Ball at the Palazzo Rezzonico in Venice in 1967, called 'the most elegant costume ball of the century,' was justified as providing help for Venice's flooded artisans. But other than the minor work done in costume repairs for the drenched guests, the affair raised little money for the artisans, although much fear in the guests from a false telephone call: 'We put a bomb in the palace – Vive Mao.'

Yet no bomb was put in the palace. And if the thoughts of Mao did inspire widespread student activism across Europe, they only inspired the smarter aristocrats like Prince Dado Ruspoli to wear silk Mao jackets at their *soirées*. Even revolutionaries can set a style, if not a content. For in the age of democracy, fashions can rise from the bottom as well as fall from the top. From Marie Antoinette onwards, the well-born have shown a certain taste for elegant peasant dress. The Italian-style clothes of the 'mod' gangs of London in the 1950's have altered the style of Savile Row a decade later. The economic changes which have made the European rich relatively poorer and the European poor relatively richer, have turned even the High Fashion dress-designers to the pursuit of the mass rather than the millionaire market. For them, the purses of millions of young people outweigh the little fortunes of the titled few.

The penetrating Louise de Vilmorin quite rightly sees the end of the old aristocratic ways less in the actual lowering of her class's standards than in the indifference and change of all the other classes, deliberately exploited by the great merchandisers of our time. When the rich and the well-born controlled the fashion-houses of Paris and even the Hollywood films of the depression spoke of a nostalgia for dressing-up like Melvyn Douglas, then the mass dream was of long evening gowns and tail coats and the style of a duchess. But after the Second World War, relaxed American styles and intense American exploitation followed the American troops. Opportunity follows the army. And just as the British Empire was lost the day the first British colonial officer sat down to dinner in shorts, so the principle that the aristocrats should set the mass fashions was lost when the Americans came to Paris. As Louise de Vilmorin says:

Those awful Americans, they invented the teenager. All part of the money-making machinery – very clever, but diabolical. I remember the first time I saw a pair of jeans in Paris. I said then, This is the end. Yes, jeans was the beginning of the end. . . . The great revolt against everything – parents, manners, schools. It's all terrible, and it ends in nothing.

Great revolts, particularly of young people, always grow small and old. And the imminent end of the aristocracy has been announced so frequently since the French Revolution that the warning cry has come to sound like an accolade. As in the case of the surviving European Jews, the difficulty for the European aristocrats now is less their coming extinction than their rapid absorption. If they adapt too well to the mechanisms of publicity, how will they be distinguished from the other common publicists of screen and television? If the young aristocrats join in the revolt of the young against everything they have inherited, how will they be able to claim their inheritance when they become older?

Of course, conservatism grows with age, revolts turn into reactions, and a sense of being better than others normally increases with each birthday. Thus as long as the young aristocrats survive to become older ones and as long as governments are not provoked into an attack on meaningless names and as long as the general public retains its sense of snobbery, then the title will die a slow and lingering death through overexposed insignificance.

For snobbery has a longer history than any pedigree. A snob is merely a cannibal who eats with a fork. The most primitive society has its social gradations and exclusions. And snobbery is the slave of hierarchy, just as it is the bastard child of aristocracy. 'I attach but little value to rank or wealth,' W. S. Gilbert wrote in *H.M.S. Pinafore*, 'but the line must be drawn somewhere.' There is scarcely anyone who does not draw a line somewhere, and put himself above it.

Evelyn Waugh was the most perfect observer of English social gradations in this century, and thus the most perfect plotter of snobbery. In Israel, he had asked the heterogeneous immigrants who exactly was a Jew, and they had replied that anyone who believed himself to be a Jew was a Jew. The same rule, Evelyn Waugh thought, applied to English society. Everybody believed that he was a gentleman; but also everybody drew the line just below his social grouping, saying that gentlemen stopped there. The professions looked down on trade, the army on the professions, the Brigade of Guards on the regiments of the line, those with stately homes in London and the country on those who only had one large house, and so on to the infinite frontiers of exclusion. In fact, the definition of a gentleman was merely a series of negatives based on a keen observation of what to avoid in the habits of all inferiors.

The demarcations of snobbery below the line have much to do with the admirations of snobbery above the line. The poor white in the Southern backwoods of the United States respects the aristocratic owner of the plantation because he can despise the nigger. If one feels oneself superior to many, it is easier to accept a few men's superiority in their turn. It is only the position at the bottom of the ladder that makes a man want to throw it all down. Otherwise there is the hope of social climbing, the search after status. For that search after the high position which most men think they deserve is one of the motors of human industry, even if the original meaning of status was 'the height or acme of a disease'.

Not even the aristocrats, who can rise little further in the social scale, are free from the taints of snobbery. As the aristocratic and misanthropic Chamfort wrote before turning with disgust from the follies of his own class to the follies of the French Revolution:

Society, that which one calls the World, is only the struggle of a thousand little opposed interests, an eternal struggle of all the vanities which cross, clash, wound and are wounded, humiliated one by the other, which expiate the next day in the disgust of a defeat the triumph of yesterday. To live alone, not to be bruised in this miserable clash, where one attracts attention for an instant to be crushed the instant afterwards, that is what people call being nothing, not having any life at all. Poor humanity.

In Emerson's opinion, society was 'a hospital of incurables'. Its routine was snobbery and its disease ambition and few wanted a cure. The majority, indeed, do prefer to remain diseased, for most men are doomed by the structure of society to remain relative failures. There is not much room at the top. Thus a form of snobbery becomes a kind of necessity, because the contemplation of the inferiority of those below and a spurious identification with those above can disguise the personal failure to rise.

Of course, the more numerous the group of supposed inferiors, the better for self-esteem. Women, children, all foreigners, all poor people, all coloured people, Catholics, Protestants, Jews, Masons, slum-dwellers, subordinates, neighbours . . . the chosen inferiors can number the distant billions or merely the family next door. But without them to despise, his own inadequacy would stare a man in his face. Rather than that, he would spit down at the many and bow down to the few above him and call them aristocrats and dream of joining them, privileged and apart.

No society, however large and however much 'of the people', has yet done away with snobbery altogether. Even communist countries have their New Class of privileged Party members and their reactionaries to despise. Rid the country of the aristocrats and the *kulaks* rise to take their place. Rid the country of the *kulaks* and the enemies of the people are still trying to displace the régime which is lording it over the people. Yet unquestionably in the socialist republics, snobbery is a mere itch compared to the scarlet fever that rampages across the United States and western Europe, the societies which might do well to remember the wise remark made in *Tin Pan Alley*, that snobbery was but a point in time, and that patience was needed with our inferiors, for they were ourselves of yesterday. Such prudence was also noticeable in the counsel of Lady Ailesbury: 'Always be nice with young girls, one never knows whom they might not marry.'

As snobbery is nearly universal and as it demands its aristocracy, then the mass media are bound to supply the demand. Three stories illustrate how a perfect symbiosis is taking place between snobbery and aristocracy as they feed off each other, the world audience giving the mass approbation and cash that nobility needs for its proof of its worth. The first story concerns Baroness Maria von Trapp, who became mere Mrs Trapp when she fled from Austria to the United States with her singing family and dropped the title to become a citizen of that democratic country; now that *The Sound of Music* has grossed a tidy fortune from the applauding masses, she has told her lawyers to put back the *von* on her name. Her station has improved.

The second story concerns a competition run in *Queen* magazine in England, entitled 'Win a millionaire'. The millionaire whom any girl could win was the fifth Earl of Lichfield, photographed by the fifth Earl of Lichfield. To win the millionaire, each girl entrant had to send a photograph of herself and tick off in order of desirability the eight most important traits of her dream millionaire from nine listed assets, Education, Houses, Wealth, Title, Looks, Business, Interests, Land, and Cars. The winner was chosen by the model Twiggy and had dinner with the Earl, who then gave her a photographic session in his studio. 'After that,' Queen said, 'it's up to you ... ,' And the earl gallantly added, 'I've obviously had lots of affairs – not necessarily with models. But I really don't care about breeding and class. It has ceased to matter with me.'[7]

The third story concerns one of the great technological breakthroughs in mass communications, the transmission of the first still picture ever transmitted via two satellites in space. When the first telegraph message was sent by its inventor, Samuel Morse, over a forty mile line between Washington and Baltimore, his message read: 'What hath God wrought?' The first picture transmitted by the two satellites was sent more than seven thousand miles between Honolulu and London. It was of Waikiki beach, where Carl Gustaf, Crown Prince of Sweden, was shown democratically ogling an American girl student in her bikini.

[7] *Queen*, 14 February 1968.

Ten

THE POLITICS OF DIFFERENCE

As Heraclitus wrote, all is flux. Even the great conservative Edmund Burke could add, 'Nothing in progression can rest on its original plan. We may as well think of rocking a grown man in the cradle of an infant.' The principle of hereditary aristocracy, however, is based on the resistance to change or the reluctant adaptation to it. With slow change, aristocracy may survive a few generations; with quick change, it must go soon.

In this century of social revolution, the political forces of the aristocracy have been beating a retreat. Yet it has remained more powerful in hiding than the believers in the myth of the business conspiracy would wish to believe. In 1914 the decisions taken by Austria and Russia and Germany that led to the world war had more to do with nationalism and expansionism, and with dynastic and aristocratic values than with the plottings of the trusts or the armament manufacturers. Plutocrats, even in modern times, do not and did not wholly control the political decisions of nations, certainly not in France under General de Gaulle nor in England under Harold Macmillan and Sir Alec Douglas-Home. There the old aristocratic conceptions still played a large part in shaping the political decisions of modern nations.

Before modern revolutionary times saw things in terms of opposites, as Hannah Arendt pointed out, aristocracy was not thought to be the *opposite* of democracy but 'two sides of the same event'. Aristocrats suffered when they became the scapegoats of the ills of society instead of part of the settled ruling order. They have survived if they have avoided the role of scapegoat, either through finding alternative whipping boys for the ills of society in the Jews or the plutocrats or the reds, or by overstating their insignificance in and irrelevance to modern life. Absence of conspicuous consumption is their most conspicuous camouflage to distinguish themselves from the rotten rich.

Yet the qualities that the aristocrats prize are not the qualities that the modern political party prizes in its search for people to join the political élite. A modern political party must seek to recruit its members from the whole people, not from a small hereditary group. If a noble name is still of advantage in politics in Spain and France, it is a temporary advantage, due to Generals Franco and de Gaulle. Even in England, where the hereditary principle was important for so long in Conservative Party and ruling circles, an inherited name is at last becoming of little help in politics.

That process has been slow, but instructive. Until the early years of this decade, Britain remained the last major defender of the importance of the principle of hereditary aristocracy in politics. The leadership of the Conservative Party in the post-war years passed from aristocrat to the relations of aristocrats, from Winston Churchill to Anthony Eden to Harold Macmillan. Macmillan had married into the Cavendish and the Cecil families and had thus joined himself to blood groups who thought politics was 'almost a hereditary profession'. He was Prime Minister for the longest period of any man since the 'sleeping dog' days of Sir Robert Walpole. Part of the reason for his rise and his survival in office was his habit of keeping on good terms with his influential Tory relations and of giving them good jobs, where noble Lords could still be employed. Macmillan never went in for government by crony, because he had very few and powerless cronies. He did go in for government by family, because his family connections were numerous and powerful.

Yet if aristocratic habits and relations accounted for something of Macmillan's success, aristocratic philandering led to the beginning of his downfall. The notorious Profumo scandal's lesser effect was the downfall of the Minister of War and the travels of Viscount Astor. Its chief damage was to the all-important myth of the Conservative Party, that the Tory leaders were somehow better than most people and were born to rule, while the leaders of the Labour Party were just a lot of politicians little better than the man in the street.

In fact, Macmillan had won successive general elections on the aristocratic myth. Yet that myth could not survive the scandals of petty whores claiming that they were doing no more than Lady Hamilton had done for Admiral Nelson, of Russian officers sharing the favours of the War Minister's mistress, and of week-end orgies being provided at one of the leading stately homes of England. The self-admitted relation of dukes, Harold Macmillan, suddenly found himself in shoddy company. The people born at the top, who were meant to set a good example, could not be setting a worse one. Harold Macmillan sniffed the winds of change, and like his predecessor after Suez, fell ill for the good of his party.

It was fortunate for Macmillan that the most dangerous scandal of his life, his clearance of the traitor Kim Philby in the House of Commons, did not break until he had long given up power in the government. Philby had been able to be the leading Soviet agent within British intelligence for many long years, because of his aristocratic connections and mistresses, and because of his right behaviour in the right places. Macmillan cleared Philby since he thought the intelligence services should do their own dirty work rather than get nasty questions asked in the Commons. As the acute commentators on the Philby affair noted, Macmillan's patrician attitude was summed up in the remark: 'I don't expect the gamekeeper to come and tell me every time he catches a fox.' More important, however, than Macmillan's white-washing of Russia's chief spy were reasons why the British Secret Service, with a long list of impressive intelligence victories over the Nazis, could have suspected Philby for so long and yet allowed him to continue to betray them. The only answer lies in the idiotic trust they put in the honour of a fellow gentleman and club member. John le Carré, himself an ex-professional in such matters, brilliantly summed up the whole business of aristocratic overconfidence in its own sort:

Both Philby and Profumo, significantly, enjoyed Macmillan's professional confidence on the floor of the House of Commons. Each, in his own sphere, was so much a part of the Establishment he betrayed that it was impossible for his colleagues to judge him. Each was incompetently tried in private and incompetently exonerated in public. Each held out, with astonishing gall, against what seemed to be a foregone conclusion. Each ultimately knew the great weakness of the Establishment: '*This club does not elect liars, therefore Profumo is not a liar; this Club does not elect traitors, therefore Kim is not a traitor.*' This Establishment is a self-proving proposition. [1]

Yet the curious thing was that the Tory party, once its aristocratic element had let it down so badly in the Macmillan years, reverted to one of the most aristocratic of them all to lead it out of its troubles. The choice of the fourteenth Earl of Home as Foreign Secretary by Harold Macmillan had seemed rather anachronistic; but his choice by the bosses of his party and by the Queen to form a new government after Macmillan's withdrawal seemed positively antediluvian. Some of his opponents such as Macleod and Bevins thought that his selection as the leader of the party would be electoral suicide; but they knew their conservative country less than the shrewd party bosses, who had helped to steer the choice towards the Earl of Home. For the Earl's irreproachable private life and his quitting of his title to serve in the Commons as plain Sir Alec Douglas-Home, his easy drawling manner and his quiet dry jokes almost carried his party to another electoral victory. If Macmillan's subordinates and noble associates had smashed the Humpty-Dumpty myth of aristocratic merit, Sir Alec Douglas-Home made a pretty fair attempt to do the impossible and put the eggshell back together again.

[1] See John le Carré's introduction to B. Page, D. Leitch, and P. Knightley : *Philby: The Spy who Betrayed a Generation* (London, 1968).

The last noble Prime Minister of Britain, however, had no stomach for criticism within his own party, and he soon handed over power to a grammar-school boy, Edward Heath, who seemed to represent the future of the party without anyone being really satisfied with him at the present. Douglas-Home's greatest contribution to the aristocratic code lay in his distaste for clinging on to mere power for the sake of it, and the final closing of the question of snobbery over mere matters of lineage. With his immortal remark on the family tree of Harold Wilson, he put the whole question of the importance of genealogy into its proper perspective. If he was the fourteenth Earl of Home, was not Harold Wilson the fourteenth Mister Wilson? And if so, the peer implied that people should choose between them on their merits. What was certain in the future, however, was that not even the Tory party was likely to choose an aristocrat again to lead it, for the power of nominating a party leader was forever removed from the hands of the old Conservative families into the hands of the party's elected members.

The long survival of the aristocratic principle in Conservative circles merely highlighted the chief paradox of Britain. How could the nation which unleashed the industrial revolution on the world not give up feudalism at home? Its forwardness seemed to ensure the survival of its backwardness. As late as December 1957, politics in Westminster could still be concerned with a debate on whether certain families were born to rule or not. The debate in the House of Lords at the time when the Conservative government proposed to appoint Life Peers to join the hereditary peers provided the most pithy discussion of whether an aristocracy should rule since the great days of Athens and Rome. The debate had nothing to do with modern times, but still used classical allusions. As the Earl of Dundee so aptly observed, referring to the advantage of a House of Lords:

It is very difficult to be a non-professional in the House of Commons unless you have large private means; and that is a great pity. Fifty years ago, a man like Cincinnatus could have sat in the House of Commons. Now I do not think he could. He would not have enough time to attend to his plough. But in the House of Lords Cincinnatus can serve a highly useful purpose, and can do a real service for his country.

The Bill providing for Life Peerages aimed to ensure the survival of the House of Lords, not its destruction. As Lord Brand saw so clearly in the debate, the hereditary principle originally derived from a feudal society and from a powerful land-owning class. But the 'days of landed splendour were over.' Therefore, if the House of Lords was to survive with any political power or meaning, Life Peers had now to be admitted. The next question was, of course, how many Life Peers should be admitted and how many hereditary peers should be excluded? In fact the Bill gave no answer to this question, except that the elected House of Commons would certainly not allow all hereditary peers to be excluded, in case the House of Lords really were to become a senate of wise men and a rival to the Commons itself, as once it had been.

No noble lord in the debate dared to defend the hereditary principle on the grounds of genetics or better blood. The more favoured defences were pragmatism, history, the Constitution, the independence of the peers, their specialism and amateurism and occasional youth, their support by the great British public, and the final plea that the lords were not really noble after all. Peer after peer rose to say that the House of Lords did not make sense, but it worked. 'Anybody, of course,' Viscount Bridgeman admitted, 'can make a perfectly good case in saying that the hereditary principle is illogical. So it is. But the question is not whether or not it is logical, but whether it supplies something of which this House is in need.' Viscount Bridgeman's answer to that was, logically, yes. Even the leader of the socialists in the Lords, Earl Attlee, once had admitted that 'against all probability this House works extremely well, as things in England do, and that we should be unwise to be too logical.'

Lord Teviot believed that it was 'a natural result of history that the hereditary principle should go on. In the days when it originated, of course, there was no Labour Party at all.' By this view, the merit of an institution depended on its longevity –

which would make Methuselah a better man than Jesus. An appeal to the Constitution was on more certain ground. Lord Elton saw the creation of Life Peers as the first step in getting rid of the House of Lords altogether and in giving 'some future Government – presumably a Labour Government – a blank cheque to rewrite the English Constitution,' although this is actually not set down in a written document.

The independence of the peerage seemed another bulwark of the hereditary principle. The Earl of Mansfield accused the members of the House of Commons, particularly the socialists there, of being mere 'Lobby Fodder'. But the nobility had been taught to speak out.

This independence of thought and expression is largely due to the preponderant hereditary element in your Lordship's House. We have been brought up to think as individuals, and to speak as individuals; and we continue to do so. And I am certain that to substitute any other form of Second Chamber for one that is predominantly hereditary would be to lower both its effectiveness and its prestige at home and abroad.

The next defence of the House of Lords was its command of specialists. There was never a point so obscure that some back-woods peer might not appear from his castle hermitage and deliver an erudite speech on the problem, only to disappear from the House and not to be seen again in his lifetime. More serious than this myth was the fact that in the House of Lords sat specialists in science, the law, the church, the civil service, and in many of the professions, for a peerage was the logical reward of a well-spent life in public service. All in all, the Earl of Airlie suggested that the House had 'proved itself to be a pretty good Second Chamber and that, with all its incongruity, the country might do well to leave it alone'.

The next defence of the House of Lords was exactly the opposite, that it represented the common man more than the House of Commons did, because there were so many hereditary peers of moderate mental capacity. As Lord Winster said when quoting Lord Mount Ararat in *Iolanthe*: 'Now that the Peers are to be recruited from persons of intelligence I do not really see what use we are.' Lord Teynham was even more plain-spoken about the ordinariness of the average peer as compared to the average Member of Parliament 'in another place' – the Lords' euphemism for the House of Commons, a phrase once used by Victorians when referring to Hell.

I would say that our strength and prestige are bound up in the fact that we are really a group of ordinary people – in fact, of men in the street – and that we have not sought political membership like those in another place in any way at all. Therefore, I think we can claim to delay a controversial measure to enable the people of the country to think again.

More strange was the defence of hereditary selection by the fact that it gave young men the chance to speak out, as though a youthful peer was somehow representative of his generation. This point was most forcibly put by the blunt speech of the self-styled 'typical hereditary peer', Lord Lovat, who felt that he should speak out for the backwoods peers who spent all their time running their estates and thus could rarely come up to London to run the House of Lords. To Lord Lovat, the images of the grouse moor were the natural way to express the need for having young lords to act as the spokesmen of their age group.

It is considered by good keepers that old birds often become vermin. They are inclined to drive out healthy young stock; and young stock is as necessary in your Lordships' House, as a cross-section of public opinion, as it is on the grouse moor. My Lords, that is all I have to say in supporting this Bill. I am grateful to Her Majesty's Government for retaining the position that noble Lords in our situation, of Peers who cannot appear too often, are accepted on the hereditary principle.

A few lords even thought that the Upper House was more popular than the House of Commons, which seemed to spend most of its time discrediting itself. More specifically, these peers considered that the delaying and revising powers of the House of Lords were a good check on an elected government, which might otherwise try to push through the Commons measures which had never been aired before the people in an election. In the most notable clash of the debate, Lord Balfour of Burleigh rebuked the Labour peer, Viscount Alexander of Hillsborough, for questioning 'the divine right' of the House of Lords to check the excesses of the Commons.

Lord Balfour of Burleigh: . . . Where does the House of Commons get its mandate from?
Viscount Alexander of Hillsborough: The people.
Lord Balfour of Burleigh : The people, quite so; and when they exceed the mandate it is for this House to say, 'Stop a minute. Have the people considered this?
Viscount Alexander of Hillsborough: I am asking the noble Lord, where do you get your mandate from?
Lord Balfour of Burleigh: From the ancient Constitution of this country. And please God the noble Lords opposite will never have the temerity to alter it!

The final defence of the hereditary principle in the House of Lords was that the noble body was not really very noble after all – a sentiment which the pedigree-conscious European aristocrats would have applauded heartily. Titles were quite easily available in Britain, as Lord Moran pointed out :

When I spoke of the travesty of facts, I had in mind in particular the hereditary principle. A quarter of the peerage at the present time are first creations, and more than half of those who regularly attend the House are also new creations. The hereditary element is already in a minority in the proceedings of the House.

Such arguments concluded the defence of the hereditary principle – except for a determined attack on the possibility of women peers, as if somehow women had nothing to do with heredity. This attack was led by the Earl of Airlie, although Viscount Massereene and Ferrard produced its best lines. 'It was beyond my wildest dreams that we should find the fair sex amongst us . . . the ladies are seeking admission under cover of the Trojan Horse of Life Peers.' The Earl of Home gently defended the surrender of the last male bastion of hereditary privilege with the remarks:

The need to keep this House up to date is perhaps the most powerful argument for the introduction of women. There are some of your Lordships who may contend – indeed, some have – that women have not made the mark on the political life of this country that was expected of them. Some of our instincts against surrendering this, one of the last sanctuaries of the male, may be very strong. Some may say that women do not understand how golden is silence, particularly when seven o'clock in the evening is approaching. My trouble is that I cannot see any argument in logic or in reason, why, if women are in another place, they should not be here.

Of course, every defence leads naturally to a form of attack, and the outnumbered Labour peers, aided by a few young and dissident Conservatives, assaulted the hereditary principle on exactly the same grounds as it had been defended. Since few of the Labour peers had inherited their position in the Lords, there was not a reason in the world that they should accept anything but the virtues of the self-made man who had earned his title.

As for the fact that the House of Lords worked pretty well as it was, that was dealt with by Lord Darwen.

I am not going to defend the hereditary principle. It cannot be defended in the context of a liberal democracy. Nor do I think it can be justified with the convenient assertion that it works. In my submission, your Lordships' House works in spite of, and not because of, the hereditary principle. At the moment the effective functioning of your Lordships' House depends on half a dozen – or, not to be invidious, let me say, a dozen – Peers with the necessary energy, time, experience and devotion to duty to provide at least the semblance of an Opposition.

It was well known that the vast majority of the peers were Conservative, and even the smattering of Labour peers created to oppose them was merely a drop of red blood in the blue sea of the House.

The aged Earl Attlee, Prime Minister of Britain after the Second World War and architect of the failed social revolution of the post-war years, gave the best speech against the inheritance of titles, which he had done nothing to destroy when he had the opportunity. To him, the sanction of time was meaningless.

Whatever may have been the position in historic times, we do not consider that the hereditary principle today stands up to criticism. We think it as much an anomaly as the hereditary principle in the State of Nepal, in which every member of the Royal Family is born a major-general. The qualities of a major-general are very great; so are the qualities for a legislator, and we do not think either of them is necessarily born. Therefore the hereditary principle is one which we consider should be abolished.

As for the Constitution, every Labour peer knew very well that the House of Commons had almost total power to change the Constitution through any law it could pass. And as for the vaunted independence of the individual peer, Earl Attlee waspishly observed that in his experience, anyone who called himself an Independent in politics always turned out to be a Conservative in the end. In fact, that noble independence did not amount to much in terms of representing national feeling, as Lord Conesford admitted, quoting the remark: 'The Lords represent nobody but themselves and have the entire confidence of their constituents.'

The opponents of the hereditary principle found nothing wrong in the specialist knowledge available in the House of Lords; they wished to increase it through Life Peerages. They deplored the amateurism of the backwoods peers, who might appear any time in their hundreds to swamp learning with inherited ignorance and massed prejudice. As for the argument that the peerage allowed the young to voice the complaints of their generation, that was as spurious as the argument that the Lords fairly represented the Labour Party. The plain fact was that most of the peers were old, and that the older the peer grew the more conservative he grew. According to Viscount Stansgate, this was 'due to mental and spiritual decay'.

The supposed popularity of the House of Lords was derisory to the Labour peers. In fact, the ancient political body was only tolerated because the average man had not the least idea nor interest in what was taking place there. As Lord Lloyd noted:

Men like Lord Derby and Lord Lonsdale were well known, but I doubt whether the average man in the street today is aware that your Lordships are sitting here at all. Anyway, if he does, he is a clever fellow, because certainly his newspaper tells him nothing about it.

Obscurity was a greater preservative of the noble institution than popularity. And as to the claim that the House of Lords was not really very lordly after all, that was a good thing. To the young Viscount Stansgate, who was not yet allowed to renounce his title and rejoin the House of Commons, an inherited title was an 'incubus' rather than a privilege. In fact, the best thing which could be said for the House of Lords by the Labour opposition was that its existence made their party able to reward its elderly supporters in their declining years. As Earl Attlee finally admitted at the end of his long critique of the Second Chamber, in which he was a member:

I believe that we need a body like your Lordships' House to get valuable work done, relieving an overloaded House of Commons; and, if I may say so, it is not entirely an unfortunate thing that this House affords what I think one noble Lord has described as a chance for an 'old war horse' to be put out to grass and to graze over some of the political pastures to which he has been accustomed for many years.

After the defence and the attack, the truce. Few in the House of Lords really wanted to get rid of their cosy body, which had its small importance in the political system and its great prestige. The introduction of Life Peers would add new blood without forcing out the old. As the aged and wise Viscount Samuel said so well, he was 'more concerned to get the right people in than to get the wrong people out'. A partial reform of the Lords was better than none at all. No wholly hereditary body was tolerable in the modern state, despite the best defence of the lottery of birth by the Earl of Dundee, whose speech along with the Marquess of Salisbury's was the proof that the hereditary principle might still throw up the brilliant legislator. As he so wittily said:

Of course, the right to legislate by the accident of birth is less democratic than the right to legislate by the accident of popular approval. But it is not entirely undemocratic. After all, birth is one of the most democratic things in the world, and the accident of birth is an accident which happens to everybody at one time or another. It is not an accident which requires any great intellectual attainments – or, at least, not on behalf of the person who is born. Neither does it require any great intellectual attainments to be elected to the House of Commons. I have been elected to the House of Commons twice and I have been born once; and I do not remember any particular difficulty about either operation.

Yet compromise was certain. The British peerage has always preferred accommodation to annihilation. Lord Noel Buxton even thought that a compromise between a life and a hereditary peerage was justified by the principles of the new technology. 'In the launching of the satellites a great many principles must have been involved – not merely one principle such as that of gravity – and I cannot see why we might not launch this revitalized House of Lords on more than one principle.' Looking to the future, the Earl of Home hoped that the present concession of the hereditary peers in admitting Life Peers would lead the Labour Party in later reforms 'to include in a reformed House an element of hereditary peers'. The English genius was, after all, a matter of working things out without extremism. The hereditary Peers should be allowed to hang on a little longer by conceding their exclusiveness now – although as the Earl of Woolton gloomily observed, high taxation would eliminate the peerage anyway, whatever political manoeuvres might do for its temporary preservation.

It was left to the Lord Chancellor to put realistically the reasons for the survival of the Upper House. First, the House of Commons did not want to reform the House of Lords too well, because an elected Second Chamber might well become a formidable rival or even a superior rival in the manner of the Senate of the United States. Secondly, the House of Lords had to include enough experienced and willing lords to do its work of revising and initiating and debating legislation. Thirdly, the peers had to remain truly independent and moderately representative, which actually meant more Labour peers. Fourthly, more peers had to come from common people who had proved their worth, in order to fit legislation 'to the ordinary round, the common task'. And fifthly, the Upper House needed constant refreshment to remain vital and important.

After such a speech, there was nothing left to do but to pass the Bill to admit Life Peers and to erode the last stronghold of the male hereditary Peer. Women and temporary lords were inside the gates. In fact, those peers who said that this measure was merely the first step in limiting the political power and the numbers of the hereditary peers in the Upper House were proved right when the Labour government of Harold Wilson produced in 1967 a proposal to limit the number of hereditary peers allowed to sit in the House. The principle of heredity was, indeed, fighting a losing battle. The wonder was that it had survived in an industrial and democratic nation for so long.

In a country whose chief political text seems often to be *Alice Through the Looking Glass*, it was no wonder that the Queen herself pronounced the verdict that the axe would indeed fall on the hereditary peers – who had often termed themselves 'the King Charles's head' of the Labour party. Of course, the Queen did not write her speech herself; it was written for her delivery by her Labour ministers. But through her mouth at the Opening of Parliament in October 1967 came the declaration that legislation would be 'introduced to reduce the powers of the House of Lords and to eliminate its present hereditary basis'. She must have been conscious that the monarch might well be eliminating the hereditary basis of the throne at some future date, for royal birth is hardly more than a step up from noble birth. But monarchs, like prime ministers, have always sacrificed their peers and their cabinets before themselves.

The Queen's Speech did not say how many hereditary peers, if any, would be allowed to debate and vote in the revised House of Lords. Despite headlines such as GUY FAWKES WILSON BLOWS UP THE LORDS and THAT WAS THE LORDS THAT WAS! the reform seemed more likely to strengthen the power of the Upper House than to diminish it. The *Daily Express*, which came out for an elected House of Lords as a curb on the power of the Prime Minister and the Commons, thought that the reform would not go far enough. In the country as a whole, a poll showed 23 per cent of the voters in favour of the abolition of the Lords and 70 per cent in favour of a change in it, either by reform or abolition. Only 19 per cent were satisfied with the working of the Lords after the piecemeal reform of ten years before. A majority of voters, indeed, supported an elected Second Chamber – but this reform would never be sanctioned by a jealous House of Commons, which still wanted to reduce the powers of the reformed Upper House.

What the people wanted, the Lords certainly did not want. Another poll of their attitudes showed a bare majority of them favoured a mild reform of the Upper House, while only 3 per cent of the Conservative peers and 14 per cent of the Labour peers wanted to axe all hereditary peers at once. Only 6 per cent of the peers wanted to be elected, so that, for once, the great majority of them agreed with the Commons that the rough and tumble of democracy should not be for them.[2] They would rather preserve a little power which they had left than risk winning a greater power in a popularity contest.

Perhaps the greatest irony of the abolition of the hereditary peerage would be that it would remove the only Communist who sits in either House of Parliament. Lord Milford is unique in either House and he made it quite clear in his major maiden speech in 1963 that he and his party stood for the total abolition of his forum. He questioned both the hereditary principle and its political workings.

My Lords, what, in fact, are we supposed to inherit? Is it some special ability or talent which enables us to function as legislators? No. What we inherit is wealth and privilege based on wealth – a principle which cuts right across every conception of democracy. . . . Britain is the only industrial country in which the hereditary principle of choosing legislators still survives; a principle which belongs to the age of the Divine Right of Kings, and which is entirely out of place in this age

[2] See the *Sunday Times*, 5 November 1967.

of automation, space flights, sweeping technological changes; the age of the advance of socialism, the democratic rights of the common people and the national liberation of the colonial people.

It was a good speech, except for the devastating reply of Earl Attlee immediately after its conclusion.

There are many anomalies in this country. One curious one is that the voice of the Communist Party can be heard only in this House. That is the advantage of hereditary representation.

The recent Queen's Speech has made it certain that the legislative power of the hereditary peers will be severely curtailed, if not withdrawn altogether. This may happen very soon, since the House of Lords had the temerity to defeat the government's policy on Rhodesia in June 1968. Harold Wilson's immediate response was to promise 'comprehensive and radical' legislation to cut deeply into the hereditary principle and to strip the peers of most of their powers to interfere with the work of the House of Commons. As with the great estates – the real basis of an aristocracy – the British peerage is in a period of rapid decline. The *Daily Sketch*, indeed, was sorry for Harold Wilson's attack on the House of Lords, calling it 'the tamest and most timid of bodies in the land'. Since the Second World War, the holders of titles have learned that their only way of survival lies in lying as low as they can – except when they need the advertisement to attract tourists and cash to their stately homes. Total detachment is the best camouflage, even to the extent of Lord Feversham's remark about his own country, 'I have not a clue what Britain is and where it is going, if it has not gone already.'

Eleven

A SPORTING DIFFERENCE

War was the original reason for the creation of the aristocracy and hunting their recreation. Most of the other recreations of the aristocracy derive from these traditional forms of soldiering and hunting – agriculture, and even service to the state. In the earliest days, a leader fought off his clan's enemies and brought in its meat. With the first function gone to governments and the second to butchers, the aristocracy now hunts for sport and smart restaurants. Habits long outlive reasons, and rituals necessity.

In the golden days of the aristocracy before the First World War and its silver age in certain areas until the Second World War, the mass slaughter of the lesser beasts was a highly organized affair. While regretting his inability to go to Baron de Hirsch's shoots in Austria, where 10,000 head could be killed in a day, the late Earl of Rosslyn liked to remember helping to kill 2,000 pheasants and 600 hares in one shoot and 1,600 brace of partridges in another. Armies of beaters comprising the population of whole villages would go out to drive the game in the direction of the corpulent slayers. Beating could be a very tiring and dangerous business, almost as bad as for the game. As Pascal once pointed out, a gentleman sincerely believed that hunting was great and royal sport ; but a beater was not of that opinion.

Game flourished only on the larger European estates when the men were away killing each other in war. As late as 1932, a shooting party organized by Count Lónyay in Hungary killed 2,384 hares, 159 partridges, 4 roebuck and 6 pheasants. The aristocrats behind the guns did not have to move, for not only did the beaters drive the game towards them in their hidden blinds, but loaders would keep a gun always loaded and ready to hand, so that not a second of slaughter should be missed. Once the birds came so thick and fast over the Duke of Sutherland that his loader was heard to cry out, 'Grace, Your Grouse.'

The reasons for indulging in these set-piece massacres of beasts and birds were hardly ever examined by the aristocrats. The passion for the chase was an expected part of their lives and came to them with their titles. As Count Alfred Potocki observed of the old life of his class, 'The pleasures pursued were inherited and not merely invented to kill time, as has since become common.' Hunting was a hereditary affair, and like heredity could only be accepted, not questioned. In Spain just before the Spanish Civil War, a politician asked the Count de Rodezno, the leader of the Carlist Party in the Cortès, who would be Prime Minister if the King came back. 'You or one of these gentlemen,' the Count replied, 'it is a matter of secretaries.' He himself would 'stay with the King and we should talk of the chase.'

The education in the art of the chase began at a very early age. Sir Edward Cadogan grew up with the largest rocking-horse he had ever seen, bequeathed by the elder members of his family who had given it up for real horseflesh. That notable killer of big and small game, the Duke of Sutherland, who slowly progressed to the butchery of lions and tigers and elephants and even a white rhinoceros, was begun on his education in the family tradition at an early age.

Like my father, I have always loved the wilder type of open air life where one sees Nature in the raw, untamed by man. Of all my childhood memories those which stand out among the clearest are of days spent tramping the moors with my father's gamekeepers learning the art of deer-stalking and grouse-shooting, and of my delight when my father first allowed me to take a gun. I must have been very young at the time for, as I have mentioned before, I shot my first stag when I was ten; but though we often trekked very great distances I was always far too excited to be conscious of tiredness. . . . I have now shot well over a thousand stags.[1]

[1] The Duke of Sutherland, *Looking Back* (London, 1957) p. 55.

The time to stop and consider the reason why such fanatic and repetitious slaughter should be pursued was rarely taken. What could the Marquess of Ripon say for himself at the end of his extraordinary shooting career from 1867 to 1923, by which time he had killed over half a million head of game, stretching from two hundred thousand pheasants to a pig? He was so mad about his blood sports, indeed, that he was reputed to roll about in the cart full of the dead game at the end of the day. And yet hardly a hunter will confess to merely satisfying an instinct to kill. Every other reason is given which may be acceptable to civilization, but not the joy of murder. For if that was confessed, men might begin to enjoy murdering each other in peace as well as war.

The taboo against confessing the truth is evident even in the more intelligent aristocratic memoirs, such as the Earl of Bessborough's, who calls his autobiography *Return to the Forest*, yet cannot admit that his nature is red in tooth and claw. He has to excuse his hunting by inventing an aesthetic, and sprinkle the holy water of beauty over the thrill of dealing out destruction.

The rabbit was running at full tilt. The shot of the twenty-bore bowled him over. The pigeon diving towards a stook of corn collapsed in flight. Why do we so often kill that which we love most? From the age of eleven, when the lure of the chase first captured the imagination, the paradox was pondered. The hunt lured you on. The possibility of killing a duck at dawn made you rise at three, might keep you out all night or all day. But it is not merely the killing which is remembered. It is the old-man's-beard in the hedgerows; the berries on the shrubs around the clumps in the garden; the crisp drag of the shooting shoe over the stubble; the elegance of the trees and the variety of the weather. ... Those days are remembered perhaps above the heavy thud of the pheasant fallen from high – dead before it reached the ground – or the plop of the duck – equally dead – in a clearing among the reeds in the pond. Those were the days which made you forget the dull tedium – sometimes the anguish and fear – of the return to school, to the war or merely to humdrum work. Only this kind of outdoor sport made you forget, almost all the day through, what was soon to come.[2]

[2] Earl of Bessborough, *Return to the Forest* (London, 1962) p. 4.

This confusion of the joys of walking at all hours and seasons in the country with the satisfactions of killing birds and beasts *to forget war*, is a normal confusion in the hunter seeking to justify his wish to kill. But no rationalization can take the blood out of blood sports.

Perhaps the most interesting contribution to the subject came from the late Duke of Bedford. A hatred of the army and of 'the Eton bully type' had made him spend the First World War working for the Young Men's Christian Association; later, he became an extreme evangelical and a pacifist enough to support accommodation with Hitler at all costs. Yet the duke combined his pacifism and hatred of violence with a traditional sporting outlook. He fished salmon and shot stags, pointing out that the preservation of game fish leads to an attack on the pollution of rivers, and that the 'weeding-out' of bad deer increases the beauty of the stock that is left. In fact, the wild stream and moor used for sport also conserve nature and aid selective breeding. As if to prove his interest in preserving rather than slaughtering animals, he set up a zoo in the grounds of Woburn Abbey.

The duke admitted that the opponents of blood sports had a strong case on moral and humanitarian grounds; but he accused them of practical ignorance. Firstly, he denied that sportsmen took any pleasure in the suffering of their quarry. A clean kill was a pretty one and a proof of skill, a botched kill a nasty business and a proof of ineptitude. He quoted J. G. Millais to prove the paradox that the sportsman and the naturalist were blood brothers under the skin, the man behind the shotgun loving and studying his victims, protecting them from their natural enemies and taking good care that they never became wholly extinct, which would ruin his sport.

Like Turgenev in *A Sportsman's Notebook*, the duke claimed that hunters were true nature-lovers, having particular bonds with landscape, seasons, keepers, countryfolk, horses and dogs. The expert shot killed more cleanly than nature's tooth and claw or an internal parasite, while keeping numbers down sufficiently to prevent the slow starvation of a species through overpopulation.

The hunting of deer and foxes from horseback gave them a certain sport and was more merciful than shooting them messily or trapping them. Birds quickly recovered from shot wounds or died, salmon probably preferred twenty minutes on the hook and the gaff to the slow death of Salmon Disease or by exhaustion after spawning. In all, man was no crueller to nature than nature was to herself. So the duke's strong moral case against blood sports became a strong practical case for preserving them; what the spirit denied, the hand should do.

Even the more sensitive of the aristocrats could hardly oppose one of the hereditary obsessions of his class. No less than the sheltered Consuelo Vanderbilt, who became Duchess of Marlborough, could praise the aesthetics of a good kill. 'The Duke of York was a beautiful shot, and it was a pleasure to watch the clean way he killed his birds. I hated to see birds maimed, but a high pheasant plummeting to the ground or a partridge winged as it passed was exciting.'[3]

Yes, it was exciting. This word gave away the whole rationale of hunting. There was a thrill in it, and moral reasons or social reasons for hunting were secondary. As in heredity, the blood was the thing. In an interesting letter to the *Sunday Telegraph* after an article examining the ritual slaughter of game birds that begins on August the Twelfth, an ex-hunter turned vegetarian was very precise on the issue:

The killer instinct is in us, and the special thrill the gunman derives from hitting a bird is because it is fundamentally different from hitting an inanimate target like a clay pigeon.

The setting of moor or mud flat does indeed provide a backcloth which arouses the emotions, even the manly camaraderie of the picnic lunch or feel of the vibrant saddle is in part emotional, but all these emotions can be experienced without the additional emotion which the hunter derives from killing. And what is that if not blood lust?

The emotion I feel when hunters justify their sport on grounds of being cruel to be kind, or on the grounds that nature itself is cruel, is that of any reasonable man confronted by blatant hypocrisy. Why

[3] *The Glitter and the Gold*, p. 90.

don't sporting killers admit to their bloody pleasure without the invariable bilge about the social service they are providing to nature?[4]

Hunting the fox from horseback has an even stronger mystique than killing birds and beasts on foot. The fox is obviously a wily and dangerous killer in his own right and the number of foxes in farming country has to be controlled, by gun or hunt. The ritual and excuse for riding provided by a fox-hunt is a reasonable way of combining a steeplechase with the control of vermin. Any social function which can also be made a pleasure is obviously no bad thing.

Although high society has always pursued fox-hunting, snobbery is not the reason for its success. Fox-hunting is a true obsession for its devotees. How else would a supremely witty woman such as Margot Asquith stick at the sport? As she said of herself:

Physically I have done pretty well for myself. I ride better than most people and have spent or wasted more time on it than any woman of intellect ought to. I have broken both collar-bones, my nose, my ribs, and my knee-cap; dislocated my jaw, fractured my skull, and had five concussions of the brain; but – though my horses are to be sold next week – I have not lost my nerve.[5]

Of the many eulogies on the subject of hunting, the one which came from the pen of Lady Augusta Fane seems to sum up best the obsession of her inarticulate group.

To the uninitiated it is a mystery why men and women are so passionately devoted to hunting and are ready to sacrifice time, money and everything to the sport they love. But if you are lucky enough to be born with a delight in riding, and can feel the blood racing through your veins from excitement when galloping and jumping fences, and add to that the interest of understanding the science of the game, you need not worry about the sneers of those poor creatures who do not possess your good luck. Probably their objection to the finest sport in the world comes from jealousy – which is the root of most ob-

[4] N. A. Gray in the *Sunday Telegraph*, 14 August 1966.
[5] *The Autobiography of Margot Asquith* (London, 1962) p. 214.

jections! So what they say can be of no importance. Rather go down
on your knee and thank God you 'are not one of these!'

> Not for the lust of killing,
> Not for the places of pride,
> Not for the hate of the hunted
> We English saddle and ride,
> But because in the gift of our fathers
> The blood in our veins that flows
> Must answer for ever and ever
> The challenge of 'Yonder he goes.' [6]

But the great social days of fox-hunting before the First World
War are vanished. Then, when Lady Augusta Fane was riding and
many of the European aristocrats turned up in the English Mid-
lands for the society and the sport, the hunt could seem the last
resort of noble life and true patriotism. The mystique has gone.
Now the diminishing fox-hunts of the shires are supported chiefly
by farmers. The Masters of the Hunt are no longer inevitably
aristocrats or even country gentry; they are frequently retired
industrialists who wish to spend their increasing fortunes and
declining years playing the squire. This process was noticed by
Baroness Ravensdale even before the Second World War, when
she saw the farmers putting up wire instead of hedges, and noted
the tarmac roads crossing the green acres of the chase. Already
there was a 'shabbiness' hanging over it all.

Yet fox-hunting, like the aristocracy, dies hard. The Duke of
Beaufort managed to hold up for some time the building of one
of England's larger motorways, the M4, because it broke up his
hunt. As he says, 'The M4 and other motorways are the greatest
nightmares to Masters of Foxhounds. Foxes are not barred from
crossing motorways, but horses and hounds are.' Some maps of
England in the shires still show no roads and cities, only the whole
area of the country divided up into hunts. But urbanism and the
tarmac strips are holding down the shires and dividing the hunts,
as once the Roman roads held down and divided the rebellious
Celtic tribes.

[6] Lady Augusta Fane, *Chit-Chat* (London, 1926) p. 199.

In France, however, the hunts are fewer and remain more aristocratic. In a famous ceremony at Bonnelles in the Forest of Rambouillet, staghounds are brought into the church for the Mass of St Hubert and are blessed by the priest. Hunting horns sound tunes throughout the ceremony. The French aristocracy, made gamey by a judicious mixture of the plutocracy, still runs the hunts, and there are more packs out now than there were before the Second World War. The women riders are very elegantly dressed in scarlet coats trimmed with blue-and-gold, tricorne hats sporting black ostrich feathers, and blue aprons over their breeches. To see a meet of the Rambouillet hunt under the direction of the Duke de Cossé-Brissac is to see the last meet of the *ancien régime*.

The duke himself is a famous killer of stags. He inherited his tastes from his grandmother, who had killed over two thousand stags with her pack before she died at the age of eighty-six. The walls of the duke's hunting-lodge are so full of stag-horns that they seem to be growing thickets of curling bone. As the duke says, 'One antler is bourgeois, two thousand four hundred more or less chic.' To kill beasts in quantity separates the aristocrat from the herd.

France is not only the last home of the aristocratic stag-hunt other than a rare outpost on Exmoor, it is also the mecca of the aristocratic stud, closely followed by England and Ireland. Hunting and racing have always gone hoof and hoof. Although the horses bred for one sport are different from those bred for the other except for steeplechasing, the facilities for both are the same. France and Ireland still have flourishing studs which raid England to carry off its richer racing prizes, while the English studs sell the better of their horses to the United States and even to Japan. Horse-racing has always been a rich man's game, and there is no question that the high direct taxation of England has been bleeding its horseowners and thus its bloodstock to a slow death.

If hunting and racing in England are paralleling the decline of the aristocracy, what will happen to Adam Lindsay Gordon's warning?

> Yet if once we efface the joys of the chase
> From the land, and outroot the Stud,
> Good-bye to the Anglo-Saxon race!
> Farewell to the Norman blood!

Frankly, nobody in England really knows just how much Anglo-Saxon or Norman blood he has in him. Miscegenation between Celt, Jute, Angle, Saxon, Dane, Norman and all comers has long since solved any question of blood differences in the little offshore European island. Curiously enough, the people who will force something to be done to save English bloodstock, although not the English well born, are the masses of punters, who make England lead the world in gambling. It is strange that a democracy can be so concerned over the pedigree of horses and so little concerned over the pedigree of their owners. But then, the horses give the people more pleasure, profit and loss than the owners do.

In one way, hunting on foot or on horseback will remain a more aristocratic sport in Britain than in Europe. For the opportunity to hunt in Britain is severely restricted by the lack of wilderness. All the good shoots and rivers are owned by wealthy people, either singly or in groups. While hundreds of thousands of Frenchmen traipse around the fields, killing with a gun anything which moves wing or furry foot, the islanders are usually reduced to stealthy poaching with a snare to get their game. Meanwhile, one aristocrat, Sir John Whitmore, has taken to killing stags even faster by the use of scrambling motor-cycles to pursue them over the Scottish highlands.

The aristocrats love the chase. This love is inbred. And as long as they love the chase, they will love the land which is the basis for their titles. And they will live on that land and care for its people and its preservation. It is odd that a passion for blood sports should lead to such a responsibility for conservation. Yet how else can a heritage be maintained without a love for its traditional ways?

In Longleat, that masterpiece of Renaissance architecture, there is a cemetery for pet dogs, used for hunting. One poem is inscribed over the grave of a bitch called Pansy, which shows the ultimate hold the chase has over the hearts of the aristocrats.

Brave little huntress ever true
Engraved upon my heart are you
No one can fill your special place
My Pansy with a sooty face

Darling I hope they give to you
Budgerigars to hunt of blue
Rabbits of black and white in cages
And rats to shake throughout the ages

And when I stand alone and grey
Outside the forest Lord I pray
That I may hear her little bark
To lead me through the unknown dark.

Twelve

༄ི༅ི

A WORLD OF DIFFERENCE

As in the case of nationalism, Europe is recovering from the disease
of an overwhelming aristocracy supported by an excessive snobbery just at the time that these phenomena rage in other parts of
the world, based on the old European example. In Latin America,
where the heritage of the conquistadors makes most wealthy
people of Spanish or Portuguese descent still treat the racially-
mixed and the Negroes and the Indians like serfs, a straight feudalism exists. This form of arrogant behaviour is imitated by the
wealthy and recent immigrants from Europe. In Argentina, names
are all important, particularly those dating from early colonial days
such as Anchorena and Bustamente and Ortiz. Those who bear these
names call themselves *los apellidos*, and they have accepted into the
ranks of the named ones the great Jewish names of Bemberg and
Tannenberg and Bunge. High society is totally exclusive there,
based on the possession of vast wealth and country estates. As the
half-Argentinian and wealthy Honourable David Ward says,
Argentinian life is unlivable for a European aristocrat. 'The upper
class is all wrapped up in its own scene ... not willing to be influenced by anything new.'

As in Argentina, so across the continent to the banana republics
of Central America. The upper classes remain wrapped up in
their own scene and refuse to allow anything new to happen. If it
looks like happening, the army is called in to repress it. The
reactionary feudalism of that continent, the unrestrained arrogance
and frivolity of its wealthy people, and the huge difference
between the rich and the poor can only lead to a bloody ending
of aristocracy there if Cuba has its way, or to the slow emergence

of a new Indianized aristocracy if the example of Mexico is followed. In Mexico, the possession of some Indian blood is considered a sign of Aztec or Mayan aristocracy, just as some Inca blood is prized in Peru and Bolivia. For it was the rabble of Spain, posing as gentlemen and *hidalgos*, who supplanted a genuine aristocracy in the New World. And the descendants of those same Indians will rise in their turn to supplant their conquerors.

In North America, the influence of Europe has always been paramount. The principle of aristocracy was imported there with the *Mayflower*, as the descendants of those hardy pioneers would recognize. The first common stock that farmed New England and Virginia now provides an authentic breed of native aristocrats, as do the heirs of those families who fought at the time of the American Revolution. In certain parts of the old thirteen colonies, the study of genealogy is second only to the study of the Bible, and certainly more satisfactory. For few are descended from the old revolutionary families, but all from Adam and Eve. Societies to hallow early differences of origin abound in New England and the Old South. A new Voltaire might well ask of the Daughters of the American Revolution as he once asked of the Holy Roman Empire – In what are they Daughters? In what are they Revolutionary? And he would receive the answer that they were merely all American.

When Andrew Jackson was elected President and ushered in the so-called age of the common man, the United States seemed at last to have put off its aristocratic pretences for ever. Two major works of social history were written of his time, the 1830's. One was cleverly called *Democracy in America* and gave its author, the aristocratic Alexis de Tocqueville, a lasting reputation as a sage. The other was called *Aristocracy in America* and gave its author, the democratic Francis J. Grund, little reputation until a recent revival of his work. For de Tocqueville had produced a brilliant analysis of the egalitarian new society which most Americans believed was there; Grund had produced a sound analysis of the European influence on America which most Americans believed they had escaped. The United States was then and is now a democracy deeply divided by considerations of place and race and origin and religion and caste, some of which can be called aristocratic preoccupations, if the rule of the best is considered to be the rule of the first immigrants to America.

Grund was chiefly horrified by the spirit of persecution and exclusiveness shown by the ruling classes in the United States. He loathed the pretensions of an upper class, which appointed itself by the criterion of wealth without any sense of *noblesse oblige* from the inheritance of a title, yet which tried to act in a free democracy exactly like the worst of the European aristocrats. 'Here is a free people,' Grund complained, 'voluntarily reducing itself to a state of the most odious social bondage, for no other object but to maintain an imaginary superiority over those classes in whom, according to the Constitution of their country, all real power is vested. And here are the labouring classes, probably for the first time permitted to legislate for themselves, worshipping wealth in its most hideous colours.'

There was not even the saving grace of inherited titles among the American wealthy, for at least gentility, as Bacon had pointed out, came from ancient riches. New riches did not soften the impact of rule by fresh millionaires, who were too insecure about their self-made claim to power to be nice about keeping it or insisting upon its dues. As Grund noted:

We have 'lots' of aristocracy in our country, cheap, and plenty as bank-bills and credit, and equally subject to fluctuation. Today it is worth so much, – tomorrow more or less, – and, in a month, no one will take it on any terms. We have, in fact, at all times, a *vast deal* of aristocracy; the only difficulty consists in retaining it. Neither is the position of our aristocrats much to be envied. Amidst the general happiness and prosperity of our people, their incessant cravings after artificial distinctions are never satisfied.

As the wise Oliver Wendell Holmes was to point out later, there was to be only one safety for great wealth in the United States, a new version of the Old World axiom – *richesse oblige*. And luckily, as the sons of the first billionaires inherited wealth and the leisure it entailed, they took on the habits of the European aristocracy which their fathers had not had time to acquire in the scurry after fortunes. In fact, they began to behave better from the point of view of philanthropy than the European aristocracy had done since the Middle Ages. The great American philanthropic foundations, Carnegie and Harkness and Rockefeller and Ford, distributed a *largesse* to the deserving that the Kings of the Old World had never done even on the days of their coronations, and they played a role of patron to the arts that would have beggared Maecenas in a week.

Yet as inherited riches became more common in the United States, so gentility flourished. The Marquis de Lafayette and the troops of the *ancien régime* of France had, after all, been one of the reasons for the original victory of the Republic, while the nearest thing to titles ever achieved in the United States after the Revolution, the Society of the Cincinnati made up from revolutionary and foreign officers and patronised by Louis XVI, still exists and has the ranks of those officers' descendants printed in annuals listing the nobility of Europe. One annual goes so far as to state that it is 'no exaggeration to affirm that the best and most significant example of Franco-American friendship is the existence today of the Society of the Cincinnati' with its many American members and its few French ones. If so, relationships between France and the United States must have sunk to an abyss beyond even a Gaullist dream. As for the American chapter of the Knights of Malta, *Time* magazine had the answer: each member must have substituted twenty-four company directorships for the twenty-four titled ancestors necessary for each true Knight.

Deprived of honours by the official republicanism of their nation, those Americans who have achieved or yearned for distinction have found titles all the same. One of the more fascinating sides of American social history is the national urge to profess equality while seeking for honours. The contradiction is partially explained by the fact that the United States only claims to provide each American with an equal start to make himself as unequal as he likes, echoing the recent dictum of Lord Mancroft, 'All men are born equal, but quite a few eventually get over it.' The result is that the complimentary title flourishes everywhere, with each backwoods state legislator an Honourable, every veteran of a shooting club a Colonel, and many a connoisseur of good southwestern whisky a Judge. As one American replied to an Austrian enquirer about his patent of nobility, 'Sir, my country is a republic; if it had been a monarchy, I would have been the Duke of Pennsylvania.'

In the United States, a title is something to be assumed by anybody who wishes one. A courtly air will earn the soubriquet in the South, as Mark Twain knew only too well in *Huckleberry Finn*, when he called his two performing rogues King and Duke. Huck's comments on the King sum up the democratic feeling for those who have inherited titles: 'All I can say is, kings is kings, and you got to make allowances. Take them all around, they're a mighty ornery lot. It's the way they're raised.' Twain's sympathies are all with the *natural* aristocrat, Colonel Sherburn, who can face down a mob with pride and scorn and a readiness to kill. The Colonel has achieved his position of dominance without trickery.

This feeling that anyone should have a title who feels he wants one in a country where opportunity is supposed to knock on every door has led jazz musicians to name themselves like aristocrats – Count Basie and Duke Ellington. In a way, they are right to arrogate these titles to themselves, for a genuine mass respect is paid to them for their musical talents. They are the best in their field, and so they deserve the titles. Showmen can do even better, as Prince Littler's name demonstrates. But even he is overtopped by the greatest creation of them all – King Kong, the monster who spawned a thousand horror movies and bestrode New York more majestic than a royal colossus.

That a genuine American aristocracy now exists is incontestable. The Cabots and the Lodges and the Biddles and the Whitneys have far longer and more distinguished pedigrees, not to mention greater wealth, than most Europeans who bear titles, for most titles in Europe date from no more than the nineteenth century. And even the origins of the older European titles do not bear much examination – four of the older English dukedoms alone date from King Charles the Second's tumbles with his mistresses. The possession of titles, as Jonathan Swift so savagely pointed out, has little to do with good behaviour in the past or the present; Gulliver found this out quickly when he reached the new world of Glubbdubdrib.

I HAD the Curiosity to enquire in a particular Manner, by what Method great Numbers had procured to themselves high Titles of Honour, and prodigious Estates; and I confined my Enquiry to a very modern Period. . . . A great Number of Persons concerned were called up, and upon a very slight Examination, discovered such a Scene of Infamy, that I cannot reflect upon it without some Seriousness. Perjury, Oppression, Subordination, Fraud, Pandarism, and the like *Infirmities* were amongst the most excusable Arts they had to mention; and for these I gave, as it was reasonable, due Allowance. But when some confessed, they owed their Greatness and Wealth to Sodomy or Incest; others to the prostituting of their own Wives and Daughters; others to the betraying their Country or their Prince; some to poisoning, more to the perverting of Justice in order to destroy the Innocent: I hope I may be pardoned if these Discoveries inclined me a little to abate of that profound Veneration which I am naturally apt to pay to Persons of high Rank, who ought to be treated with the utmost Respect due to their sublime Dignity, by us their Inferiors.

So much for titles, when not accompanied by better behaviour than the rest of mankind. The American aristocrats may well feel proud at not possessing such horrible attributes. In fact, their lucky inability to acquire titles except by marrying their daughters to the European nobility has left them with the possibility of retaining some political influence. In the politics of Massachusetts, the Lodges and the Saltonstalls still count; in Virginia, the aristocratic Byrds long controlled the state. The new aristocracy of the Tafts of Ohio and the Rockefellers of New York is assured politically, not to mention the national hold of the Kennedys.

This political influence, however, has been acquired and kept by practising the democratic virtues in public. John F. Kennedy began with a shy gentlemanly manner as he sought votes on the

Boston streets and ended with the crowds jumping and screaming to see him. Nelson Rockefeller now *likes* eating the obligatory blintzes on his vote-gathering tours of Manhattan. The crowds delight in seeing an aristocrat behave as they do on their best behaviour.

Many Americans have bemoaned the fact that the American aristocracy has not been able to distinguish itself successfully from café society. As Mrs Price 'Emily' Post complained in the seventy-seventh edition of her book on *Etiquette* in 1950:

In the general picture of this modern day, the smart and the near-smart, the distinguished and the merely conspicuous, the real and the sham, and the unknown general public, are all mixed up together. The walls that used to enclose the world that was fashionable are all down. Even the car tracks that divided cities into smart and not-smart sections are torn up. . . . There is nowhere to go to see Best Society on Parade.

Yet this development in American society was a healthy one, a return to the simplicity of that society before the extravagances of the Gilded Age. The last tendencies towards conspicuous consumption by the American wealthy aristocrats have been dropped with the Great Depression. These were not forced abstinences despite the comment of the *Financial Chronicle* that 'the wealthy and cultured have all suffered and been compelled to make sacrifices' because 'the greater the amount of wealth any individual has, the greater has been his loss'. The consequent shunning of display was a matter of guilt, caution, and tactics. Ostentation was dangerous, if not downright wrong, in a country where millions were poor and jobless. Even in the flush years after the Second World War, conspicuous consumption has remained unpopular in the more aristocratic circles of the United States, particularly in those families with political ambitions.

For the American people still admire simplicity in the wealthy and will not forgive *hauteur*. Henry Cabot Lodge failed as a national politician because his manner was too aristocratic. As Scott Fitzgerald so rightly pointed out in *The Great Gatsby*, Americans, while occasionally willing to be serfs, have always been obstinate about being peasantry. While they are sometimes prepared to be oppressed without complaint, they will never tug their forelock to anyone. Sir Denis Brogan also noted the lack of the deferential attitude:

American fox-hunting may be a far better sport than English hunting; the foxes and hounds alike may be finer animals; but where is the loyal tenantry? Where the grumbling but really delighted farmers? The real trouble is that American society has never developed any indigenous standards of its own except in small areas. It has been parasitic on Europe, especially on England, for its ideas as well as for its butlers. [2]

Yet what the American people lack in deference, they make up in snobbery. That insidious and overpowering American invention, mass advertising, has long exploited snobbery as one of its more penetrating weapons. All the major car companies sport coats-of-arms, so that the Cadillac or the Chrysler may be confused with a princely charger. All the cosmetics companies use aristocratic titles on their products, and the greatest cosmetician of them all, the late Elizabeth Arden, used to say disarmingly, 'There's only one Elizabeth like me, and that's the Queen.' Such brainwashing has merely stimulated the national search after honours in the republic. One of the sadder examples of this was in a recent letter to *Playboy* from Chicago, stating that some Americans were called The Honourable in print, and asking, 'Who decides who's honourable, anyway, and how can I get this title?'

When the Japanese imperial government capitulated to the Americans at the close of the Second World War, the Emperor and the royal house did not lose their titles, although the aristocrats did. Powerless and respected and discreet, the Emperor of Japan still lives in the human honours of his past glory, although he has shed his divine attributes. Most of his nobles have quietly slipped into private life; very few are in business, next to none in politics. Their titles are no longer used, except in formal ceremony when one noble nostalgically meets another in the aristocrats' club

[2] Sir Denis Brogan, *American Themes* (London, 1948) p. 87.

recently begun on one floor of a Tokyo skyscraper. In that respect, Japan has become even more Americanized than the Americans. Now that aristocratic titles are unreal there and unlinked to power on the ground, they are rapidly forgotten and paid little false respect.

The Chinese Revolution first begun by Sun Yat-sen and completed by Mao Tse-tung swept away many thousand years of imperial and mandarin rule. While Europe was a barbarous congeries of tribes, the patterns of hereditary court rule and the mass worship of ancestors had made China the most civilized place on earth. It was this worship of the past which was one of Mao's chief enemies. More important than destroying the remnants of the feudal landlords and the ancient power structure, which had survived the Kuomintang years and the Japanese occupation, was the replacing of the cult of the dead family in the Chinese mind. Progress here has been slow and sporadic, for the Chinese are even more wedded to the worship of their ancestors than most of the present members of the English House of Lords.

The last Emperor of China, 'Henry' Pu-Yi, ended as an official supporter of the Maoist régime. Emperor as a child until Sun Yat-sen's revolution and again Japanese puppet Emperor of Manchuria in the 1930's, he was later imprisoned by the Russians, then made to rethink his ways by the Chinese communists. His ability to forget his imperial heritage and to speak the Maoist line raised him again from a prison camp to a gardener's job and finally to the post of researcher into his own family's past. So the last Manchu emperor ended by rewriting the history which he had helped to make.

In the rest of Asia, the hereditary principle still survives, where governments have been able to use western aid to keep out the pressures of eastern communism. Royal families still rule in Cambodia and Thailand and even in parts of Laos, and aristocrats still survive near the throne. Malaysia has its Tungku at its head, although the rule of the nationalist generals in Indonesia and Burma has set the same alternative to communist domination that is present in the Arab world, where the new governments of the army officers stand opposed to the *anciens régimes* of the hereditary rulers.

Socialism and democracy in India has allowed the old autocratic princes there a new chance. Their British education has opened their eyes to the possibility of survival and limited power within the democratic framework. The leaders of the two hundred and more princes are setting themselves up as a successful opposition to the ruling Congress Party, gradually declining under the pressure of rising right-wing and left-wing extremist groups. In Orissa, the princelings have destroyed the Congress Party; in Bihar, the Maharajah of Ramgarh is powerful in the state government opposed to Delhi; in Madhya Pradesh, the Dowager Maharani of Gwalior and her son have toppled the Congress Party, while the Maharani of Jaipur is influential in the opposition Swatantra Party.

Some of the princes such as the Minister of Tourism, the Maharajah of Kashmir, and the Gaekwar of Baroda support the Congress Party; but in general, they pin their hopes on the rise of a right-wing nationalist government. When Nehru took over India at the time of independence, he never expected the Indian princes to be more than decorative aids to the tourist trade. But the later attacks of the Congress Party on property and private business have persuaded the princes to enter politics in the Swatantra and Jan Singh Parties, in order to conserve something of their estates and fortunes, now oriented towards industrial investment.

As elections in India become more and more expensive, and as the slow pace of education seems to do little to change the Indian peasants' fatalistic acceptance of past ways, the princes have a great advantage in political campaigns. They are known and can buy themselves advertising space to become better known. Instead of living in their old extravagant style, they are learning to live more inconspicuously and to hide their wealth, especially as the Congress Party has begun to attack their remaining privileges. The future of the Indian princes seems most threatened by the national rise of true socialism; but unless an accommodation is reached with China, a right-wing solution to India's ills may well provide a further lease of life to the aristocracy of India.

Kings still rule in Afghanistan and a Shah in Iran; there are kings in Arabia and Jordan and Morocco, princes and sheikhs in the little states of the Persian Gulf. Under all these rulers, hereditary aristocracies still wield great powers. Most of those who have inherited greatness in these countries have used the west to buy arms to defend themselves, also to serve as bankers against the day of exile. The American arms and aid agreement and the Swiss or London private bank account are the twin securities of the surviving aristocracies of the Middle East and Southern Mediterranean; they will fight to stay or live comfortably if they have to go.

Against them stand the governments of the Arab army officers led by Nasser; these are dedicated to reform through Arab socialism. In every Arab country still led by the old aristocrats, a Nasserite opposition exists, sometimes powerful as in Jordan where King Hussein's survival imitates the Perils of Pauline, and sometimes weak as in Saudi Arabia, which has barely left the Middle Ages outside the areas where oil is being exploited. In the Yemen, the new republican government, despite long-term assistance from Egypt and Russia, seems unable to defeat royalist tribesmen. The principle of hereditary rule is tenacious in the deserts, for longevity in a family in those harsh conditions seems the greatest of virtues and almost proof of the blessing of Allah.

One westernized outpost exists in the Eastern Mediterranean; Lebanon. It has long been the haven of deposed rulers and aristocrats, with its efficient and discreet banking system and its blend of Asian and European ways. The wealthy Sursock family – commemorated by a popular song expressing the wish to be one of their pampered horses and live on pistachio nuts – has taken the opportunity to ally itself to many aristocrats passing through or down on their luck. Through marriage, the Sursocks are allied to the families of the Counts de Zogheb and de Lareinthy-Tholozan, Sir Desmond Cochrane, Bart., the Emir Loutfallah, the Marquis di Sambucci, the Dukes de Cervinara and de Serra Cassano and di Santo Pietro, and Prince Colonna. Beirut rivals Lisbon as the last haven of the deposed rulers of yesteryear, still looking for the vanished respect and wealth of the old days.

The problem of aristocracy in Africa is less that of the Duke of Montrose, a rebel against the English Crown like his famous ancestor and a minister of the white supremacist régime of Rhodesia, than the tribal kings and chieftains who present the chief threat to African nationalism. The problem for the rulers of the African nations is exactly the same that the European kings had to face in the sixteenth and seventeenth centuries, how to use the power of the expanding cities to break the power of the tribal rulers of the countryside. Slowly, nationalism and urban technology are destroying the tribal system that still divides so many of the new nations. Sometimes terrible bloodshed may be the result of the clash, as in the Congo and Nigeria; sometimes, breakaway states may form on tribal lines, such as Katanga and Biafra. But under their new leaders, who can sometimes make a successful switch like Seretse Khama of Botswana from being a deposed tribal chief to becoming President of the new state, the surviving tribes of Africa are already headed for the same slow process of amalgamation that made nations out of the warring tribes of Europe.

One hereditary ruler has refuted de Tocqueville's dictum that the true basis of aristocracy is land; in his case, it is religion. The Aga Khan holds a unique position among the world's aristocrats. Hereditary leader of fifteen million Ismaili Moslems scattered over Asia and Africa, he controls a vast fortune, ever-increasing from shrewd investment and the contributions of the faithful. More European than the most European aristocrat in manner, the young Aga Khan has never lost the authority of the religious leader of his sect. He sees his function as 'somewhere between that of a Head of State and that of a Pope', and he spends four months a year visiting the various communities of the faithful in Asia and Africa and looking after their spiritual and social welfare, fuelled with capital from the large industrial fortune which he controls. The rest of the year he spends mainly in Europe, looking after the growth of that fortune, after his racehorses near Paris, and after his huge tourist development in the Costa Smeralda, Sardinia.

The Aga Khan most nearly corresponds to the ideal of the modern aristocrat. He sees no conflict at all in being a religious leader, a big businessman for his people's welfare, and a race-horse owner. As he says, an Imam such as himself 'can lead an absolutely everyday life. Our Prophet, Mohammed, was himself after all both a business man and a leader of the army. In the Christian world you have this heartrending dichotomy between what is narrowly good and what is worldly. We try to attribute goodness to each of these areas, in proper balance.' As the most influential aristocrat remaining in the world, and as probably the most useful and best-balanced man among them, the young Aga Khan is the only argument for the continuance of aristo-cratic rule – and unique.

Finale

Finale

The late Joseph Schumpeter, one of the more brilliant critics of Karl Marx, once defined the political and social significance of class.

It is an essential property ... of the phenomenon of class that the members of one class behave toward one another in a characteristically different manner than they do toward members of other classes; that they maintain closer connections among each other, understand each other better, co-operate more easily, join together among themselves and close ranks against outsiders; that they are looking with similarly predisposed eyes from similar points of view in the same direction into the same segment of the world. ... Social intercourse within the boundaries of class is fostered by the influence of the identity of manners, of habits, of things valued positively or negatively and considered interesting. In communication across class boundaries, on the contrary, there are differences in all these respects, which repel and inhibit sympathy, so that there is always a larger or smaller territory of delicate topics which must be avoided, and of matters which appear strange or even ridiculous, and which must be laboured or paraded and become unnatural and forced. The difference between communication among members of the same class and communication with outsiders is that between swimming with the current and swimming against it.[1]

By this definition, the nobility of Europe still was a class up until the time of the Second World War. The characteristics of the nobility of France tabulated by Ferré in the 1930's and mentioned earlier endorse Schumpeter's definition. Thirty years later, these

[1] Joseph Schumpeter, 'Die sozialen Klassen im ethnisch homogenen Milieu', *Aufsätze zur Soziologie*, p. 152, quoted in K. Deutsch and L. Edinger, *Germany Rejoins the Powers* (Stanford, California, 1959) p. 125.

phenomena seem to be under erosion, and the end of the aristocracy as a class very near.

Firstly, there is the question of the different manner which the
aristocrats have towards each other and towards the rest of the
world. Naturally, all people are more relaxed within the company
of those they know, their manner is slightly different, and they
have their private jokes and references. But the actual marks of
behaviour which used to distinguish an aristocrat from a com-
moner – an arcane slang, a weary disdain, a freezing politeness,
and an expectation of immediate service – are disappearing. The
young aristocrats are now more likely to pick up the slang coined
by the makers of pop music, than the undertones of their class.
In Edwardian days, aristocrats liked to use a bit of slang from the
grooms in the stables; now their grandchildren turn from
raciness to the disc jockeys. But in general, the young aristocrats
would prefer not to be distinct by their speech or dress from their
contemporaries, in case they were thought to be behaving like
the aristocrats they were born to be.

Again the aristocrats are marrying each other less often,
putting a lower value on questions of pedigree, and becoming
less exclusive. Their hostility towards intrusion by strangers and
their excessive concentration on their ancestors has become an
unwilling acceptance of successful commoners in their midst and
a nostalgia for times past, rather like the reaction of most modern
white Southerners in the United States to the integration of the
Negroes. The aristocrats still do understand one another better
than the rest of the world, but they never have co-operated with
each other against the pressures of society. It is an open scandal
that one of the premier earls of Scotland was recently reduced to
penury in England. Not one of his wealthy ilk sent him a penny;
he died in poverty. A Jewish charity would have done better.

As has been noticed, a similar predisposition by the aristocrats
in their views of the world has almost disappeared. Their views
are fragmented, personal, independent. In Britain, no unanimity
could be found among the peers on questions like the death
penalty or the reform of the penal laws against male homosexuals,

which had once condemned Oscar Wilde. Answers ranged from
the Earl of Westmeath's, 'I'm for hanging and the cat, look at
England since the cat was given up, murder is getting a national
pastime,' to Lord Arran's successful defence of homosexual
reform in the House of Lords, when he denied that one lot of
privileged people were helping to legalize the position of another.

Lest the opponents of the Bill think that a new freedom, a new
privileged class, has been created, let me remind them that no amount
of legislation will prevent homosexuals from being objects of dislike
and derision or, at best, of pity. We shall always, I fear, resent the
odd man out. That is their burden for all time and they must shoulder
it like men.

The possibility of resentment at the odd man out has led the
aristocracy to – in the reverse of Sam Goldwyn's famous phrase
– exclude itself in. It masks its desire for isolation, its identity of
habits and values and interests, in so far as these still exist. On
private country estates, something like the old life can still be
led, and often is. But in the city or the public eye, a genial democracy is practised. In Europe today is what de Tocqueville noticed
in the United States at the time of President Jackson, 'The picture
of American society has . . . a surface covering of democracy,
beneath which the old aristocratic colours sometimes peep out.'

But de Tocqueville also noticed, when he was considering the
ancient aristocracy of France, that value attached to high birth
declined just as fast as new avenues to power were discovered.
In the eleventh century, for instance, nobility was beyond all
price; by the thirteenth century, it might be bought for gold or
land. Nobility was conferred by gift in France in 1270, and equality
was thus introduced into the government by the aristocracy
itself. By the nineteenth century, de Tocqueville thought that
titles were already worthless. 'We have destroyed an aristocracy,'
he wrote, 'and we seem inclined to survey its ruins with complacency and to accept them.'

In fact, he was speaking a century too soon. The aristocracy
had another hundred years to run before the widespread creation

and assumption and buying of titles had made them all seem rather ridiculous and somewhat insignificant. Not only has socialism and democracy made titles out of date, but the aristocrats have debased their own coinage. Emerson always saw the British peerage as 'an aristocracy with the door open', but now the walls are down all across Europe for the nobility. The reason does not lie entirely in social change, but partially in the aristocrats' own failure to live up to their ideal of the rule of the best. As Machiavelli once pointed out so shrewdly, it is not titles that reflect honour on men, but men on their titles.

There are those responsible aristocrats who talk of the continuing role of the aristocracy, from Lord Mowbray's feeling that it represents the continuity of history and a real detachment from material things, to the Duke de Cossé-Brissac's old-fashioned assertion that 'the mark of aristocracy is the hereditary ability to command, an ability which tarnishes through lack of practice when one is content with the mere remembrance of past power'. Yet that ability to command may not be given the chance to command; opportunity is no longer the inevitable legacy of a noble father. In fact, he may regret passing on a heritage to the unworthy. 'It seems unfair that a son who has done nothing,' the Marquess of Hertford says, 'should inherit everything.' It does indeed. But those who live by the hereditary principle must also die by the hereditary principle. All they can do is counsel their heirs to do better than they themselves have done, in order to survive longer. 'I find one has to convince the younger generation,' the Count Draskovich says, 'not to make the same mistakes as we and our fathers made.'

But the same mistakes will be made. For it would be extraordinary if the aristocracy, still brought up in its traditions, should wholly deny its upbringing. It will adapt partially, but only enough to coast along for the length of time that governments and mass snobbery tolerate its existence. Of course, new aristocracies will and have arisen, which will benefit their sons and grandsons. As Baroness Pauline de Rothschild noticed on her recent tour of Russia, Soviet scientists have the social privileges of English dukes. But these new ruling classes will remain aristocracies without hereditary title – unless acquired by worth.

For the meritocracy has already taken over from the aristocracy. The rule of the best at technology and finance has already taken over from the rule of the best at landowning and hunting. Privilege exists and will continue to exist in every society; but that privilege is no longer to be inherited by blood, but won by brains. Feudalism was the basis of title, and feudalism is dead or dying in Europe. The French Revolution was its first grave, the First World War its burial ground, and the Second World War its requiem. The aristocracy is tenacious and well-publicized, but it is also doomed by the advance of technology and mass democracy. Nothing will do it more honour than if it chooses elegance in its own passing.

On the Fourteenth of July, the French people have their great national holiday and dance in the streets to celebrate their Revolution and their Republic. Only a small and impotent group do not celebrate, the members of the Association of the French Nobility. 'We have nothing to do with it,' its spokesman said recently. 'Of course, in that aristocrats work nowadays, we take advantage of the holiday. We rest.'

Index

Wollaston, Nicholas, 151n.
Woolton, Lord, 249
working class, Austrian, 79
Wurttemberg, Duke of, 44

Xenia, Grand Duchess, 99

Yemen, 273
York, Duke of, 257
Yorkshire, 114

Young Men's Christian Association, 50, 256
Ypres, 44
Yugoslavia, 64, 89, 177

Zamoyski, Count, 85
Zborowski, Count, 14
Zichy, Countess Anita de, 166
Zitzewitz, Baron von, 134
Zogheb, Count de, 273